D1282959

# Neville Chamberlain, appeasement and the British road to war

In this controversial re-evaluation of Neville Chamberlain and appeasement, Frank McDonough draws on a fascinating range of primary and secondary sources to make his case. He argues that Chamberlain believed a second world war would be disastrous for Britain, and focused all his energies to avoid it. In doing so, he used and abused the 'mood of the age', which favoured a collective international drive to preserve peace, and not the nationally self-interested policy which Chamberlain followed.

It was Hitler's entry into Prague in March 1939 which exposed appeasement as a fantasy and forced Chamberlain, under pressure from national opinion, to make a half-hearted and muddled attempt to stand up to the dictator in 1939. It was a task to which Chamberlain's flawed political judgement was even more ill-suited and which ultimately led to the outbreak of war in September 1939.

The book differs from other studies of the subject by setting Chamberlain's actions within a wider chronological framework and by taking a fresh look at the underlying influences on the policy of appeasement within British society.

Frank McDonough is Senior Lecturer in Modern Political History at Liverpool John Moores University.

MANCHESTER
UNIVERSITY PRESS

# NEW FRONTIERS IN HISTORY

*series editors*

Mark Greengrass
Department of History, Sheffield University

John Stevenson
Worcester College, Oxford

This important series reflects the substantial expansion that has occurred in the scope of history syllabuses. As new subject areas have emerged and syllabuses have come to focus more upon methods of historical enquiry and knowledge of source materials, a growing need has arisen for correspondingly broad-ranging textbooks.

*New Frontiers in History* provides up-to-date overviews of key topics in British, European and world history, together with accompanying source material and appendices. Authors focus upon subjects where revisionist work is being undertaken, providing a fresh viewpoint which will be welcomed by students and sixth-formers. The series also explores established topics which have attracted much conflicting analysis and require a synthesis of the state of the debate.

**Published titles**

C. J. Bartlett   Defence and diplomacy: Britain and the Great Powers, 1815–1914
*Jeremy Black*   The politics of Britain
*Paul Bookbinder*   Weimar Germany
*Michael Braddick*   The nerves of state: taxation and the financing of the English state, 1558–1714
*Michael Broers*   Europe after Napoleon
*David Brooks*   The age of upheaval: Edwardian politics, 1899–1914
*Carl Chinn*   Poverty amidst prosperity
*Conan Fischer*   The rise of the Nazis
*T. A. Jenkins*   Parliament, party and politics in Victorian Britain
*Keith Laybourn*   The General Strike of 1926
*Panikos Panayi*   Immigrants, racism and ethnicity 1815–1945
*Daniel Szechi*   The Jacobites
*David Taylor*   The New Police
*John Whittam*   Fascist Italy

**Forthcoming titles**

*David Andress*   French society in revolution 1789–1799
*Ciaran Brady*   The unplanned conquest: social changes and political conflict in sixteenth-century Ireland
*John Childs*   The army, state and society 1500–1800
*Barry Coward*   The Cromwellian protectorate
*Simon Ditchfield*   The Jesuits in early modern Europe
*Bruce Gordon*   The Swiss Reformation
*Susan-Mary Grant*   The American Civil War and Reconstruction
*Neville Kirk*   The rise of Labour, 1850–1920
*Tony Kushner*   The Holocaust and its aftermath
*Alan Marshall*   The age of faction
*Keith Mason*   Slavery and emancipation
*Evan Mawdsley*   The Stalin years: the Soviet Union 1922–1956
*Alan O'Day*   Irish Home Rule
*Michael Turner*   British politics in the age of reform
*Alexandra Walsham*   Persecution and toleration in England 1530–1660

# Neville Chamberlain, appeasement and the British road to war

## Frank McDonough

Manchester University Press

Manchester and New York

Distributed exclusively in the USA by St. Martin's Press

Copyright © Frank McDonough 1998

*Published by* Manchester University Press
Oxford Road, Manchester M13 9NR, UK
*and* Room 400, 175 Fifth Avenue, New York, NY 10010, USA

*Distributed exclusively in the USA by*
St. Martin's Press, Inc., 175 Fifth Avenue, New York,
NY 10010, USA

*Distributed exclusively in Canada by*
UBC Press, University of British Columbia, 6344 Memorial Road,
Vancouver, BC, Canada V6T 1Z2

*British Library Cataloguing-in-Publication Data*
A catalogue record for this book is available from the British Library

*Library of Congress Cataloging-in-Publication Data*
McDonough, Frank.
    Chamberlain, appeasement and the British road to war / Frank McDonough.
        p. cm. — (New frontiers in history)
    Includes bibliographical references and index.
    ISBN 0-7190-4831-1. — ISBN 0-7190-4832-X (pbk.)
    1. Great Britain–Foreign relations–Germany.   2. Great Britain–
Politics and government–1936–1945.   3. Great Britain—Foreign
relations–1936–1945.   4. Chamberlain, Neville, 1869–1940.   5. World
War, 1939–1945–Causes.   6. World politics—1900–1945.   I. Title.
II. Series.
DA47.2.M26   1998
324.41043'09'043—dc21                                           97-15519
                                                                    CIP


ISBN   0 7190 4831 1 *hardback*
       0 7190 4832 X *paperback*

First published 1998

03  02  01  00  99  98        10 9 8 7 6 5 4 3 2 1




Printed by Bell and Bain Ltd, Glasgow

120298-4156X8

# Contents

# Acknowledgements

It was R. A. C. Parker who first made me especially interested in Neville Chamberlain and the policy of appeasement when I attended his famous Special Subject at Oxford many years ago. I must also thank him for his inspiration and for his advice on this project at the outset. I must also pay tribute to Maurice Keen, John Prest, and Jon Powis from Balliol College, Oxford, who taught me never to be afraid to defend a controversial position. I was, therefore, delighted when the editors of the New Frontiers in History series, John Stevenson and Mark Greengrass, invited me to contribute a book on this topic. I am also greatly indebted to a multitude of scholars whose work has increased my understanding of this subject. I must also thank the staff at the various archives I have visited during the extensive research for this book. I have acknowledged these debts in the footnotes and in the bibliography as far as possible. What follows, however, is my own post-revisionist interpretation of the subject.

I am also very grateful for the financial assistance provided in the form of research expenses from Professor David McEvoy, Director of the School of Social Science, and in the form of relief from teaching from the Research Committee of the School of Social Science at Liverpool John Moores University and its chairman, Professor John Vogler. I would like to acknowledge the research assistance provided by Linda Walsh on Board of Trade journals for the chapter on economic appeasement. I have also been greatly helped by the staff in the library at John Moores University –

## Acknowledgements

especially in gaining important items on inter-library loan, and by the typist, Sue Barlow. I would also like to thank Ralph Footring for his excellent copy-editing of the typescript, and Carolyn Hand, Vanessa Graham and Gemma Marren at Manchester University Press for their efficiency. The continued support of my colleagues Nick White and Rex Li deserves a special mention, but I would also like to pay tribute to all my close colleagues, my friends and the students who have listened to many of the views expressed here over the years. I owe a special debt of gratitude to my brother Michael, whose inspiration was vital in my formative years. Finally, I must reserve my deepest thanks of all for Ann and Emily for their help, their love and their support.

F. X. *McDonough*
Liverpool

# Abbreviations

## Abbreviations used for sources

AC       Austen Chamberlain papers, University of Birmingham
BP       Broadlands papers (Lord Mount Temple papers), Hartley
         Library, University of Southampton
CAB 2    Committee of Imperial Defence, minutes and reports,
         Public Record Office, London (PRO)
CAB 23   Cabinet minutes (PRO)
CAB 24   Cabinet memoranda (PRO)
CAB 27   Cabinet committee on foreign policy, minutes and memo-
         randa (PRO)
CAB 29   Proceedings of the London reparations conference (PRO)
CAB 53   Chiefs of staff sub-committee, minutes (PRO)
CPA      Conservative Party archive, Bodleian Library, Oxford
*DBFP*     *Documents on British Foreign Policy* third series, London,
         HMSO (1949–57) (followed by volume and document
         numbers)
FO 371   Foreign office, general correspondence (PRO)
FO 800   Foreign office, private papers series (PRO)
FO 954   Foreign office, Avon papers (i.e. Sir Anthony Eden's)
         (PRO)
MRC      Modern Records Centre (i.e. Federation of British Indus-
         try Papers), University of Warwick
NC       Neville Chamberlain papers, University of Birmingham
T        Treasury papers (PRO)
TA       Times archive, London

## Abbreviations for organisations

| | |
|---|---|
| AGF | Anglo-German Fellowship |
| BBC | British Broadcasting Corporation |
| BUF | British Union of Fascists |
| CID | committee of imperial defence |
| DEG | Deutsch Englische Gesellschaft |
| DRC | defence requirements committee |
| FBI | Federation of British Industry |
| ICI | Imperial Chemical Industries |
| PPU | Peace Pledge Union |
| RAF | Royal Air Force |
| RI | Reichsgruppe Industrie |
| SIS | secret intelligence service |
| TUC | Trades Union Congress |

# 1

# Introduction: the changing debate

Neville Chamberlain is always remembered in the popular mind as a deluded politician who believed a second world war could be prevented through a policy known as appeasement. The policy prevented a world war in 1938 through the signing of the Munich agreement, but ended in humiliating failure when war broke out in 1939, and is enshrined in folklore as the epitome of cowardice and illusion. Yet appeasement was no invention of Chamberlain alone. From 1918 to 1933 it was viewed as a noble and magnanimous search for just solutions to international problems by the use of negotiation. Appeasement grew originally from a desire to solve the legitimate grievances of nations dissatisfied with the peace settlement of 1919. From 1931 to 1937 it has been claimed the British national government followed a form of 'passive appeasement' which accepted treaty revision by Japan, Italy and Germany without resort to arms. Under Neville Chamberlain, its most famous practitioner, from 1937 to 1939, it has been argued appeasement became an 'active' policy, pursued with energetic vigour, which attempted to satisfy specific demands of Germany in the hope that this might prevent war.

There are many historians who view appeasement as a popular policy.[1] However, to claim the appeasement of Nazi Germany was universally popular is somewhat misleading. It ignores the wider context of British society and public opinion in which the policy operated. In fact, as we shall see, Chamberlain's appeasement of Hitler and Mussolini in the late 1930s was extremely controversial, and provoked opposition from a large group of opponents.

1

Chamberlain's appeasement became so controversial that it brought foreign policy to the centre of political debate. During the Czech crisis of 1938, for example, Chamberlain's frantic and impromptu attempts to gain emergency compliance by Czechoslovakia to the demands of Hitler aroused deep opposition. In 1939, appeasement was described as 'a clever plan of selling off your friends in order to buy off your enemies'.[2] In 1950, Winston Churchill made a distinction between appeasement from weakness and fear, which he saw as 'futile and fatal', and appeasement from a position of strength, which he defined as 'magnanimous and noble'.[3] Such was the impact of Chamberlain on the very meaning of appeasement that even dictionary definitions changed. Before 1937, appeasement was defined in positive terms such as 'soothing' and 'calming' with the central aim of reducing tension and producing harmony. After 1939, appeasement was viewed as involving negative acts such as 'buying off' or 'sacrificing principles' to satisfy 'a potential aggressor'.[4]

The initial historical judgements on Neville Chamberlain were negative. The most influential was *The Guilty Men*, written in 1940 by a group of Labour supporters, including Michael Foot, Frank Owen and Peter Howard, under the pseudonym 'Cato'.[5] The guilty men – most of whom were leading figures in the national government – were charged with failing to stop Nazi aggression in Europe and bringing Britain near to military collapse.[6] Chamberlain was singled out for the greatest share of the blame. As chancellor of the exchequer (1931–7), he was accused of starving the armed forces of cash. As prime minister (1937–40) he was castigated for pushing forward his own deeply personal form of appeasement at a time when all logic suggested that it had little hope of success. *The Guilty Men* indicated that Chamberlain knew what he was doing, knew the risks, rejected the alternatives and brushed aside opposition, and therefore it was only right and proper he should accept the blame. *The Guilty Men* portrayed appeasement as a combination of calculated deception, incompetent leadership, a lack of principles, diplomatic bungling and poor military planning. In spite of its 'I told you so' form of expression, *The Guilty Men* thesis enjoyed a great deal of support in the immediate post-war years.

When the full horrors of the Nazi death camps were revealed in 1945, most people speculated about why Hitler was not stopped earlier. The ghost of Neville Chamberlain evoked a spirit of shame and regret. A key feature of the immediate post-war era was the practice of historians, with a clear memory of events and no access to government archives, passing instant historical judgements. Contemporary history was born. In one of the first post-war studies of British foreign policy, John Wheeler-Bennett described Munich as 'a case study in the disease of political myopia which afflicted the leaders and the peoples of Europe in the years between the wars'. He viewed appeasement as a policy of delusion, championed by an ineffective leader who failed to tackle the moral issues inherent in negotiating with the Nazi dictatorship. A moral was drawn from the tragic events which led to the Munich agreement: war is often preferable to peace at any price.[7]

Alongside the rush to instant judgement, there was a stream of memoirs from politicians, diplomats, army, navy and air force chiefs, journalists, and newspaper editors. Most of these fallible recollections also denounced Chamberlain and appeasement.[8] The most influential memoirs were those of Winston Churchill, who showed how Chamberlain led Britain to 'the bull's eye of disaster' and who explained 'how easily the tragedy of the Second World War could have been prevented',[9] and those of Anthony Eden, who presented appeasement as the misguided personal policy of Chamberlain which was opposed by many leading figures in the cabinet and the foreign office.[10]

The very notions that Chamberlain was a competent leader and appeasement a sensible policy seemed to contradict the instant judgements of contemporary historians, and of those with first-hand experience of the events leading to war. Yet the object of historical study is to explain the past outside a moral framework. This was certainly the view adopted by A. J. P. Taylor in his classic book *The Origins of the Second World War*, published in 1961. Taylor rejected the orthodox idea of Hitler as a monster, a messiah or a systematic planner, following a blueprint for European domination laid out in his book *Mein Kampf* ('My Struggle'); rather, he viewed him as a coffee-house dreamer, a man of improvisation, following a foreign policy which, while unclear, was very little different from the policy of the Weimar era. In other words, Hitler was an 'ordinary German statesman'. In fact, Taylor did not view Hitler's aggression as the main cause of the war, attributing this instead to the failure of the peacemakers in 1919 to solve the 'German problem' and create a genuine balance of power in Europe.

Taylor also argued that Chamberlain's policy of appeasement was a logical and realistic choice in the circumstances. It recognised the failings of the past and was a well meaning attempt to solve them. According to Taylor, the Munich agreement was 'a triumph for all that was best and enlightened in British life', as it solved a German grievance and aimed to prevent war. Indeed, Taylor thought Chamberlain should not have lost his nerve and abandoned the policy in March 1939. He suggests that, after appeasement was dropped, serious errors of judgement were made by Chamberlain which made war inevitable. The first mistake was the decision to offer a unilateral military guarantee to Poland in March 1939. This left the British decision for war in the hands of Poland. The second error was the failure of the British government to secure a swift Anglo-Soviet agreement, which was vital if war stood any chance of being prevented. In Taylor's view, Hitler would have gladly accepted another Munich-style peace settlement over the Polish crisis, and he concluded that the major reason for the outbreak of war was Chamberlain's decision, pushed along by the momentum of the national will, to meet force with force when Britain was in no position to do so.[11]

It was not, however, until 1967, when the Public Records Act reduced the traditional fifty-year embargo on the release of official documents to thirty years, that a full-blown revisionist school on Neville Chamberlain and appeasement emerged. The revisionists suggested that concentration on the guilt and incompetence of Chamberlain obscured the importance of a complex range of factors which made a policy based on standing up to the dictators impractical, and a policy based on peace, even at considerable moral cost, preferable to a war in which the odds were heavily stacked against Britain and France.[12] They argued that the decision makers had become prisoners of circumstance.

For the revisionists, Chamberlain was not a weak and ineffective leader, but a strong-willed, realistic and able politician who saw that Britain and France were in no position economically or militarily to keep order in the world, and wanted Britain to retain its independent power and influence within the world power system, which he thought could be achieved only if a second world war could be avoided. It was for these reasons that Chamberlain refused to go cap in hand to the communist Soviet Union, which he disliked more than Nazi Germany, or the United States, which he felt had no desire to become involved in European problems.

According to this view, appeasement under Chamberlain was a far-sighted attempt to ensure Britain remained a major world economic and imperial power.[13]

David Dilks has played a very important role in making judgements on Chamberlain increasingly more sympathetic. Dilks views appeasement as a sensible policy which tried to find out whether German aims could be satisfied without bloodshed or war, while attempting to improve Britain's national defences to fight a war if the policy failed. In other words, Chamberlain hoped for the best and prepared for the worst. The hope was that face-to-face contact with Hitler might both flatter him and induce him to solve his grievances through negotiations and written agreements. The preparation for the worst involved a massive surge of spending on armaments.

Neville Chamberlain, as presented by Dilks, is no deluded politician, but a complex character with a sharp mind who weighed up all the possibilities and took detailed military and economic advice before pursuing foreign policy. He wrestled with doubts over whether Hitler's aims were vast or limited and wanted peace, not purely for narrow domestic political, economic or imperial reasons, but because he genuinely hated the whole idea of plunging Britain into war. According to Dilks, appeasement was designed to revise the Treaty of Versailles by peaceful means in favour of Germany, *en route* to a new general settlement of European problems. It was no policy of abject surrender, but one based on the view that if Germany intended to dominate Europe by force then Britain would go to war. This prospect was seen as more or less certain only after the occupation of Czechoslovakia in March 1939, when, according to Dilks, Chamberlain promptly abandoned the policy for a commitment to meet force by force.[14]

As a result of exemplary research, revisionists have held the historiographical high ground for many years and have enabled the negative contemporary view of Chamberlain, and the policy of appeasement, to be overturned. The revisionists view appeasement as a realistic policy, adopted by a strong and capable leader in Chamberlain, who based his policy on a detailed assessment of Britain's economic and military weakness and a clear realisation of its declining power and influence in the world. Another key argument of the revisionists is that Chamberlain pursued a policy supported by public opinion.

Yet the revisionist drive to rehabilitate Chamberlain and the policy of appeasement has not gone unchallenged. Many historians still adopt a very critical stance. On such critic is Keith Middlemass, who views Chamberlain's appeasement as a 'diplomacy of illusion'. The major issue for Middlemass is not whether it was immoral to appease Hitler, but whether it was advisable to do so when all logic suggested the policy would fail. He argues that it failed because of deluded thinking, poor planning and poor timing, and that Chamberlain should be singled out for special blame because he ran foreign policy as a one-man band, used the cabinet as lap dogs, muzzled the foreign office, brushed aside all opposition and fed the public scraps of untrue information about the prospects for lasting peace. This might not have mattered if the policy had been based on solid military planning and a workable defence strategy. According to Middlemass, it was based on a wholly defensive military strategy, which neither protected Britain adequately from air attack nor offered a deterrent to Hitler. It was also based on the illusion that Hitler's aims were limited to a revision of the Treaty of Versailles, and could be satisfied by face-to-face negotiations and written agreements.[15]

More recently, Alistair Parker has produced a hugely impressive and detailed study of Chamberlain and appeasement which skilfully combines elements of the old orthodoxy with insights from the revisionists to produce what should be regarded as the beginnings of a post-revisionist interpretation. It will no doubt inspire a fresh wave of research. Parker fully accepts the revisionist view of Chamberlain as a competent, able and clear-sighted politician who exerted the most powerful influence over British policy; but he rejects the other central view of the revisionists, namely that the type of appeasement Chamberlain followed was dictated by economic and military weakness. On the contrary, Parker argues that the appeasement followed by Chamberlain was chosen from a range of alternatives, which were skilfully dismissed, and was pursued with zeal. It seems Chamberlain began his mission to appease Hitler and Mussolini with a great deal of cabinet support, but as the policy was put into effect many in the cabinet began to hesitate and to doubt its morality. Such was the supremacy of Chamberlain that he was often able to find ways of manoeuvring his way free to continue the policy. For Parker, Chamberlain pursued appeasement with obstinacy, rejecting expert advice as well as the hostility of critics, and in the process 'stifled serious chances of preventing the Second World War'.[16]

A major problem with the whole debate has been the extent to which it has revolved around very different interpretations of largely the same official documents. The quantity of this material is enormous. For example, the foreign office papers for 1938 alone contain well over 250,000 items. The numbers of papers of the cabinet, the chiefs of staff and the various committees concerned with foreign affairs and national defence are equally large. But there remain some major gaps. Papers relating to the dominions have been destroyed and the documents of the intelligence services – the so-called 'mission dimension' – relating to foreign policy during the inter-war period remain classified.[17] In fact, the well arranged and lucid documents of the major departments of state hold treasures and dangers.

The chief danger of these documents is that they were drafted, collected and selected by state officials who were deeply involved in the very events they seek to record. Such documents can all too easily delude the historian into writing a naive official version of events, which can often exonerate or provide a self-justification for the actions of state officials. It is too easy to be seduced into believing the path followed was the only path or the most logical path available. The reality of foreign policy making was much more complex. The parameters of government decision making, and the artifice of minute taking and report writing, rarely give any real indication of how the decisions were reached, gloss over bitter arguments by the use of polite language and give little idea of the tactics and methods which surrounded decision making. Official documents nearly always underestimate, and even totally ignore, because of the conventions surrounding their creation, the importance of outside forces – especially party politics, business, public opinion and organised labour. They also give little account of the prejudices, emotions, personal friendships and networking which underpin a great deal of the daily grind of political life. The lack of real humanity and outside pressures in the neatly ordered official documents of the British government in the 1930s leave many historians extremely doubtful whether a study exclusively based on official sources can ever provide a completely satisfactory picture of the broader context of the society in which the decisions were taken.

It seems that the time is ripe for a study of Neville Chamberlain and appeasement which shows how central foreign policy became within British politics and society during the inter-war years, and which broadens its scope to ask searching questions about the interrelationship between foreign policy and society – a study which not only explores the 'official mind' but looks at the 'public mind'. This book offers such an approach, by setting Chamberlain's actions within a longer chronological framework, which takes in the whole period 1918 to 1939 and analyses appeasement from 'above', within the British government, and from 'below', within British society, in an attempt to show why the policy provoked such passion and opposition. To achieve these objectives, the book is divided into two parts.

In the first part of the book, a chronological pattern is followed to explain the development of British foreign policy and the imperatives underpinning national defence policy for the period 1918 to 1939, using a narrative/interpretative framework with sources drawn primarily from government archives, private papers and the work of many noted historians. Chapter 2 briefly surveys the major features of foreign policy from 1918 to 1937. Chapter 3 explores the military strategy which underpinned British policy during the inter-war years. The aim of these chapters is to trace and explain the development of British foreign policy before Chamberlain became prime minister, and to explain the role of national defence on policy formation. Chapters 4, 5, and 6 provide a comprehensive and original analysis of Neville Chamberlain and the conduct of foreign policy from 1937 until the outbreak of war in 1939. These chapters explore Chamberlain's motives and the formal and informal methods he employed, and examine the relationships he enjoyed with his close advisers, notably the foreign secretaries Eden and Halifax, officials in the foreign office and colleagues in the cabinet.

In the second part of the book, a thematic/analytical framework is employed to examine the effect of appeasement on British society in three important areas. Chapter 7 examines the position, attitudes and methods used by the appeasers in British society to promote the idea of appeasing Germany and examines the views of the major critics of appeasement, with special emphasis on the views of Labour and Liberal Parties, and an analysis of anti-appeasers in the Conservative Party. Chapter 8 examines how the leading forums of the mass media – the press, radio and cinema – covered foreign policy during the inter-wars years, and explores the extent to which the government attempted to manipulate the mass media and public opinion to portray appeasement as a popular policy by examining evidence from opinion polls and elections. In chapter 9 the efforts made by government and business groups to pursue economic appeasement during the inter-war period is fully investigated. Finally, in chapter 10, an attempt will be made to evaluate Neville Chamberlain's role in the events which led to war in the light of the insights provided by a detailed analysis of the broader domestic situation in which British foreign policy operated.

## Notes

1  A. Roberts, *The Holy Fox: A Biography of Lord Halifax* (London, 1991), pp. 44–5.

2  *Manchester Guardian*, 25 February 1939.

3  *Hansard*, 14 December 1950, col. 1367.

4  See W. Rock, *British Appeasement in the 1930s* (London, 1977), pp. 1–7.

5  Cato cleaned the sewers in Rome.

6  Cato, *The Guilty Men* (London, 1940). The controversy surrounding the book is discussed in S. Aster, '"Guilty Men": The Case of Neville Chamberlain', in R. Boyce and E. Robertson (eds), *Paths to War: New Essays on the Origins of the Second World War* (London, 1989). See also P. M. Taylor, 'Appeasement: Guilty Men or Guilty Conscience', *Modern History Review* (1989).

7  J. Wheeler-Bennett, *Munich: Prologue to Tragedy* (London 1948), p. 437.

8  A major exception is Sir Samuel Hoare, *Nine Troubled Years* (London, 1957), which offers a very sympathetic treatment of Chamberlain's motives and actions.

9  W. S. Churchill, *The Gathering Storm* (London, 1948), p. 31.

10  Earl of Avon, *Facing the Dictators* (London, 1962).

11  A. J. P. Taylor, *The Origins of the Second World War* (London, 1961). The whole A. J. P. Taylor controversy is discussed in G. Martel (ed.), *The Origins of the Second World War Reconsidered: The A. J. P. Taylor Debate After 25 Years* (Boston, 1986).

12  See J. Charmley, *Chamberlain and the Lost Peace* (London, 1989), for a spirited polemical defence of Neville Chamberlain and the policy of appeasement.

13  See D. C. Watt, 'Appeasement: The Rise of Revisionist School', *Political Quarterly* (1965); P. M. Kennedy, *The Rise and Fall of the Great Powers* (London, 1987), pp. 355–431; P. M. Kennedy, 'Appeasement', in

G. Martel (ed.), *The Origins of the Second World War Reconsidered: The A. J. P. Taylor Debate After 25 Years* (Boston, 1986); P. M. Kennedy, *The Realities Behind Diplomacy* (London, 1980). New thinking on appeasement is discussed extensively in V. Mommsen and L. Kettenacker (eds), *The Fascist Challenge and the Policy of Appeasement* (London, 1983).

**14** D. Dilks, '"We Must Hope for the Best and Prepare for the Worst": The Prime Minister, the Cabinet and Hitler's Germany 1937–1939', *Proceedings of the British Academy* (1987).

**15** K. Middlemass, *The Diplomacy of Illusion: The British Government and Germany, 1937–1939* (London, 1972). Other critical accounts include: L. W. Fuchser, *Neville Chamberlain and Appeasement, a Study in the Politics of History* (London, 1982); W. Rock, *British Appeasement in the 1930s* (London, 1977); R. J. Q. Adams, *British Politics and Foreign Policy in the Age of Appeasement 1935–39* (Stanford, 1993); R. Cockett, *Twilight of Truth: Chamberlain, Appeasement and the Manipulation of the Press 1937–1940* (London, 1989).

**16** R. A. C. Parker, *Chamberlain and Appeasement: British Policy and the Coming of the Second World War* (London, 1993), p. 347.

**17** See D. Dilks, 'Appeasement and Intelligence', in D. Dilks (ed.), *Retreat from Power, Studies in Foreign Policy in the Twentieth Century, vol. 1, 1906–39* (London, 1981), pp. 139–69.

# Part I
# Appeasement and British government
# 1918–1939

# 2

# British foreign policy, 1918–1937

The First World War, which ended on 11 November 1918, ruined the old balance of power, altered the map of Europe and paved the way for major changes in the international system. Four major monarchical empires lay shattered: Imperial Germany (Hohenzollern), Austria–Hungary (Hapsburg), Turkey (Ottoman) and Romanov (Russia). A bewildering mixture of national groups demanded self-determination. The Russian revolution of 1917 spawned great anxiety about the possibility of a spread of communism elsewhere. Only the United States and Japan actually profited from the war economically.

For Britain, the 'Great War' was an economic disaster. The world export trade collapsed, and nearly 1 million soldiers of the British empire had been killed, while another 2 million were wounded or disabled. It was little wonder that the popular press screamed the headline 'Make Germany Pay'. At the 1918 general election, David Lloyd George, leader of the wartime coalition, promised the British people: 'We propose to demand the whole cost of the war from Germany'.[1] Once the initial euphoria had subsided, it was soon apparent to the foreign office that the defeat of Germany, combined with the weak state of the Soviet Union, held out the distinct possibility of Britain returning to relative isolation from European affairs.

The most immediate problem was to find a viable peace settlement. For this purpose, the Paris peace conference opened on 12 January 1919. Delegates were optimistic that they would be able to bring political order to Europe and prevent a major war ever happening again. Leaders from the thirty-two victorious nations were present. But all the vital decisions were taken by a 'Council of Four' – Woodrow Wilson, US president, Georges Cleameaceau, French premier, Vittorio Orlando, the Italian premier, and, of course, David Lloyd George, described by Churchill as 'the master in the art of getting things done'.[2] The British delegation stayed at the sumptuous Hotel Majestic. They wanted military restrictions placed on Germany and financial compensation to satisfy public opinion, but not a punitive settlement which would leave Germany resentful, vengeful and in economic misery.

After six long months of compromise, complex legal argument and wrangling, the five treaties which made up the Paris peace settlement were finally agreed upon. The most important was the infamous treaty of Versailles, presented to the German delegation on 28 June 1919. The German army was reduced to 100,000, conscription was banned, and tanks and aircraft were prohibited. The German navy was reduced to a coastal force and the building of battleships and submarines was not allowed. By these measures alone, Germany was reduced to the level of Greece as a military power and ranked on a par with Argentina in naval strength. In addition, Germany lost 13 per cent of its territory, including Danzig, which became a free city, and a corridor was created which gave Poland an outlet to the sea by cutting through the territory of west Prussia. These latter decisions provoked bitter recriminations from German nationalists. In western Europe, the Rhineland was turned into a demilitarised zone for the purpose of easing French anxiety about a German military revival. All the former German colonies were confiscated and placed under the 'mandate' of the victorious allies. On the financial side, Germany was required to pay, after much protest, the seemingly mind-boggling figure of £6,600,000 as compensation for the damage and death caused by the war. A union between Germany and Austria was also strictly forbidden. Under article 231 of the treaty, Germany was obliged to accept full responsibility for the outbreak of the war (the infamous 'war guilt clause'). Every German greeted Versailles with a mixture of disbelief, horror and disgust, and most of the ills Germany suffered after the First World War and most of the conflict Germany engaged in with other countries were linked, in one way or another, to specific clauses contained in the Versailles treaty.

All those in Britain who advocated appeasement came to believe Versailles had punished Germany too harshly and required revision. It was equally clear that Germany would seek treaty revision and, so long as 'legitimate' German grievances were being appeased, this was not something British foreign policy opposed. The appeasement of legitimate grievances was viewed as a magnanimous gesture by a major power to a forlorn and greatly weakened one. This was appeasement from a position of relative strength and was not viewed as cowardly, silly or gullible. For Lloyd George, appeasement was a necessary antidote to French hatred of Germany. John Maynard Keynes, the noted British economist, believed the appeasement of Germany made economic sense, and in 1920 he warned in the deeply influential *Economic Consequences of the Peace* that the financial demands made on Germany by the reparations clauses would cause great damage to the international trade and payments system, destabilise the German economy and bring economic collapse. When these predictions came true, blaming the sorry economic plight of Germany on the architects of the treaty of Versailles seemed logical.[3]

The subsidiary treaties dealt with Austria–Hungary, Bulgaria and Turkey, and also created enormous problems. A major aim of the peacemakers was to ensure that the principle of national self-determination was applied to the diverse ethnic and national groupings of central and eastern Europe. This proved incredibly difficult, and few ethnic groups were ever satisfied with the place they had been assigned on the new maps decided by the peacemakers.

The creation of two new states – Czechoslovakia and Yugoslavia – at the expense of Austria–Hungary and Bulgaria, and the expansion of Poland at the expense of Germany and Russia, left eastern Europe more unstable than ever before. All the successor states were weak, politically and ethically divided, and in a sorry economic condition. They could never even get along with each other, and never fully grasped the ideals of democracy and free trade. 'I cannot imagine any greater cause of future war,' claimed Lloyd George, 'than that the German people, who have proved themselves one of the most powerful and vigorous races in the world should be surrounded by a number of small states, many of them consisting of peoples who have never previously set up a stable government for themselves'.[4] The British government took very little interest in the affairs of the small and vulnerable states of eastern Europe. The only country greatly interested in their well-being was France, which signed treaties of mutual assistance with Poland (1921), Czechoslovakia (1924), Rumania (1926) and Yugoslavia (1927).

The only initiative decided upon by the peacemakers in 1919 that at least gave some grounds for optimism was the creation of the League of Nations. Woodrow Wilson is usually credited with founding this completely new international body, but the idea had long been suggested by liberals in Britain as a useful means of ending old diplomacy and finding a new framework in which to settle international disputes without resort to war. The League had an agreed constitution, outlined in its covenant, which pledged to preserve against external aggression the territorial integrity and existing political independence of all members and to undertake collective action by economic and military means to punish any member guilty of unprovoked aggression. But the League faced enormous problems from the very beginning. The defeated powers were denied entry until they had shown a willingness to abide by the treaties imposed upon them. The Soviet Union, racked by civil war, was also denied entry. Even worse, the United States, a leading architect of the organisation, never actually became a member of it, which deprived the League of the most powerful non-European power. Apart from Japan and China, the League of Nations was overwhelmingly composed of the victorious European powers which had established it.

In the 1920s Britain and France were the two most dominant powers in Europe. Without a firm guarantee of military support, no alliance with the Soviet Union and a strong belief that Germany would not accept Versailles lying down, and would eventually launch a revenge mission, the French still felt extremely anxious. The British did not share these anxieties. This left Anglo-French relations in a state of jealousy, suspicion and resentment for most of the inter-war years. In 1920, a Channel tunnel project was rejected by the foreign office on the grounds that 'our relations with France never have been, are not, and probably never will be, sufficiently stable and friendly to justify the building of a channel tunnel'.[5] In fact, foreign office officials feared French dominance in Europe during the 1920s far more than the possibility of a German revival.

The major aims of British foreign policy during the inter-war years were to encourage the reconciliation of the defeated powers and to promote international co-operation and disarmament. In July 1921, Churchill saw the chief aim of British policy as the 'appeasement of the fearful hatreds and antagonisms which exist in Europe and to enable the world to settle down'.[6] From 1920 to 1922, Lloyd George participated in twenty-three conferences designed to tackle problems left unresolved by the peace conference, concerning issues as diverse as naval disarmament, reparations, the League of Nations and territorial adjustments. But the key issue of Britain's relations with Europe in the 1920s remained the German problem. To nearly all British politicians, Europe would finally settle down only if Germany was reconciled to the new international order. This was an extremely difficult task. Germany emerged from the First World War in a deeply unstable position. The Weimar Republic was born in defeat, cradled in disorder and eventually died during the depression. From 1918 to 1933, Weimar democracy consisted of a series of unstable coalition governments, beset by political violence between extremists on the left and right. In such a deeply unstable political environment, economic problems were bound to prove disastrous. From 1918 to 1923, the German mark collapsed, inflation rose to unmanageable levels, political violence flared on the streets and there seemed no end in sight to German misery.

The battle between Germany and France over the payment of reparations was the most dominant issue in international affairs during the early 1920s. The German government saw reparations as a symbol of everything they hated about Versailles, but the French saw their payment as vital to their own economic well-being. A clash over the issue was inevitable. The British government came quickly to dislike French anti-Germanism and expressed more sympathy with Germany as the underdog in this bitter struggle. The whole sorry crisis came to a head in the winter of 1922–23. Raymond Poincaré, the French premier, outraged at successive failures by Germany to meet its payments, ordered the occupation of the industrial Ruhr region and was supported by Belgium. This strained Anglo-French relations to breaking point. 'If the French and ourselves permanently fall out,' Lord Curzon, the British foreign secretary commented, 'I see no prospect for the recovery of Europe or the pacification of the world'.[7] The British government believed the use of brute force by the French to extract payment from a severely weakened Germany was likely to prove counter-productive and ultimately fruitless.

The occupation of the Ruhr, which lasted nine months in 1923, proved a major political blunder, but also a turning point. It showed that the French government, acting without British support and against strong German resistance, could never hope to enforce payment. It was finally agreed by Britain, France and the United States to establish an inter-allied reparations committee of financial experts, chaired by Charles G. Dawes, a US banker, to find a means of enabling Germany to pay. At the London reparations conference of July–August 1924, the Dawes plan, the first major act of appeasement, gained German agreement to make regular annual reparations payments in return for a substantial US loan.

A lasting solution to the Franco-German dispute seemed the one sure route to security. In April 1924, the French government asked the British government to sign a pact of mutual assistance, but this offer was rejected on the grounds that it might encourage France to continue in its overbearing and unaccommodating attitude towards Germany. A treaty of mutual assistance to guarantee the security of all members of the League against unprovoked aggression was then championed by the French, but this was also rejected by the British government. In 1924 Ramsay MacDonald, the first Labour prime minister, gave qualified support to the Geneva protocol, an ingenious plan which linked collective security with compulsory arbitration in international disputes and set out a format to determine the aggressor and impose penalties in disputes between nations. But after the Conservatives won the 1924 general election, Austen Chamberlain, the Tory foreign secretary, rejected this idea because it might involve Britain in all manner of conflicts.

In 1925 Austen Chamberlain told the King that his chief foreign policy aim was 'to make the new position of Germany tolerable to the German people in the hope that, as they gain prosperity under it, they may in time become reconciled to it, and unwilling to put their fortunes again to the desperate hazard of war'.[8] This type of appeasement did not mean allowing an increase in German military power but was an attempt to influence the German government willingly to accept a new security arrangement in western Europe which would ease French fears and preserve the status quo.

In October 1925, the German government decided to sign a reciprocal security pact with Britain, France, Italy and Belgium at the Swiss lakeside town of Locarno. The Locarno treaty seemed to mark an end to the bitter European conflict of the early 1920s. Germany agreed to accept the western frontiers laid down at Versailles, as well as the de-militarisation of the Rhineland (both of which were guaranteed by Britain, France, Italy, Belgium and Germany). In return, the German government was promised an early end to the military occupation of the Rhineland (this took place in 1930) and the end of the allied military inspection committee (curtailed in 1927). As a further symbol of reconciliation, Germany agreed to join the League of Nations. This new mood also influenced the celebrated Kellogg–Briand pact of August 1928, when fifteen nations agreed to renounce war as a legitimate weapon for a nation state, to be joined by over forty others before the end of the 1920s.

Shortly after the signing of the Locarno treaty, Sir Austen Chamberlain and his German and French counterparts, foreign ministers Gustav Stresemann and Aristide Briand, reportedly wept tears of joy. All three were later jointly awarded the Nobel prize for peace. Most contemporaries saw Locarno as a major reconciliation between Germany and the western allies. This was an over-optimistic assessment. The German government may have accepted the western frontiers of Versailles, in return for important concessions, but gave no similar assurance about its eastern frontiers. Locarno showed that the British would not stand by and see France crushed in western Europe but equally that they offered no promise to defend the small states of eastern Europe. Sir Austen Chamberlain viewed Locarno as a treaty of peace which had cemented the military balance in Europe in favour of France and fostered the ideas of 'compromise and cooperation in European affairs over bitterness and revenge'.[9] It seems self-interest played an important part in the endeavour. A healing of the Franco-German rift would allow Britain to adopt a semidetached position towards the problems of eastern Europe. In the late 1920s, the policy of appeasement appeared to German and French ministers as a shrewd device to further British interests by allowing Britain to free itself from any European alliance system, and specific military entanglements, in order to concentrate on domestic politics and the empire. Hence, the 'Locarno spirit' was something of an illusion. Britain saw the agreement as an opportunity to retreat from Europe, the German government viewed it as a first step towards further treaty revision and the French were too anxious about a German revival to

consider using the agreement to establish a Franco-German reconciliation.

In any case, economic reality soon dented the high hopes raised
by Locarno. In October 1929, the Wall Street stock market crashed,
producing a far-reaching economic depression. The first consequence
of the US financial collapse was the ending of US loans to Europe,
which had been vital in stimulating recovery. The cold wind of
depression chilled the era of international co-operation. It is important to stress how much the depression damaged international
co-operation. Unemployment rose everywhere, banks failed, industrial output fell alarmingly and agricultural prices collapsed. The
widespread optimism in the free market, democracy and international co-operation of the mid-1920s gave way to the pessimism,
totalitarianism and self-preservation of the 'hungry thirties'.

During the depression, all the major powers became obsessed
with domestic problems. In 1931, there was a British financial crisis
and rising unemployment, which led to the fall of the Labour
government and the formation of the national government led by
Ramsay MacDonald, who deserted his party during the crisis to
lead a coalition government dominated by the Conservative
Party. Neville Chamberlain, the chancellor of the exchequer,
introduced import duties ranging from 10 to 50 per cent on a wide
range of goods. This was followed by the Ottawa conference of
1932, which allowed imperial goods entering Britain to remain free
of the tariff.

MacDonald was branded a traitor by the left, but he retained a
foreign policy which was very much in the British socialist tradition.
MacDonald sympathised, as did most of the Labour Party in the
1920s, with the sorry economic plight of Germany. 'If German
militarism is to be crushed,' MacDonald wrote in 1915, 'Germany
must not be given as an inheritance from this war, the spirit of
revenge'.[10] MacDonald also believed no European power should
resist 'the German claim that the Treaty of Versailles must in some
respects be reconsidered'.[11] The removal of reparations, support for
disarmament and the finding of peaceful solutions to international
problems remained central objectives of British foreign policy under
MacDonald. In 1930, MacDonald gained an agreement with Japan,
Italy and the United States to limit naval building. In 1931, he
agreed to Britain signing the act for the pacific settlement of
international disputes.[12]

Above all, MacDonald wanted to find a world-wide agreement on disarmament. In 1932, the celebrated world disarmament conference opened in a blaze of publicity and optimism. It was attended by sixty-one League member nations, including Britain, France, Germany, Italy and Japan, and five non-members, most notably the Soviet Union and the United States. It was largely convened through the persuasive efforts of MacDonald and Arthur Henderson, the ex-Labour foreign secretary who chaired the conference. The British government had taken the lead in naval disarmament, and helped persuade Japan, the United States and Italy to participate in two key arms limitation agreements on naval building at Washington in 1922 and London in 1930. The world disarmament conference was designed to extend this process to all weapons and armies.

The British government wanted world disarmament and was supported in this endeavour by most of the smaller powers, but Germany, France, Italy and the Soviet Union opposed any wide-ranging agreements. A British proposal to place strict limits on the production of offensive weapons, including tanks, bomber aircraft, submarines and poison gas and chemical weapons, was rejected. A French idea for the creation of a League of Nations army also foundered. The most vexed issue at the conference was German rearmament. The German delegation argued for equality of treatment, which found support from Britain, but the French could not accept this proposal. In September 1932, the German delegation, led by Franz von Papen, withdrew from the conference. In December 1932, a second German delegation returned after Britain, France and Italy had agreed to grant Germany equality provided the German government would first agree to a new system of security. The German delegation went on wrangling for equality and the French kept raising objections. In October 1993, Adolf Hitler withdrew Germany permanently from the disarmament conference on the grounds that it could never treat Germany fairly. The futile world disarmament conference, the great hope of many appeasers, dragged on until 1934, but achieved no agreement.

The rise of Adolf Hitler from corporal in the German army during the First World War, to leader of the right-wing National Socialist German Workers' Party (NSDAP, or Nazi Party) and finally to the pinnacle of German power in January 1933 once more raised worries about the prospects of European peace. Hitler's rise was primarily due to the depth of the economic depression, which paralysed the German political system and made the strong government the Nazi leader promised seem attractive, especially to groups hit by the depression. Although Hitler was the most well known and most popular opponent of the treaty of Versailles in Germany, he came to power with a promise to drag Germany out of the depression.

The appointment of Hitler as Chancellor of Germany did lead to some soul searching concerning the policy of appeasement. After all, a key justification for appeasement up until 1933 had been the attempt to support a democracy along the path of peace and reconciliation. What supporters of appeasement had to argue after 1933 was that it could succeed with a dictator pledged to restore Germany to military greatness. It might have been expected that the policy of appeasement would now have to be dropped. There were many involved in British foreign policy in the 1930s who doubted whether appeasement was the best policy to deal with 'a half mad and ridiculously dangerous demagogue'.[13]

The first signs from Nazi Germany hardly gave grounds for believing Hitler wanted a quiet life. In 1933, the cruelty of the Nazi regime was greeted with a sense of anxiety in Britain. Sir Austen Chamberlain, the ex-foreign secretary and a key architect of Locarno, felt the Nazi regime consisted of 'The worst of all Prussian militarism, with an added savagery,' and he opposed the policy of appeasement being applied to the 'new' Germany.[14] At the foreign office, Sir Robert Vansittart, permanent under-secretary, also opposed an active policy of appeasement directed at Nazi Germany and commented that on past and present form Germany would launch a European war 'just as soon as it feels strong enough'.[15] However, the arrival of Hitler did not lead to the abandonment of appeasement. For many, the policy still seemed a justifiable response to the alleged severity of Versailles and the best way to prevent a German war of revenge.

From 1933 to 1935, the British government showed little enthusiasm for an active policy of appeasement, but equally displayed little inclination to present a strong military challenge to Germany. In many ways, British policy makers were unsure of the best way to deal with Hitler. MacDonald recognised the danger Hitler posed to European peace and saw the appeasement of Germany as a risky proposition. The foreign office cited French intransigence in the

1920s as the key cause of the rise of Nazism, but initially favoured keeping Hitler at arm's length and wished to cement British friendship with Mussolini. To this end, MacDonald paid an official visit to Italy in March 1933 to encourage close Anglo-Italian relations.

It was the question of German rearmament which dominated Anglo-German relations in the early period of Hitler's rule. In February 1934, Anthony Eden, a rising Tory star in foreign affairs, visited Germany and discussed German demands for rearmament. On his return, Eden described Hitler as 'sincere in desiring a disarmament convention'. In April 1934, the British government conveyed Hitler's rearmament demands to the French government and urged their acceptance. But the French rejected them, which prompted a foreign office official to lament, 'We always urged the French to make a bargain with the Germans while there was yet time'.[16]

Meanwhile, alarming news circulated Europe concerning a possible Nazi take-over in Austria. Engelbert Dollfuss, Austrian chancellor, banned the Nazi Party in June 1934. Less than a few weeks later he was killed by Nazi thugs. Mussolini sent four army divisions to the Austrian border as a demonstration of his opposition to any Nazi-inspired putsch. The French government also issued a declaration of support for Austrian independence. In the face of this opposition, Hitler was forced publicly to deny any plan for a Nazi seizure in Austria. In June 1934, news broke of Germany's so-called 'night of the long knives' – the merciless and lawless eradication of leading figures in the socialist wing of the Nazi Party, and among the Sturmabteiling (the Nazi's paramilitary wing) and political opponents. On 2 August 1934, president Paul von Hindenburg died, which greatly strengthened Hitler's power.

These events prompted further worries about German intentions. The French response was to seek fresh agreements with Italy, the Soviet Union and the small nations of eastern Europe. In July 1934, the Soviet Union emerged from years of diplomatic obscurity to join the League on Nations. In January 1935, France and Italy signed a new diplomatic agreement, pledging mutual military support in the event of German aggression. The British response was to push forward plans for rearmament while searching for agreements to limit German air and naval strength.

On 4 March 1935, MacDonald, the great believer in disarmament, put his signature on a white paper entitled *Statement Relating to*

*Defence*, which admitted that, despite of the League of Nations, 'adequate defences are still required'. Only days later, Hitler officially announced the existence of a German air force and promised to expand the army, navy and air force way beyond the limits imposed under Versailles. In response, Sir John Simon, the foreign secretary, met Hitler in Berlin on 25–26 March 1935 and informed him that the major aims of British policy were to preserve general peace by helping to secure co-operation among all European countries, to try to prevent the division of Europe into two armed camps and to seek close association with Germany 'without prejudice to relations with France'. In reply, Hitler claimed Versailles could never be revised while Germany remained in a position of military inferiority, without colonies and disarmed. At the same time, Hitler offered the olive branch of an Anglo-German naval agreement.[17]

In 1935, British policy makers could not fully decide whether to deter or appease Nazi Germany. In April 1935, for example, the emphasis in British policy was on deterrence when the leaders of Britain, France and Italy met at Stresa and issued what sounded like a strong joint declaration, opposing by 'all practical means any unilateral repudiation of treaties which may endanger the peace of Europe' and promised collaboration for this purpose. It was dubbed the 'Stresa front' but there was no agreement on how to restrain Germany. Each signatory pursued disparate aims. France wanted to encircle Germany, and signed pacts with the Soviet Union and Czechoslovakia to this end. Italy was preparing for unilateral aggression of its own and was not keen to uphold the principles outlined at Stresa.

In June 1935, the emphasis in British policy shifted back to appeasement. On 21 June the Anglo-German naval agreement was signed. It limited the German navy to 35 per cent of the British royal navy's ship strength and to 45 per cent of its submarine strength. The British attitude towards the agreement was self-interested and pragmatic. From a strategic point of view, it eased pressure on the admiralty, which was already concerned about the naval threat posed by Japan in the far east, and saw the agreement as bringing Germany into the existing British framework on naval disarmament rather than something radically new. The Anglo-German naval agreement made plain that the British government had no objection to German rearmament provided it was kept within some arms limitation framework.

In June 1935, Stanley Baldwin became prime minister of the national government. He was a moderate consensus politician who had juggled conflicting principles all his political life. He was happy to leave foreign policy to the foreign secretary, Sir Samuel Hoare, and the foreign office. Only days after Baldwin became prime minister, the results of the 'peace ballot' were published. In the final months of 1934, volunteers from the National Declaration Committee, a group associated with the League of Nations Union, canvassed the opinions of nearly 12 million British voters on foreign policy. The results showed quite incredible support for the policy of collective security, the League of Nations and disarmament. Baldwin was deeply impressed and decided to appoint Sir Anthony Eden as minister for the League of Nations.

Unfortunately, this dramatic surge of enthusiasm for the League coincided with a major test of its credibility. Early in 1935, Mussolini's desire to create a large Italian empire in north Africa was an open secret. On 8 June 1935, Vansittart informed Hoare bluntly: 'Italy will have to be bought off – let us use and face ugly words – in some form or Abyssinia will perish'.[18] In June 1935, the cabinet decided to buy off Mussolini by offering him the Ogadon province of Abyssinia, a twelve-mile corridor to the Gulf of Aden, and the port of Zeila in British Somaliland. On 24 June 1935, Eden went to Italy to present these proposals to Mussolini, but he rejected them and promised to 'wipe the name of Abyssinia from the map'.[19]

In Britain, public opinion wanted a strong stand to be taken in the League of Nations to prevent Italy occupying Abyssinia. The cabinet realised satisfying public opinion might alienate the Italian dictator. This put British policy in an ambivalent situation: in public, supportive of the League; in private, determined not to alienate Mussolini. On 11 September 1935, Hoare told the League of Nations assembly: 'The League stands, and my country stands with it for the collective maintenance of the Covenant in its entirety, and particularly for steady and collective resistance to all acts of unprovoked aggression'.[20] Mussolini guessed that the British were talking tough to satisfy public opinion but were still willing to find a compromise in a suitable smoke-filled room.

On 3 October 1935, Italy attacked Abyssinia. The British government immediately supported an overwhelming vote in the League of Nations to impose economic sanctions. In November 1935,

Baldwin gained support for this tough stand against unprovoked aggression by winning the 1935 general election. This eased Baldwin's domestic worries but did nothing to solve the dilemma facing British policy makers over Abyssinia. News filtered through the diplomatic grapevine from Rome to Paris which indicated that Mussolini might accept an Anglo-French peace plan, provided it left him with most of Abyssinia.

On 2 December 1935, the cabinet agreed that Hoare should go to Paris to discuss a compromise over Abyssinia with Pierre Laval, the French foreign secretary. It was later claimed by the British government that Hoare, tired and ill, acted on his own initiative, but this was a lie designed to placate an outraged British public.[21] On 7 December 1935, Hoare met Laval in Paris. The next evening, the two ministers had agreed Italy should receive over three-fifths of Abyssinian territory, except what *The Times* later dubbed 'a corridor for camels' which led to the sea at Assab. To the horror of the British government, news of the Hoare–Laval plan was leaked to the press and the public was rightly outraged. On 19 December 1935, Hoare, vilified in the press and abandoned by the cabinet, was forced to resign.

In many ways, the Abyssinian affair was a bitter blow to the credibility of the League of Nations. It certainly damaged the integrity of British foreign policy by showing that the British government paid lip service to the ideals of the League in public, in order to court popularity, but was privately willing to engage in a secretive and quite cynical abandonment of those principles. In diplomatic terms, the Abyssinian affair was also unfortunate. Far from being bought off, Mussolini felt betrayed and drifted out of the Anglo-French orbit and moved closer to Hitler.

Hoare was replaced by Eden, at thirty-eight the youngest foreign secretary since 1851. Eden had built up his reputation as a firm supporter of the League but he was aware of the difficult task he faced. The Abyssinian affair greatly damaged relations with Italy and was not counter-balanced by any improvement of Anglo-German relations. Eden was relatively inexperienced in high office and he knew his policies would come under intense scrutiny from more experienced colleagues.

In the early months of 1936, the whole question of improving Anglo-German relations came sharply into focus. Nazi Germany was no longer viewed as a weak and defeated power but as a menacing threat. In January, Eden concluded that Hitler was aiming at 'the destruction of the peace settlement and the re-establishment of Germany as the dominant power in Europe', and he advocated two policies to cope with this: firstly, a new programme of rearmament to provide some form of deterrence to Germany; secondly, a *modus vivendi* with Nazi Germany to lessen the tension caused by 'the growth of Germany's strength and ambitions'.[22]

The foreign office also examined the prospects for appeasement. In February 1936, Vansittart wrote a long memorandum on the subject, which stated that 'Germany was armed from top to bottom in a way never before contemplated by any state'. To deal with this, Britain must encourage 'effective rearmament of all members of the League', and modify those parts of Versailles known to be 'untenable', in a process of give and take with Germany arranged through the League of Nations. He suggested the return of German colonies and economic aid as two ways of opening up a dialogue, but in return Germany was expected to return to the League and sign a new security pact.[23] It was finally agreed that any settlement with Germany could not be unilateral but must be part of a general European settlement.[24] The only concrete proposal to emerge from these discussions was to establish a sub-committee to examine ways of finding agreement with Nazi Germany.

These discussions were soon overtaken by a new menacing event. On 7 March 1936, German troops marched into the demilitarised Rhineland. This came as no real surprise. In December 1935, Sir Eric Phipps, British ambassador in Berlin, warned the march of German troops into the Rhineland would occur 'whenever a suitable opportunity presents itself'.[25] In a speech to the Reichstag, Hitler claimed the decision of France to ratify its treaty with the Soviet Union on 27 February 1936 had freed Germany from its obligations under Locarno. The British government accepted Hitler's Rhineland coup as a *fait accompli*. Eden, in his first real test as foreign secretary, informed the French that the British government was not prepared to support military action. The chiefs of staff felt Britain was in no position to go to war with Germany over the issue. By and large, British public opinion agreed with the view of Eden's taxi driver, who claimed that 'Hitler was only going into his own back garden'.[26]

The Rhineland episode was not seen by the British government as an act of unprovoked aggression but as the righting of an

27

injustice left behind by the Versailles treaty. The prospect of military action over the Rhineland received no support from the majority of dominions, except New Zealand, which recommended taking action through the League. On 26 March 1936, Eden told the Commons that the occupation was as an 'accomplished fact' and claimed British policy remained committed to seeking peaceful and agreed solutions by the 'appeasement of justified grievances'.[27] On 30 March 1936, Eden sent Hitler a polite questionnaire, which asked what terms Germany required to act as a law-abiding power, but Hitler did not reply.

Meanwhile, another European crisis was erupting elsewhere. On 18 July 1936, the bitter and bloody Spanish civil war began. It lasted three years. It grew out of a familiar inter-war theme – a fragile European democracy threatened with the rise of fascism. In the Spanish general election of February 1936, right-wing nationalist factions became the largest group in the Cortes. They were denied office by a coalition popular front consisting of liberal republicans, socialists and communists. Nationalists, led by General Francisco Franco, supported by land owners, business people, the church, the monarchy and the army in north and west Spain set up an alternative government in Burgos. The republicans – or loyalists – of the popular front, supported by a rag-bag 'people's militia', held Madrid and central and eastern Spain. The actual issues were very complicated and produced deep division on both sides.

The Spanish civil war did not remain a private matter. Hitler and Mussolini gave military support to Franco, in order to prevent the spread of communism, while Stalin offered limited military aid to the communists (but not the Trotskyists) in the popular front. The reaction of the British government to the Spanish imbroglio was to adopt a policy of non-intervention. This was viewed by the left as another form of appeasing Hitler and Mussolini. But there was no ground-swell of public support to send British troops to Spain. British policy attempted to prevent the conflict escalating. There is a strong, almost mythical, belief, that British ministers virtually blackmailed the French into following non-intervention.[28] The evidence for this is patchy and inconclusive. It appears the French were reluctant to become involved, not only out of fear of losing British support in a future European war, but because the Blum coalition was weak and feared active French involvement might precipitate a civil war on the streets of France, and a possible European war.

The policy of non-intervention weakened the ability of the popular front to resist the nationalists and further damaged the credibility of the League. Mussolini and Hitler drew closer as a result of their military collaboration in Spain and signed the Rome–Berlin axis of October 1936. Anglo-Italian relations continued to deteriorate and were not greatly improved by the decision to drop economic sanctions against Italy in July 1936, or the Anglo-Italian 'gentleman's agreement' of January 1937, which affirmed mutual British and Italian interests in the Mediterranean and pledged both governments to uphold the existing status quo in the national sovereignty of territories in the area.[29] However, Eden was firmly opposed to any new initiative of appeasement towards Mussolini, whom he now regarded as a major mischief maker in European affairs.

In the summer of 1936, Eden admitted to the cabinet that 'The international situation is so serious that from day to day there was risk of some dangerous incident arising and even an outbreak of war could not be excluded'. He stressed the two main aims of British policy remained 'to secure peace' and 'keep this country out of war'. Eden believed Britain had to search for some agreement with Germany.[30] One possible means of enticing Germany to open negotiations was the return of German colonies. It was agreed by the cabinet to set up a committee under Lord Plymouth to investigate the issue. The Plymouth committee eventually concluded that the return of German colonies would not improve the economic position of Germany. On 27 July 1936, the British government announced in the Commons that it would not support the return of colonies to Germany.[31]

By the end of 1936, there was gloom about the poor state of the international situation. Germany and Italy were engaging in unilateral repudiations of international law and were linked as allies. A bitter civil war was under way in Spain, which seemed like a dress rehearsal for a larger ideological war between communism and fascism. Japan and China were on the verge of war in the far east. In the United States there were plenty of strong words of protest uttered by president Roosevelt, but the US neutrality laws gave no promise of US military or economic aid. British rearmament had only just begun.

On 31 December 1936, Vansittart argued that the only sensible policy for Britain in these circumstances was to attempt to 'hold the situation to at least 1939', and continue to urge conciliation until rearmament was complete.[32] In a similar pessimistic tone, Eden told the Commons on 19 January 1937 that Germany had a choice in its foreign policy between force and co-operation and he suggested that if Hitler decided to choose the latter 'there is nobody in this country who will not assist whole-heartedly to remove misunderstandings'.[33] In reply, Hitler questioned whether any co-operation with Britain was possible until all outstanding German grievances had been resolved and Germany was treated as a full and equal member of the international community. On 18 March 1937, Eden told the foreign policy committee that the prospects of a general settlement with Germany 'were very small'.[34] In the spring of 1937, it was difficult to be optimistic about the prospects of improved Anglo-German relations.

The foreign office was strong on outlining the dangers of Nazi Germany but could not decide whether offering Germany colonies or economic aid might improve relations. No coherent policy had emerged to deal with the Hitler peril except to continue to 'search for peace' and keep the dictators guessing about whether Britain would use force. The dominant themes of British foreign policy from 1918 to 1937 – conciliation and compromise – still prevailed on the eve of Baldwin's resignation as prime minister in May 1937. By and large, British foreign policy in 1937 still remained a diplomacy without arms in a dangerous world situation. Without arms, Britain had to hold the situation and this involved either passive or active acceptance of treaty revision or some active attempt to halt military aggression by force.

It was widely appreciated by British policy makers that the system built at Versailles was designed for co-operative nations, not antagonistic ones. By May 1937, the world order established at Versailles had virtually collapsed, and the revisionists held the military initiative. A set of difficult decisions faced Neville Chamberlain, the new prime minister. It was very difficult for British foreign policy makers to contemplate an integrated policy of deterrence and alliances. It would have seemed an admission of defeat and a return to past failures. It is only by understanding this essential fact that Chamberlain's conduct of foreign policy from 1937 to 1939 becomes intelligible.

## Notes

1   *The Times*, 12 December 1918.

2   W. S. Churchill, *Thoughts and Adventures* (New York, 1952), p. 60.

3   J. M. Keynes, *The Economic Consequences of the Peace* (London, 1920).

4   M. Gilbert, *The Roots of Appeasement* (London, 1966), pp. 189–96.

5   A. Sharp, 'Britain and the Channel Tunnel 1919–1920', *Australian Journal of Politics and History* (1979), p. 210.

6   Gilbert, *Appeasement*, p. xi.

7   Cabinet papers (Public Record Office), Reports of imperical conferences before 1939, imperial conference, October 1923.

8   Gilbert, *Appeasement*, p. 112.

9   C. T. Emerson, *The Rhineland Crisis, 7 March 1936, A Study in Multilateral Diplomacy* (London, 1977), p. 24.

10   Gilbert, *Appeasement*, p. 106.

11   MacDonald to Herriot, 10 October 1932. Quoted in A. Adamthwaite, *The Making of the Second World War* (London, 1979, 2nd edn), pp. 113–14.

12   *Ibid.*, p. 37.

13   I. Colvin, *Vansittart in Office* (London, 1965), p. 19.

14   Gilbert, *Appeasement*, p. 139.

15   M. Gilbert, *Britain and Germany Between the Wars* (London, 1964), p. 76.

16   R. A. C. Parker, *Chamberlain and Appeasement: British Policy and the Coming of the Second World War* (London, 1993), p. 18.

17   E. L. Woodward and R. Butler (eds), *Documents on British Foreign Policy*, third series (London, 1949–57) (hereafter *DBFP*), vol. 21, no. 654.

18   N. Rose, *Vansittart. Study of a Diplomat* (London, 1978), p. 165.

19   Earl of Avon, *Facing the Dictators* (London, 1962), p. 255.

20   *The Times*, 12 September 1935.

21   Parker, *Appeasement*, p. 52.

22   *DBFP*, vol. 15, no. 460.

23   Cabinet foreign policy committee, minutes and memoranda (Public Record Office) (hereafter CAB 27), 3 February 1936.

24   Parker, *Appeasement*, p. 61.

25   R. Kee, *Munich, The Eleventh Hour* (London, 1988), pp. 83–4.

26   This remark was reportedly made by Sir Anthony Eden's taxi driver – not exactly the man on the Clapham omnibus, but the nearest thing to it.

27   *Hansard*, 26 March 1936.

28   G. C. Bowers, *My Mission to Spain* (London, 1954), p. 281.

29   A. R. Peters, *Anthony Eden at the Foreign Office 1931–1938* (Aldershot, 1986), p. 235.

30   Cabinet minutes (Public Record Office) (hereafter CAB 23), cabinet meeting, 6 July 1936.

**31**  Parker, *Appeasement*, pp. 70–1.
**32**  *DBFP*, vol. 17, appendix 2.
**33**  *Hansard*, 19 January 1937, cols 93–108.
**34**  *DBFP*, vol. 17, no. 307.

# 3

# National defence

Military force plays a crucial role in the type of foreign policy a nation follows. This is certainly true for any nation contemplating war. It seems clear that the poor state of Britain's military forces had some influence on the policy of appeasement. However, it is unwise to believe the weakness of Britain's forces alone dictated a conciliatory stance. The relationship between military strength and appeasement is extremely complex. Economic resources and political considerations also played important roles in influencing the pace of the rearmament programme.

British military weakness in the 1930s can be traced back to the impact of the First World War. This led to a disenchantment with the use of military force. Finding peaceful solutions to international conflict became a central aim of British policy. In 1919, Lloyd George informed British military chiefs to plan defence spending on the assumption that no major war would occur for ten years. This 'ten-year rule' was in force until 1932. It was accompanied by a dramatic fall in defence expenditure. In 1913, 30 per cent of British government expenditure went on defence, but in 1933 a mere 10 per cent was set aside for military spending.

In such circumstances, Britain's forces were diminished in terms of equipment and strength. The key to British security from invasion was the Royal Navy, which remained one of the most powerful fleets in the world. Yet the world-wide commitments of the fleet were enormous. Battleships, cruisers and submarines were growing old and naval disarmament agreements had led to a further decline in British naval power. In this respect, two key disarmament agreements effectively ended the historic supremacy of the Royal Navy. The Washington naval agreement (1922) pronounced that all battleships under construction must be scrapped and that no new ones should be brought into service for ten years. Moreover, Britain agreed to maintain parity with the United States in the building of battleships and a margin of five to three in the same class of vessel over Japan, the third largest naval power. By the terms of the London naval agreement (1930) the Royal Navy reduced its cruisers from seventy to fifty and strict limits were imposed on the tonnage and armaments of submarines and aircraft carriers. A few battleships were scrapped, but no new construction of battleships, the so-called naval holiday, was ordered for five years. These agreements left the navy with a large but relatively out-of-date fleet. Even so, Basil Liddell Hart, a leading military expert, recalled that naval chiefs were the most important influence over national defence during the inter-war period.[1]

The role of the army was always a secondary consideration in British strategic planning. The maintenance of a large army was seen as beyond the pale of the British way of life. Only during the First World War did Britain maintain a substantial land army. At the end of the war, the army was restored to its age-old position as the 'Cinderella service'. In 1933 it numbered less than 400,000 troops, with over 75 per cent of its fighting strength devoted to the defence of the empire. Spending on the army was reduced greatly after 1918. Equipment and tactics were not updated, especially in the area of tank warfare, and the needs of the army were given the lowest priority in national defence. The creation of a vast continental-style army to fight in a future European war was hardly considered. Leading army chiefs supported the doctrine of 'limited liability' for the army in any future conflict. In effect, this meant no commitment to send a large army to fight in support of France. The chiefs of staff suggested Britain should concentrate its future war planning on the use of naval and air power. No one wanted a repeat of the high casualty rates suffered by the British army in the First World War.

The Royal Air Force (RAF), set up in April 1918, was the newest of the three services. In 1921, Giulio Douhet, an Italian military expert, wrote a portentous book which suggested that the air bombardment of civilian and military targets could deliver 'a knock-out blow' in a future war.[2] Hugh Trenchard, RAF chief of staff, made similar claims. The emphasis in RAF planning was to use air power as a deterrent to a potential aggressor through the building of bomber aircraft. This 'doctrine of deterrence' held that the RAF could bomb the enemy into submission in a few weeks. Of course, this was a view which chimed in nicely with the existing desire of the army chiefs to avoid a major infantry commitment to France. During the 1920s, with Germany disarmed and little prospect of war, the RAF was a very small organisation, primarily used for policing far and distant outposts of the empire. In 1919, the British government had refused to assign £21 million to create a home-based air force. This lack of urgency meant that by 1932 the RAF was only the fifth largest of the few air forces in the world. Yet the fear of bombing of civilians remained extremely powerful. 'I think it is well for the man in the street to realise,' Baldwin told the Commons in 1932, 'that no power on earth can protect him from being bombed. Whatever people may tell him, the bomber will always get through'.[3] This fear grew during the 1930s. In 1938, spending on the RAF was the highest priority of national defence.

The arrival of Hitler to power in 1933 slowly led to a more realistic approach to the poor condition of Britain's military forces. In March 1933, Baldwin claimed only two things frightened him: 'air attack and a rearmed Germany'.[4] Alarm bells rang when Germany withdrew from the world disarmament conference and the League of Nations. In November 1933, MacDonald created the defence requirements committee (DRC), composed of the chiefs of staff under the chairmanship of Sir Maurice Hankey, permanent secretary to the cabinet, with the aim of considering the scale and priorities of national defence. The first report of the DRC, published in February 1934, pinpointed Germany as the most likely opponent for Britain in a future European war and recommended a £70 million programme to improve national defence over a five-year period. The lion's share of this was devoted to the creation of seventy-five RAF squadrons for home defence, and an extra £19 million was given to the army. A decision on future naval expenditure was postponed in the hope of securing further limitation agreements with the United States and Japan.

In the early years of Hitler's rule, appeasement combined a modest increase in spending on the RAF with a search for arms limitations agreements. In March 1935, Baldwin said, 'This country shall no longer be in a position inferior to any country within striking distance of these shores.'[5] At sea, it was hoped Japan and Germany might agree to new limits on naval building. In April 1935, the chiefs of staff sub-committee of the committee of imperial defence (CID) warned that 'The international situation is one of instability and gives rise to constant anxiety', and they recommended a policy of seeking conciliation with Japan and Germany and improving spending on the RAF and the navy.[6] On 4 March 1935, the national government published the white paper *Statement Relating to Defence*. This was the starting point of British rearmament during the 1930s.

After March 1935, when Hitler announced German plans to rearm, the issue of rearmament began to dominate government discussions of the international situation. In November 1935, the DRC produced a secret report on the condition and requirements of Britain's national defence. It revealed an outdated navy, no longer able to defend Europe and the empire, an army so small and poorly equipped in tanks and artillery it could not hope to aid France in the event of a German assault, and an air force with few long-range bombers or modern fighters and no anti-aircraft weapons. The report blamed faith in the League of Nations, excessive cuts in defence expenditure and the general public mood against rearmament for this gloomy picture. It concluded that Britain was not only incapable of defeating a combination of Germany, Italy and Japan in a future war, but incapable of defending British cities from a German air attack. The government was advised to increase defence expenditure on the armed forces, especially on air defence, and make strenuous diplomatic efforts to avoid a situation arising whereby Britain was confronted with a combination of Germany, Italy and Japan.[7]

In all these discussions, defence chiefs urged the maintenance of British diplomatic independence and did not consider military staff talks with any other nation. No detailed military discussions concerning strategy between Britain and France were undertaken before 1939. Nor were plans made to fit British strategy within the framework of collective security through the League of Nations. By evaluating national defence through this isolationist prism, the defence chiefs were always comparing the poor condition of Britain's defence forces with more powerful rivals and nearly always excluding the benefits of potential allies or League members.

In such circumstances, offering concessions to Germany appeared a logical, sensible and justifiable policy.

It is clear British rearmament started too late and lacked the level of spending and the industrial capacity needed for an effective deterrent to Germany. The navy depended on steel and shipbuilding, two industries deeply damaged by the depression. There was a disparity between the populations of Britain and Germany. In 1935, the German population was 67 million, compared with the British figure of 47 million. The chances of Britain winning an arms race were not very high.

Skills in the British economy, especially in engineering, steel and machine tools, were in very short supply. Unemployment among skilled workers in the engineering industry was much lower than the national average and the majority of the unemployed had skills previously useful for defence but now applicable only in outdated industries. When the naval building programme began in 1936, there was a dire shortage of skilled workers. This meant that expansion of the armaments industry was dependent on poaching skilled workers from a domestic economy already experiencing difficulties in recovering from the depression.

The aircraft industry was extremely small when rearmament began. New plant and machinery had to be built, largely with government aid, before production could hope to increase. The army was in an even worse position because munitions factories had closed down after the First World War. By 1935, only one major arms manufacturer, Vickers-Armstrong, was still in business.[8]

It also proved difficult to gain the agreement of trade unions to establish new working practices to expand armament production quickly. The Trades Union Congress (TUC) opposed the idea of industrial conscription in peacetime. Thus, population size, the level of skill in the British workforce, the lack of a modern arms industry and the attitude of organised labour all combined to make rearmament a slow process. There was no quick fix to Britain's military weaknesses. This threw a heavy burden on diplomacy to buy time and reduce tension.[9]

In January 1936, Baldwin chaired a ministerial-level defence policy requirements committee, which met on nine occasions to hammer out a comprehensive rearmament programme. In February 1936, the British government finally agreed on a five-year programme of rearmament at a cost, finally estimated at £400 million

over five years, but the actual additional money spent on rearmament above the level of 1935–36 was £50 million for 1936–37.[10] It
was a late and hesitant start as Britain already lagged way behind
Germany, especially in air defence.

Chamberlain, chancellor of the exchequer from 1931 to 1937,
helped to starve the armed forces of cash. In June 1934, for example,
Chamberlain reduced the spending recommendations of the chiefs
of staff from £76 million to £50 million. In 1936, Chamberlain,
though convinced of the need to rearm, was not anxious to spend
untold millions upon it. The Treasury was equally concerned that
excessive spending on rearmament would hamper the green shoots
of economic recovery. This led Chamberlain and his Treasury
officials to urge the cheapest possible rearmament programme
which, of course, ruled out a large continental commitment.[11]

In the memoirs of the service chiefs, Chamberlain's opposition to
swift rearmament looms large. Similarly, cabinet minutes reveal that
Chamberlain wanted increased arms expenditure not to interfere
with the domestic economy (the 'fourth arm of defence') or be
larger 'than public opinion was anticipating'.[12] In 1936, most of the
new defence expenditure was devoted to the RAF, primarily to
increase offensive bomber capacity, to act as a deterrent to any
foreign power contemplating an air attack on the British Isles. The
doctrine of deterrence was based on the idea of the RAF being able
to inflict substantial damage on potential enemies. The government
hoped to demonstrate to the public that some attempt was being
made to protect against the horror of a knock-out blow being
inflicted on British cities by enemy aircraft.[13] For the navy, one
aircraft carrier and two battleships were to be commissioned and
cruiser strength was to be increased. The army was to undergo
some belated modernisation, with four new battalions added, but
on the whole did very badly from the new spending proposals. A
request by the army general staff to create a five-division regular
army, fully equipped, supplemented by a twelve-division territorial
force, was firmly rejected.

It was Chamberlain's argument, namely that the 'political temper
of people in this country is strongly opposed to continental
adventures' and preferred a 'strong offensive air force', which
carried the day. It took the intervention of Baldwin, supported by
Duff Cooper, secretary of state for war, to save any continental
commitment at all. This consisted of four infantry battalions and

one armoured division. In 1936, only two fully equipped divisions were actually in any condition to fight in Europe. A few weeks after the rearmament programme was announced, Baldwin appointed Sir Thomas Inskip, the attorney general, as minister for the co-ordination of national defence. One Tory MP described Inskip's appointment as 'the most cynical thing that has been done since Caligula appointed his horse a consul'.[14]

Quite clearly, the rearmament programme would not produce results quickly. In the meantime, the prognosis of the chiefs of staff about the German threat grew increasingly pessimistic.[15] Their report on the prospects of war with Germany written in the autumn of 1936 claimed Britain had to resist a 'knock-out blow' by the German air force to stand any chance of victory. The air chiefs gloomily, and quite wrongly, predicted 150,000 casualties in London alone during the first week of hostilities and urged the government to organise diplomacy to reduce the number of Britain's potential enemies.

Further economic pressure from the Treasury meant defence expenditure remained within strict limits. A stable economy, consisting of a strong pound, low inflation, a balance-of-trade surplus and healthy gold reserves, was seen as essential in a long war. In a 'total war' it was believed the strongest economy would ultimately prevail. In February 1937, a government white paper estimated total expenditure on rearmament would be £1.5 billion over five years and suggested this was placing enormous strain on the economy.

In May 1937, when Chamberlain became prime minister, he sought to develop a clear set of spending priorities for each of the areas of national defence. It seems his ideas were influenced, to some degree, by Basil Liddell Hart's book, *Europe in Arms*, which suggested that in the First World War a defensive ground army in the trenches had proved far superior to an offensive army that attempted futile attacks, resulting in large numbers of casualties. This doctrine of defence, which appealed to Chamberlain, implied that any attacking army would need a three-to-one advantage in numbers to stand any chance of victory. This belief led Chamberlain to think that a French army could hold a German assault virtually alone, while Britain could concentrate its war effort on mounting a naval blockade and building up its air strength. It seems Chamberlain recommended Liddell Hart's book to Hore-Belisha, Duff

Cooper's replacement as secretary of state for war, in October 1937. The desire for a more defensive strategy was also supported by the Treasury. In July 1937, Sir John Simon, chancellor of the exchequer, reported that unless rearmament spending was not rationed within a clear set of spending priorities for the three services, then economic stability was likely to be seriously threatened.

One of Chamberlain's first acts as prime minister was to ask the defence policy requirements committee, under the chairmanship of Inskip, to sketch out a clear set of spending priorities, in order to keep within the five-year £1.5 billion limit set by the Treasury. Of this figure, £1.1 billion was financed through increased taxation and £400 million financed out of government borrowing. As total government expenditure in 1936–37 was £796.9 million, the proposed figures were extremely large.[16]

The first Inskip report, presented to the cabinet in December 1937 and agreed in February 1938, was designed to make the best use of existing defence expenditure without placing intolerable pressure on the economy. It increased the rearmament programme to £1.57 billion over five years, with a further £80 million added for air-raid precautions. The four major priorities laid down by Inskip in rank order were: the direct defence of the British Isles from attack; the maintenance of sea lanes and trade routes; defence of the empire; and the co-operation of any allies 'we may have in war'.[17]

The military strategy implied by the Inskip report was insular and defensive. It confirmed that army spending would remain the lowest priority of all. The previous commitment to send five divisions to France within two weeks of the start of war was abandoned. Only two divisions would be sent, not to France but to Egypt – on 'imperial duties'. This meant France would have to fight virtually alone at the onset of war. In fact, spending on the army was so small that in October 1938 there were not even two fully equipped divisions to send anywhere.

The navy did much better from the Inskip report, being allowed enough additional spending to create a 'new standard fleet', designed to match Japan in the far east and defend home waters. By 1939, six aircraft carriers, five battleships, twenty-one cruisers and fifty destroyers were under construction. Inskip recommended concentrating expenditure on improving one service rather than spreading expenditure over three inadequate services, and the service given the greatest priority by Inskip was the RAF. However, the strategy of the RAF was also dramatically altered, much to the annoyance of air chiefs and Lord Swinton, the air minister. It is worth recalling that in the original rearmament programme, of March 1936, the emphasis was on building bomber aircraft to act as an offensive weapon. But bombers were four times more expensive to build than defensive fighter planes such the Hurricane and the Spitfire. Inskip argued the RAF could not effectively achieve a knock-out blow against Germany and should concentrate its efforts purely on defence. Sir Cyril Newall, chief of the air staff, suggested the Inskip report was using economic arguments to alter the actual defence strategy of the RAF. The cabinet decided to accept the Inskip report and rejected the strategy of the air staff. Acceptance of the Inskip doctrine confirmed that the RAF was preparing for a battle of survival.

As events moved on in the tense European situation from 1937 to 1939, the British government was repeatedly forced to accelerate the pace of the rearmament programme. Munich may have prevented war but it revealed serious deficiencies in national defence. Chamberlain was forced to concede to Halifax, then foreign secretary, in an off-guard moment on his way home from Germany, 'We must hope for the best, but prepare for the worst'. But in a speech to the House of Commons a few days later, Chamberlain made no mention of the need to prepare for the worst. In fact, he found it difficult to understand why the Munich agreement was seen by defence chiefs and his opponents as an opportunity to 'add to our rearmament programmes'.[18] Halifax took a different view and felt Munich had clearly revealed 'the unwisdom of having a foreign policy with insufficient armed strength'.[19] He supported the desires of the chiefs of staff for greater urgency to be injected into the rearmament programme.

In October 1938, new demands were made by the chiefs of staff to make more war preparations. The navy called for increased spending on small vessels to improve the defence of merchant shipping. However, the actual preparations to defend British trade or for an economic blockade of Germany were practically non-existent. Between 1919 and 1939, not one single British naval exercise to prepare for the protection of a merchant convoy against submarine or air attack ever took place.[20]

The war office urged Chamberlain to create six divisions to aid France, but this proposal was rejected and new spending was granted only for anti-aircraft weaponry and new equipment. The air ministry believed Britain was vulnerable to air attack and requested a further increase in the number of fighter aircraft. These new proposals, agreed by the cabinet in October 1938, increased the overall cost of the rearmament programme to £2.1 billion, of which £900 million was covered by borrowing.

During these discussions, Chamberlain still suggested that 'the burden of armaments might break our backs', but accepted the majority view that new expenditure, especially on the RAF, had to be supported. The economic arguments against excessive expenditure were still put to the cabinet by Chamberlain and Simon after Munich, but they started to carry much less weight. British policy was underpinned by real military preparations for war in late 1938, but Chamberlain still hoped war could be prevented by diplomacy. In January 1939, Hore-Belisha, the war minister, supported by the chiefs of staff and the majority of the cabinet, urged a change in the role of the army. In February 1939, the British government decided to raise the total strength of the army to four times its current strength and promised to prepare nineteen infantry and two cavalry divisions for the defence of France. This was the first time since the end of the First World War that a British government had opted to prepare a major land army to aid France in the style of 1914–18.

Spending on rearmament in 1939 amounted to 21.4 per cent of gross national product (GNP), compared with 8.1 per cent in 1938. This sort of expenditure did put great strain on the economy. In June 1939, Britain's gold reserves fell to £300 million, which represented a drop of £800 million from April 1938, and the pound fell in the same period from $5.02 to $4.67, thus pushing up the price of imports. By 1940, Britain was spending 51.7 per cent of GNP on armaments compared with the 38 per cent of Nazi Germany. In September 1939, Britain's aircraft production actually overtook that of Nazi Germany. Yet by the end of 1940, US financial assistance was desperately required to sustain the British war effort. This tends to suggest the British economy was never really prepared for the long struggle to which the Treasury thought it was best suited.

Quite clearly, the poor state of Britain's armed forces greatly influenced appeasement. It often justified it and helped gain support for it, but did not determine it. The military preparations which Britain embarked upon in 1936 still placed the emphasis on requiring a diplomatic rather than a military solution. Chamberlain did support rearmament but consistently felt it should be kept within the limits of a peacetime economy. He also supported a set of spending priorities which placed financial strength, naval power and air defence above all-out rearmament,

Up until Munich, Chamberlain pursued a military strategy which was increasingly defensive and insular. Diplomacy with Germany and Italy took on a far greater priority than preparing for the worst. This was a decision taken by the politicians, not the military, although they often justified it. This was essentially a defence strategy, dependent on conciliatory diplomacy, and it changed only through the pressure of events. In the end, Chamberlain's military strategy necessarily involved a type of 'phoney war' – wholly defensive – which his decisions as prime minister had largely encouraged and determined. It was a war designed to keep up economic pressure on Germany while building up armaments, which he hoped would never be used, and to 'take no offensive unless Hitler begins it.'[21] In fact, the military strategy, championed by Chamberlain – especially before Munich – defined national security in purely defensive terms and placed a heavy burden on diplomacy.

### Notes

1  B. Liddell Hart, *The Memoirs of Captain Liddell Hart*, vol. 1 (London, 1965), pp. 325–6.

2  G. Douhet, *The Command of the Air* (English translation) (London, 1943).

3  *Hansard*, 10 November 1932, col. 632.

4  R. J. Q. Adams, *British Politics and Foreign Policy in the Age of Appeasement, 1935–39* (Stanford, 1993), p. 18.

5  U. Bialer, *The Shadow of the Bomber: The Fear of Air Attack and British Politics, 1932–1939* (London, 1980), p. 46.

6  Chiefs of staff sub-committee minutes (PRO, London) (hereafter CAB 53), Report of the chiefs of staff sub-committee, 29 April 1935.

7  Cabinet memoranda (PRO, London) (hereafter CAB 24), defence policy requirements committee, third report, November 1935.

8  See M. Postan, *British War Production* (London, 1952).

9  CAB 23, cabinet meeting, 22 December 1937.

10  Treasury papers (PRO, London) (hereafter T) 161/999/S.46095, 'Defence expenditure before and during the present war', 1940.

11   See F. Coghlan, 'Armaments, Economic Policy and Appeasement: Background to British Foreign Policy 1931–37', *History* (1972); G. C. Peden, *British Rearmament and the Treasury, 1932–1939* (Edinburgh, 1979).

12   R. A. C. Parker, *Chamberlain and Appeasement: British Policy and the Coming of the Second World War* (London, 1993), p. 275.

13   Bialer, *Shadow of the Bomber*, pp. 44–8.

14   M. Gilbert, *Winston S. Churchill, Vol. V: The Prophet of Truth, 1922–1939* (London, 1976), p. 716. The reason for the attack on Inskip was that he had a legal background – and no military experience.

15   See D. Dilks, 'The Unnecessary War? Military Advice and Foreign Policy in Great Britain 1931–39', in A. Preston (ed.), *General Staffs and Diplomacy before the Second World War* (London, 1978).

16   CAB 23, cabinet meeting, 22 December 1937.

17   See Adams, *Appeasement*, pp. 58–64.

18   CAB 23, cabinet meeting, 31 October 1938.

19   J. Charmley, *Chamberlain and the Lost Peace* (London, 1989), p. 144.

20   S. Roskill, *Naval Policy Between the War, 1919–1939,* vol. II (London, 1976), p. 536.

21   Charmley, *Chamberlain*, p. 210.

# 4

# Chamberlain's new direction,
# May 1937–February 1938

Neville Chamberlain became prime minister on 28 May 1937. His personality and foreign policy actions are so crucial for understanding why Britain went to war they must be examined in some detail. He was born in Birmingham in 1869, the eldest son of Joseph Chamberlain, the famous Victorian Tory radical and imperialist, whom he 'respected and feared more than loved',[1] and Florence Kenrick, who died in 1875, when he was just six years of age. He was brought up a Unitarian,[2] attended Rugby public school, but not university, and embarked on a career in business and local politics. He spent six miserable years in the Bahamas on a failed sisal-growing enterprise before returning to Birmingham, where he worked in business and rose in local politics to become what Lloyd George claimed was: 'Not a bad Lord Mayor of Birmingham in a bad year'. He was forty when he married Ann de Vere Cole, who warmed to his aloof exterior, but who later suffered bouts of depression.

Neville Chamberlain's career in national politics did not begin until the comparatively late age of forty-nine, when he was elected Conservative MP for Birmingham Ladywood.[3] There is little doubt that Chamberlain's career was helped by the fall of Lloyd George in 1922, who disliked him (because he had proved ineffective as director of national service, a post offered to him by the prime minister during the war), and aided by Baldwin, who respected him and guided his rise when the Conservative Party finally regained its independence from the coalition under Lloyd George. As minister for health, from 1924 to 1929, he made a notable impact in the area of social reform. As chancellor of the exchequer, from 1931 to 1937, he was dubbed the man who had dragged Britain out of the depression.

He was five feet ten inches tall, thin, with a moustache. He wore dark, sensible suits, starched collars on his shirts and when he appeared in public always carried a trusty umbrella. On a personal level, he was a serious, shy and private man – seldom flippant or light-hearted, who considered himself a typical Englishman with brains and common sense. He was not anti-social, but he chose his political allies, friends and social activities with care. His hobbies confirm his image as a reliable, sober and dedicated person. He loved classical art and music, disliked the opera and was no great lover of the theatre. His favourite hobbies were solitary ones: observing birds, walking his dog Spot, fly fishing, keeping a daily diary and writing regular letters, especially to his sisters – Hilda and Ida. These letters show affection, a great deal of pride, obstinacy and streaks of vanity. His diary reveals someone who disliked sloppy sentiment, believed strongly in the policies he supported and lacked the capacity for self-criticism.[4]

In fact, Neville Chamberlain belies his traditional image as a weak and cowardly politician. It is important to recognise the reverse was true. Chamberlain was a strong-willed, intelligent and clear-sighted political tactician, who followed a foreign policy he was convinced was not only the right one but vastly superior to any of the alternatives. He sometimes wrestled with private doubts and uncertainties, but it was a confident, even obstinate, belief he was right which determined his actions.

Few prime ministers have dominated the cabinet with such supreme managerial and tactical skill. The minutes of cabinet from 1937 to 1939 reveal how Chamberlain carefully managed, manipulated and skilfully persuaded its members to turn his own views into an agreed policy.[5] Each cabinet minister was allowed to express an opinion, but the greatest weight was given to the views expressed in carefully tailored reports drawn up by the chiefs of staff, the Treasury and various defence committees, which usually fitted in with, and very often justified, Chamberlain's own preferred course. He could nearly always count on support from certain trusted cabinet ministers, particularly Lord Halifax, a shrewd conciliator, and Hoare and Simon, both ex-foreign secretaries, who were skilled in debate. Even when the cabinet sought to tie

Chamberlain down, which was exceedingly rare, he nearly always managed to wriggle free and follow his own judgement. At the outset, most of the cabinet supported his foreign policy, but, as events unfolded, doubts grew, and Chamberlain showed he was prepared to go much further in seeking peace than most of his cabinet colleagues would have done.

In many ways, it was Chamberlain's strength of will, his single-minded conviction, his management skills and obstinate persistence which allowed him to exert such a remarkable influence over events. The formal and informal methods Chamberlain favoured to achieve his foreign policy aims gave that policy a remarkably personal imprint. Chamberlain often did things and said things to foreign leaders, diplomats and semi-official contacts which had not been discussed with the cabinet, the foreign office or with the foreign secretary beforehand.

Chamberlain believed international differences could be solved by face-to-face negotiations. His faith in his own negotiating skill, honed in domestic politics and business, meant he often ignored career diplomats, disregarded foreign office advice and dismissed views at odds with his own. Lord Strang, a foreign office official, reckoned Chamberlain had a 'naive confidence in his own judgement and powers of persuasion' which most of the foreign office thought was misplaced.[6]

When Chamberlain took office he had clear views about the state of international relations, and felt British policy was drifting aimlessly when Europe had clearly entered a dangerous period. He believed the appeasement of the dictators was the policy most likely to prevent war. In Chamberlain's view, 'war wins nothing, cures nothing and ends nothing' and finding a solution to the difficulties causing tension in the hope of establishing lasting peace was his central objective.[7] He saw the likely allies of Britain in any future war as unreliable or unwanted and he wished to avoid alliances or the creation of ideological blocs. This meant he opposed an Anglo-French alliance and believed the US government was wedded to isolationism. As a lifelong anti-communist, he ruled out an Anglo-Soviet alliance.

Chamberlain also believed British politicians should 'stop parroting that we believe in the League Nations and the policy of collective security,' as he felt 'the League has failed to stop war, or protect the victim,' and it was to play no major role in his foreign policy.[8] In place of alliances and upholding the principles of the League, Chamberlain wanted Britain to act as a 'mediator and conciliator' and take a decisive role in the creation of a new system of regional pacts, similar to Locarno, which isolated danger spots and resolved them by peaceful and mutual agreement. Once this was completed, Chamberlain hoped to gain a general settlement of all European issues.[9]

The most pressing aim, however, was to get on better terms with the dictator states. In May 1937, it was clear that major territorial changes in Europe were likely to occur before rearmament was complete.[10] Yet Chamberlain did not believe this process would inevitably produce war. To the contrary, Chamberlain did not believe that Hitler aimed to dominate Europe by force, but believed his final aim was to create a racially united Germany by revising the treaty of Versailles. Thus, Chamberlain thought all that was required to relieve tension was to 'sit down at a table with the Germans and run through all their complaints with a pencil'. Another factor underlying his peace mission was the advice from the chiefs of staff, who suggested that foreign policy should aim to prevent Britain having to face a combination of Germany, Italy and Japan simultaneously.

The biggest obstacle to what Chamberlain described as a 'general scheme of appeasement', which in the short term meant appeasing Hitler and Mussolini, was the foreign office. When Chamberlain spoke of the foreign office, he often meant the influential views of Vansittart, the permanent under-secretary, who thought in power political terms and was pessimistic about the likely success of any appeasement policy aimed at the dictators. 'Van' believed Hitler was an extremist with vast territorial aims in Europe and 'very unlikely to participate in a negotiated political settlement of European problems'.[11] In such circumstances, Vansittart believed that any efforts to appease Hitler or Mussolini should be delayed 'until we are strong enough to talk'.[12]

To counteract this negative advice, Chamberlain created an informal 'inner group' of advisers, including: Sir Horace Wilson, his chief industrial adviser, who became an important sounding board, a sort of personal diplomatic envoy; Sir Joseph Ball, from the Conservative research department, who ran the Downing Street press office and wrote many of Chamberlain's foreign policy speeches; Lord Halifax, a born and bred conciliator, although as events unfolded he proved to have a strong will of his own; 'Rab' Butler, parliamentary under-secretary on foreign affairs under Halifax; Simon, the chancellor; Hoare, the home secretary (the last two proving effective and loyal supporters in cabinet); Sir Warren Fisher, who gave energetic support from the Treasury; and Neville Henderson, British ambassador in Berlin. What Chamberlain and his 'inner circle' shared was a desire to open fresh talks with Germany and Italy straightaway, but they all feared the foreign office might attempt to undermine these efforts.

In 1937, Japan presented the least immediate threat, as it was embroiled in war with China. It seems Chamberlain wished to solve tension in the Pacific in the long term, but actually gave the appeasement of Japan a very low priority. It was Germany which was regarded by Chamberlain as the primary target for the policy of appeasement. 'If only we could get on terms with the Germans,' Chamberlain told his sister, 'I would not care a rap for Musso'.[13] A chief objective in any new Anglo-German talks was 'to set out the political guarantees which we want from Germany as part of a general settlement; and if the discussions have to break down, we want the breakdown to be due to Germany's refusal to accept our reasonable requirements.'[14] The second major target for Chamberlain's appeasement was Italy. But the whole question of improving Anglo-Italian relations was problematic. Mussolini was moving closer to Nazi Germany, actively supporting Franco in the Spanish civil war, threatening British naval interests in the Mediterranean and was estranged from the League of Nations owing to his actions in Abyssinia.

There was a clear difference of opinion between the prime minister and the foreign office over the usefulness of improving Anglo-Italian relations. Sir Anthony Eden, foreign secretary, was convinced Mussolini was a 'gangster' who had shown persistent bad faith in all his dealings with the British government and he was not keen to open fresh talks,[15] but Chamberlain did and invited Count Grandi, the Italian ambassador, to Downing Street in July 1937 to discuss ways of improving relations. Grandi suggested that a personal appeal by Chamberlain to the Italian dictator might work. As a result, Chamberlain sent a friendly letter to Mussolini explaining his desire for a new understanding. The reply from Mussolini was conciliatory but there was no immediate improvement in relations. Chamberlain's letter angered Eden, who remained firmly opposed to striking a bargain with Mussolini which involved recognising Italian gains in Abyssinia. In August 1937, while Eden was away on holiday, a meeting of foreign office staff convened by Halifax agreed that the formal recognition of the Italian conquest in Abyssinia was probably the best way to improve Anglo-Italian relations. When Eden was told of this decision, he was displeased that an important foreign policy decision concerning Italy had been agreed behind his back.

On the issue of improving Anglo-German relations, Eden was much more accommodating but, in line with foreign office thinking, he was quite pessimistic about its likely success. 'Nothing could be more beneficial,' Eden told the cabinet in June 1937, 'than an improvement of Anglo-German relations, even if it is only temporary.'[16] It appears that, in the summer of 1937, Eden still believed Britain was in no position to uphold the territorial status quo in central and eastern Europe by force and needed to ensure future change came about by 'peaceful negotiation and consent'.[17] By July 1937, the cabinet had made an agreement with Germany the central goal of British foreign policy.[18]

The appointment of Sir Neville Henderson as British ambassador to Berlin also gave impetus to Chamberlain's drive for appeasement. Henderson was dubbed by foreign office critics as 'our Nazi Ambassador in Berlin'.[19] Almost as soon as he arrived in Berlin, Henderson was advising the foreign office to abandon its 'out dated theory' of maintaining the balance of power in Europe and to seek close friendship with Germany to restrain 'Russian intrigues and Italian aspirations'. In the autumn of 1937, moreover, Henderson advised the foreign office not to stand in the way of the *Anschluss*, nor prevent the peaceful incorporation of the Sudetenland into Germany, nor oppose the recovery of colonies. In November 1937, Henderson was told by Vansittart to give 'no encouragement whatsoever' to the idea that the British government would contemplate territorial concessions to Hitler in eastern Europe.[20] 'It was an international misfortune,' Eden later wrote, 'that we should have been represented in Berlin at this time by a man who, so far from warning the Nazis, was constantly making excuses for them.'[21]

The first real opportunity for face-to-face dialogue with the Nazi regime was offered to Halifax, who was invited by Prince Lowenstein, president of the German Hunting Association, to visit a hunting exhibition. Chamberlain saw the Halifax visit as an ideal opportunity to begin 'the far reaching plans I have in mind for the appeasement of Europe and Asia'.[22] Eden was surprised when first told of the visit[23] and he suspected, quite rightly, it was the product of collaboration between Henderson, Halifax and Chamberlain.[24] According to Henderson, the visit was 'designed by Chamberlain' as a means of establishing personal contact with the Nazi leaders *en route* to opening new talks.[25] A few days before his departure, Eden warned Halifax to confine any conversation with Hitler to 'a warning comment about Austria and Czechoslovakia'.[26]

Lord Halifax arrived in Berlin on 17 November 1937, determined to listen to the German point of view. In the manner of the English aristocrat abroad, he tried, with some difficulty, to blend in with the surroundings. As he got out of his car to meet Hitler at Berchtesgaden, he calmly and briefly mistook him for a footman. At the meeting, Halifax congratulated Hitler – who reportedly behaved 'like a spoilt sulky child' – for 'repulsing Bolshevism'. He found him 'sincere', but admitted 'we had a different set of values'. Halifax told the Nazi leader that British policy was not opposed to the 'peaceful evolution' of outstanding German grievances over Danzig, Austria and Czechoslovakia, provided they were achieved by methods which did not 'cause far reaching disturbances'.[27] In reply, Hitler said he was determined to crush Bolshevism, was not interested in disarmament, or returning to the League, and really wanted the British to give him a free hand to deal with problems in central and eastern Europe in his own way.

In his report of the meeting, Halifax concluded that 'The Germans had no policy of immediate adventure.... Nevertheless he would expect a beaver-like persistence in pressing their claims in Central Europe, but not in a form to give others cause – or probably occasion – to interfere'.[28] For Chamberlain, the visit was 'a great success because it achieved its object, that of creating an atmosphere in which it is possible to discuss the practical questions involved in a European settlement'. He further claimed that if Germany would agree to settle the Austrian and Czech problems by peaceful negotiation then Britain 'should accept such changes'.[29]

In December 1937, Eden gloomily predicted that the British government 'might have to acquiesce perforce in more than one *fait accompli* over German aims in central and eastern Europe'.[30] At the end of 1937, however, Eden and Chamberlain appeared to be moving in closer harmony on foreign policy.[31] This view is reinforced by two incidents which occurred in December 1937. On 23 December 1937, Eden expressed a willingness to put aside his personal dislike of Mussolini and consider finding a way to restore cordial relations. On 31 December 1937, Eden offered no objection to Chamberlain's decision to move Vansittart from his post as permanent under-secretary at the foreign office to the new and less influential post of chief diplomatic adviser. By this time, Vansittart felt increasingly divided from Eden and told him in a parting shot, 'I have to go. I don't like it. If I go, you won't last long'.[32] Chamberlain thought the removal of Vansittart, whose 'instincts were all against my policy', would make a great difference to the foreign office and help calm down 'Anthony's natural vibrations'.[33] Vansittart's replacement was Sir Alexander Cadogan, a figure recommended to Chamberlain by Eden.

As the enormously significant year of 1938 opened, Eden told Chamberlain in a very friendly tone, 'I do hope that you will never for an instant feel that any interest you take in foreign affairs, however close, could ever be resented by me'.[34] Only days later, Eden left for a holiday on the French Riviera and while he was away an incident occurred which provoked bitter conflict between him and the prime minister. Eden had long wanted to bring the United States into closer collaboration with Britain and France. In 1937, Eden had discussed with the US government the possibility of an Anglo-American trade agreement. However, Chamberlain felt that US public opinion was isolationist and he doubted whether Roosevelt could provide any real help to bring stability in Europe.

On 13 January 1938, Chamberlain was surprised to receive a personal letter from Roosevelt expressing concern about the deteriorating international situation and proposing a major international conference to establish 'generally agreed principles of international conduct'. Chamberlain said the letter contained 'preposterous proposals' and he decided, without consulting Eden, to reject its ideas because he felt the promise of a world conference would prompt derision in Italy and Germany, and delay 'full consideration of specific points which must be settled if appeasement is to be achieved'.[35]

It appears clear that Eden would have accepted the Roosevelt proposal outright. He felt the idea might be a useful means to test whether Hitler or Mussolini had any intention of participating in a new world order.[36] On his return from France, Eden was 'outraged and uneasy at the way in which this opportunity had been handled' by Chamberlain.[37] The whole incident left Eden with a feeling of being seriously at odds with the prime minister. In fact, Eden managed to secure a significant modification of Chamberlain's hostile attitude and kept Roosevelt's initiative on the table, but it was all for nothing. The US president, disappointed by Chamberlain's response, first delayed the announcement of his idea for a world conference and then dropped it, ostensibly to allow Chamberlain the opportunity to pursue his own new initiative of face-to-face negotiations.

In February 1938, news filtered through on the diplomatic grapevine from Berlin to London about Hitler's bullying of Schuschnigg, the Austrian leader, in a pretty obvious prelude to the conclusion of a union with Germany. Chamberlain's response was to investigate the prospects of offering colonial concessions to Germany in return for a peaceful settlement of the Austrian problem. By now, Eden was in no mood to smooth the path towards appeasement and he set out an extremely tough set of preconditions for opening talks with Nazi Germany, including a promise from Hitler to sign a new Locarno, a disarmament treaty and to return to the League, as well as being prepared to enter a negotiated settlement of the Austrian crisis and give a guarantee to Czechoslovakia.

Dismayed by this strong line, Chamberlain decided to open fresh talks with the Italian government. It appears that Chamberlain believed the Austrian crisis might help to bring Mussolini back into the British camp, but Eden was not so sure. He believed, quite rightly, that the fate of Austria was no longer a matter of importance to the Italian dictator. The situation was not helped by Chamberlain preferring the advice of Ivy Chamberlain, his widowed sister-in-law, resident in Rome, who optimistically predicted that Mussolini desired close Anglo-Italian cooperation, to the more pessimistic accounts from the foreign office.

On 18 February 1938, Chamberlain, accompanied by a very reluctant Eden, met Count Grandi in London, who refused to discuss the Italian position on Austria but did convey news of Mussolini's willingness to open fresh talks. The meeting was adjourned to allow Chamberlain and Eden to discuss this proposal. A furious and extremely bitter row ensued in which Eden expressed his firm view that Mussolini could not be trusted. The exchange ended with the Chamberlain shouting at his foreign secretary:

'Anthony, you have missed chance after chance. You simply cannot go on like this'.[38] Grandi, who witnessed this amazing scene, commented, 'Chamberlain and Eden were not a Prime Minister and a Foreign Secretary discussing with the Ambassador of the foreign power a delicate situation' but 'two enemies confronting each other, like two cocks in true fighting posture'.[39] It did not leave a good impression.

Over the next two days, emergency meetings of the cabinet took place to discuss the differences between Eden and Chamberlain over the question of opening new talks with Italy. It is apparent that Chamberlain, with the support of the majority of the cabinet, was determined to press ahead, but Eden was equally determined to resist. The wrangle at these cabinet meetings between Chamberlain and Eden was extremely acrimonious. Chamberlain argued that the failure to improve Anglo-Italian relations had encouraged Mussolini to move closer to Hitler. In reply, Eden questioned whether Mussolini seriously wanted an Anglo-Italian agreement, detailed on how many occasions Italy had disregarded the jurisdiction of the League of Nations and suggested it was likely that Mussolini had already agreed to the *Anschluss*. Except for Malcolm MacDonald, dominions secretary, and Walter Elliot, minister for health, the cabinet supported Chamberlain. On 20 February 1938, Sir Anthony Eden resigned.[40]

His dramatic resignation is a deeply significant moment in the development of foreign policy under Chamberlain. It is tempting to view it all as a clash of personalities – Chamberlain, the strong-willed and clear-sighted bureaucrat, versus Eden, the temperamental glamour boy with a chip on his shoulder.[41] In his resignation speech, Eden claimed there were 'fundamental differences', but Chamberlain rejected this charge and commented, 'I had no idea until the 18th. [February] that it would come to a break'.[42]

However, it is difficult to see the whole Chamberlain–Eden conflict as merely a personality clash over minor differences. A key part of the conflict was constitutional and political. It concerned the issue of whether foreign policy should result from a close collaboration between foreign secretary and prime minister, as Eden saw it, or whether the prime minister should undertake the major initiatives, sometimes in his absence, often involving intermediaries, sometimes without his knowledge, agreement or approval.[43] Differing political judgements about the international situation also played a part. Eden did not believe in February 1938 that appeasement could succeed as a form of crisis management which sought to 'buy temporary goodwill' by sacrificing principles, but only through a process of 'frank reciprocity and mutual respect'. Eden did not believe a cordial atmosphere existed between the democracies and the dictators in which any meaningful give and take could take place. He judged that these particular dictators were more than likely to prove unappeasable.[44] Eden and Chamberlain were also in disagreement about the pace of rearmament. Eden was concerned about the slowness of rearmament and he wanted the programme not to be so rigidly tied to financial restraints, but when Eden raised these objections directly with Chamberlain he was told to 'go home and take an aspirin'. By and large, Eden wanted to extend the number of Britain's potential friends and allies, as the passion he generated over the Roosevelt incident so graphically reveals, but Chamberlain wanted to reduce the number of potential enemies and concentrate exclusively on this mission. It was this overall difference in outlook which contributed to the development of the final rift.

### Notes

1  K. Feiling, *The Life of Neville Chamberlain* (London, 1946), p. 3.

2  Unitarianism valued its isolation from the orthodox Church of England. Before the nineteenth century, the Unitarians had been banned from public life for two centuries and tended to keep to themselves and developed their own teaching establishments. They strove for personal independence and strong willpower.

3  Chamberlain became an MP in 1918.

4  There are 1,200 letters to his sisters, but very few to his wife and children.

5  I. Colvin, *The Chamberlain Cabinet* (London, 1971).

6  Lord Strang, *Britain in World Affairs* (London, 1961), p. 321.

7  A. Bryant, *In Search of Peace* (London, 1939), p. 98.

8  Neville Chamberlain papers (University of Birmingham) (hereafter NC), Chamberlain diary, 27 April 1936.

9  Feiling, *Chamberlain*, p. 300.

10  *Ibid.*, p. 319.

11  R. A. C. Parker, *Chamberlain and Appeasement: British Policy and the Coming of the Second World War* (London, 1993), p. 153.

12   *Ibid.*, p. 97.

13   NC 18/1, Chamberlain to Ida Chamberlain, 4 July 1937.

14   CAB 27, cabinet memorandum, 2 April 1937.

15   A. Roberts, *The Holy Fox: A Biography of Lord Halifax* (London, 1991), p. 63.

16   *DBFP*, vol. 18, no. 566.

17   D. Carlton, *Anthony Eden* (London, 1981), pp. 102–5.

18   CAB 23, cabinet meeting, 7 July 1937.

19   *DBFP*, vol. 16, no. 16, Henderson to Eden, 5 July 1937.

20   J. Charmley, *Chamberlain and the Lost Peace* (London, 1989), pp. 6–14.

21   Earl of Avon, *Facing the Dictators* (London, 1962), p. 511.

22   NC 18/1, Chamberlain to Ida Chamberlain, 30 October 1937.

23   W. S. Churchill, *The Gathering Storm* (London, 1962, 2nd edn), p. 226.

24   J. Harvey (ed.), *The Diplomatic Diaries of Oliver Harvey, 1937–40* (London, 1970), pp. 57–9.

25   Foreign office, Avon papers (i.e. Sir Anthony Eden's papers) (PRO, London) (hereafter FO 954), 10A, Halifax to Eden, 27 October 1937.

26   Avon, *Dictators*, pp. 508–9.

27   Roberts, *Halifax*, p. 71.

28   CAB 23, cabinet meeting, 24 November 1937.

29   NC 18/1, Chamberlain to Ida Chamberlain, 26 November 1937.

30   Carlton, *Eden*, pp. 115–16.

31   Parker, *Appeasement*, p. 102.

32   I. Colvin, *Vansittart at the Foreign Office* (London, 1972), p. 172.

33   NC 18/1, Chamberlain to Ida Chamberlain, 12 December 1937.

34   Parker, *Appeasement*, p. 103.

35   A. R. Peters, *Anthony Eden at the Foreign Office 1931–1938* (Aldershot, 1986), p. 327.

36   Harvey, *Oliver Harvey*, p. 70.

37   Avon, *Dictators*, pp. 551–3.

38   Charmley, *Chamberlain*, p. 49.

39   M. Muggeride (ed.), *Ciano's Diplomatic Papers* (Oxford, 1948), pp. 164–84.

40   CAB 23, cabinet meeting, 19 February 1938.

41   Peters, *Eden*, conclusion.

42   NC 18/1, Chamberlain to Ida Chamberlain, 27 February 1938.

43   NC 7/11, Eden to Chamberlain, 9 January 1938.

44   Avon, *Dictators*, p. 576.

# 5

# The road to Munich,
# March–September 1938

The exit of Sir Anthony Eden certainly caused a political sensation but allowed Chamberlain to appoint Lord Halifax as foreign secretary. After the shock of Eden's resignation wore off, Chamberlain admitted that the ex-foreign secretary 'would never have been able to carry through the negotiations with any conviction',[1] and was soon professing great happiness in having 'a steady unruffled Foreign Secretary who never causes me any worry'.[2] Halifax was willing to support Chamberlain's diplomacy, not out of sycophancy but because he thought appeasement was a better alternative to an alliance or to the utopian ideals of collective security. As the Czech crisis developed, Halifax began to have doubts and was willing to express them. The respect which Chamberlain gave Halifax proved double edged. It was useful for Chamberlain to gain support from the cabinet for his policy, but when points of difference arose Halifax proved troublesome and showed that the most loyal colleagues can often prove the most politically dangerous when they decide to oppose.

In February 1938, however, the foreign secretary and prime minister were in harmony. The most immediate aim of the Chamberlain–Halifax team was to open talks for a settlement with Hitler. On 3 March 1938, the Nazi leader met Henderson and was offered a colonial settlement in return for a contribution to a restoration of tranquillity and confidence. In reply, Hitler claimed he could wait ten years for a return of colonies and did not want 'third parties' interfering with German policy. The reason soon became clear. On 12 March 1938, Hitler solved one 'danger spot' in his own unique style, by engineering the collapse of the Austrian government and ordering the Wehrmacht to march over the Austrian border. The union with Austria was achieved by bullying and intimidation, but without a single shot being fired. As Hitler rode in triumph through the streets of his 'beloved' Austria, Chamberlain was shocked and dismayed, but accepted the *Anschluss* as a *fait accompli*. 'The next question,' Chamberlain, told the cabinet, 'is how we prevent an occurrence of similar events in Czechoslovakia'.[3]

Czechoslovakia consisted of a number of diverse nationalities amalgamated into a multi-ethnic nation state by the peacemakers of 1919. It was one of the few democracies left in eastern Europe, led by Eduard Beneš. Yet conflict between different national groups was acute. Among these groups were approximately 3.5 million German speakers residing in a horseshoe-shaped area on the frontier with Germany and Austria, dubbed the Sudetenland. In October 1938, a Nazi-style Sudeten German Party was formed, led by Konrad Henlein, which gained financial support from Hitler and demanded greater autonomy for the region. It was clear after the *Anschluss* that Hitler would exploit the claims of Sudeten Party, and in collaboration with Henlein would seek to make demands upon the Czech government they could not possibly accept. On 24 April 1938, Henlein outlined his famous Karlsbad demands, which included the recognition of the Sudetenland as a zone of settlement and the right to profess membership 'in the German race and the German outlook in life' – in other words, complete autonomy from the Czech state. To raise the temperature further, Henlein told the Czech government there was no question of 'a peaceful solution within the framework of the Czech State.'[4]

The Czech government was prepared to offer concessions for greater autonomy in local government and to safeguard minority rights, but would not consider the kind of independence envisaged by the Karlsbad demands. After all, the Sudeten area was a border region with natural mountain defences and heavily defended fortifications, designed to prevent a German attack. However, it proved hard to deny that the Sudeten Germans had genuine grievances, which enabled Henlein to come to London in May 1938 and gain valuable support for the Sudeten case. On the other hand, the Czech government found it more difficult to arouse sympathy. Jan Masaryk, the Czech envoy in London, claimed he spent a great deal of energy trying to convince everyone Czechoslovakia was not a 'contagious disease'. But what really made the Czech crisis so important was the existence of the Franco-Czech alliance dating back to 1925 and a Czech pact of mutual assistance with France and the Soviet Union, which meant that if Germany attacked Czechoslovakia and France went to its aid, so would the Soviet Union and a European war would be the result.

In the light of this, Chamberlain believed the Czech crisis had to be resolved by negotiation. In March 1938, the cabinet discussed policy towards Czechoslovakia. During these discussions, it became clear most ministers did not see eastern Europe as a vital British interest. From the very beginning, Chamberlain saw Czechoslovakia as a sort of indefensible Humpty Dumpty state which, if Hitler wished to absorb it, was likely to fall and was very unlikely to be put back together again. 'You only have to look at the map,' he wrote in his diary, 'to see that nothing that France or we could possibly do could save Czechoslovakia from being overrun by the Germans if they wanted to do it'.[5] It seems clear that Chamberlain wanted to secure a peaceful solution and to win the French and the Czechs around to this position. First, Chamberlain had to convince the cabinet. He called on the chiefs of staff to examine the military implications of a German assault on Czechoslovakia, but advised them to exclude the Soviet Union from their calculations. Not surprisingly, the chiefs of staff produced a report which argued that German forces would defeat Czechoslovakia in weeks and could only be liberated, probably never again in its present form, by success in a long and bloody European war. Armed with this military evidence, Chamberlain easily gained cabinet support for his own position.[6] On 22 March 1938, Chamberlain summed up the agreed policy of the cabinet towards Czechoslovakia: 'We should endeavour to induce the government of Czechoslovakia to apply themselves to producing a direct settlement with the Sudeten Deutsch. We should persuade the French to use their influence to obtain such a settlement.' In other words, the British wanted the Czech government to solve these problems without the involvement of Germany. Underlying this policy were two key elements – Chamberlain's strong assumption that Britain should avoid fighting a European war for the honour of Czechoslovakia, and the desire to keep Hitler guessing about whether Britain would stand aside in the event of war over the issue.[7]

Despite outrage over the *Anschluss*, Chamberlain decided to broaden the scope of appeasement. In April 1938, an Anglo-Italian pact was signed which promised that neither country would increase naval or air strength in the Mediterranean and the Red Sea without agreement and that each power would discourage harmful propaganda. Britain further promised to support the recognition of the Italian conquest of Abyssinia. In return, Italy made a vague promise to remove troops from Spain, but the agreement was little more than polite words and was not implemented until November 1938.

Chamberlain took appeasement next in the direction of Ireland. In May 1938, the British government accepted the creation of the Republic of Ireland. Northern Ireland remained part of the United Kingdom, but other outstanding financial and trade issues were resolved, most notably an agreement to abandon a naval presence and trading rights in various Irish ports. This appeasement of Ireland was attacked by Churchill, who claimed it would mean a neutral Ireland in a future war, and make the naval defence of the Atlantic extremely difficult. For Chamberlain, the agreement gave powerful weight to his assertion that his policy was not selfishly aimed at the dictators. The offer of bank credit to Turkey served to add further weight to this assertion, as did the opening of negotiations for a trade agreement with the US government, which was signed later in the year.

But the most urgent problem remained the Czech crisis. On 28 April 1938, Édouard Daladier, the French prime minister, and Georges Bonnet, the French foreign minister, came to London. To Chamberlain's surprise, Daladier talked more like Napoleon than the leader of a deeply divided nation. He insisted German policy aimed to tear up treaties and fully intended to destroy the Czech state. In such circumstances, Daladier said what the French government really wanted was a determined policy by Britain and France to resist Hitler during the Czech crisis. Chamberlain described this view to Cadogan as 'Awful rubbish' and attempted to convince the French of the need to secure a negotiated settlement. It seems the French plan of action was not as tough as Daladier's words. The French cabinet and public opinion were bitterly divided about taking strong action over Czechoslovakia. This was especially true of Bonnet, a clear defeatist, who believed Britain and France could not 'sacrifice ten million in order to prevent 3½ million Sudetens joining the Reich'.[8]

The Czech crisis reached the first of many dangerous points in May 1938. It was reported that two Sudeten German motorcyclists had been shot dead by the Czech police. This led to rumours, largely inspired by the Czech government, of Hitler preparing to use the incident as a pretext for invasion. It is clear that the incident did not come out of the blue, but German evidence suggests there was no immediate plan for invasion. Even so, news whizzed around Europe of German troops assembling near the Czech border. The French and Soviet governments pledged support to the Czechs. Halifax sent a stiff message to Berlin which warned that if force was used Germany 'could not count upon this country being able to stand aside'. At the same time, Halifax also sent a diplomatic message which told the French they should not assume Britain would fight to save Czechoslovakia.[9] Because Hitler had no plans to attack, the crisis blew over. The two most important consequences of the 'May crisis' were: that it pushed the British government into adopting more strenuous efforts to find a peaceful solution to the Sudeten problem, and that it prompted Hitler to summon his generals on 28 May 1938 to order them to draw up plans for 'Case Green' – the invasion of Czechoslovakia, which was scheduled for 1 October 1938.

On 16 July 1938, Halifax suggested to the foreign policy committee that Britain should send a 'distinguished mediator' to investigate the Sudeten claims for self-determination. This idea was accepted by Chamberlain, who selected, on the advice of Sir Horace Wilson, Lord Runciman, a Liberal, a former president of the Board of Trade and a shipping magnate, with no experience of high-level diplomatic negotiations. Runciman was considered by Halifax as a 'safe pair of hands'. The Czech government accepted the British idea with reluctance. The declared aim of the Runciman mission, which arrived in Prague on 4 August 1938, was to find an internal solution. As Runciman investigated the problem, and saw all the major figures involved in the dispute within Czechoslovakia, he became extremely sympathetic to the Sudeten desire for home rule. In his report, Runciman placed the major share of the blame for the breakdown of talks on the Czech government and recommended that the Sudeten Germans be allowed the opportunity to join the Third Reich.

In August 1938, war over Czechoslovakia seemed to be drawing even closer, especially as the Runciman mission appeared to be floundering. Control over British policy came more and more into the hands of the prime minister. The cabinet met only once in August 1938, and little more than a handful of times in September. The foreign policy committee did not meet at all in July, August and September 1938. Parliament was not recalled until 28 September, despite opposition pressure.

During this period, Chamberlain relied heavily on his inner cabinet – especially Wilson, Halifax, Ball, Simon and Hoare – and listened, perhaps unwisely, to the advice of Henderson. 'However badly Germany behaves,' wrote Henderson from Berlin, 'does not make the rights of the Sudeten any less justifiable'.[10] Advice from those who disagreed with Chamberlain was not welcomed. An incident in the summer of 1938 adds weight to this argument. A number of German 'moderates' sent Major Edwald von Kleist-Schmenzin, a Prussian Conservative, to London as their emissary to warn Chamberlain not only of Hitler's definite plans to invade Czechoslovakia, but also of his future plans to attack France and eventually the Soviet Union. It was reported in these conversations that a strong Anglo-French line would force Hitler to back down, but Chamberlain thought these particular German moderates were exaggerating and he discounted their views because they conflicted with his own view that open threats of force would hasten the outbreak of war.[11]

In any case, Chamberlain had a bright idea of his own, rather grandly dubbed 'Plan Z', which reportedly 'rather took Halifax's breath away'. If the Runciman mission failed, Chamberlain intended to visit Hitler to make a last desperate effort to prevent war. A vital component of the plan would be surprise: Plan Z was known about in advance only by Wilson, Halifax, Simon and Henderson. The cabinet, which met in emergency session on 30 August 1938, was not told about Plan Z but unanimously agreed to support the Chamberlain line 'that we should not utter a threat to Herr Hitler that if he went into Czechoslovakia we should declare war upon him'.[12]

In September 1938, events moved at an exceptionally rapid pace. On 5 September 1938, the Czech government announced it would accept virtually all of the Karlsbad demands, but it made no difference. On 7 September, *The Times* published a notorious leading article which offered the opinion that it would be a good idea if the Czech government decided to cede the Sudetenland to Nazi

Germany.[13] On 12 September, Hitler whipped his supporters into a frenzy at the annual Nuremberg rally by claiming the Sudeten Germans were 'not alone'. Following this speech, a freshly orchestrated series of demonstrations immediately broke out throughout the Sudeten area, but they did not attract widespread local support and the Czech government was able to break them up. On 13 September, the Czech government decided to introduce martial law in the area. Henlein, who knew his lines so cleverly and acted them to perfection, fled to Germany and the protection of Hitler.

In view of the critical situation, Chamberlain put Plan Z into action by sending Hitler a telegram requesting an immediate meeting, which was promptly granted. It was the first visit by a British prime minister to Germany since Disraeli went to the Congress of Berlin in 1878 and returned proclaiming he had secured 'peace with honour'. When news reached the Czech government, they were horrified. On 14 September, the cabinet was finally given news of Plan Z and promptly gave its assent.[14] As Chamberlain prepared to leave for Germany, it is evident he was already quite prepared to sanction Hitler's demands for the transfer of the Sudetenland to Germany.

On 15 September 1938, Chamberlain, aged sixty-nine, boarded a Lockheed Electra aircraft for the seven-hour journey to Munich, followed by a three-hour car ride up the long and winding hill roads to meet Hitler at his hideaway at Berchtesgaden. It was the start of an amazing display of personal diplomacy by Chamberlain, which lasted just over a fortnight. The chief aim of British policy at this stage was to find out what Hitler's terms were for settling the crisis. It was the first extended aeroplane trip Chamberlain had ever made, though not, as is sometimes written, his first ever aeroplane trip. As with many cabinet ministers in the late 1930s, Chamberlain had been on several internal flights. He was accompanied by his trusted ally Sir Horace Wilson and Sir William Strang, a senior official at the foreign office. Lord Halifax, the foreign secretary, stayed behind, ostensibly to keep Ribbentrop, the German foreign minister, out of the discussions.

The first meeting of the British prime minister with Hitler lasted for three hours, in the company of Dr Paul Schmidt, Hitler's interpreter. Chamberlain was informed in no uncertain terms by the Nazi leader that he intended to 'stop the suffering' of the Sudeten Germans by force. After this prolonged harangue, Chamberlain asked Hitler what was required for a peaceful solution. Hitler demanded the transfer of all districts in Czechoslovakia with a 50 per cent or more German-speaking population. In reply, Chamberlain said he had nothing against the idea in principle, but would need to overcome 'practical difficulties' in order to gain acceptance of Hitler's demands.[15] 'I got the impression,' Chamberlain said of his first meeting with Hitler, 'that here was a man who could be relied upon when he had given his word'.[16]

On his return, Chamberlain met his 'inner cabinet' and informed them that Hitler wanted the transfer to German sovereignty of all German-speaking districts. On 17 September 1938, the cabinet met and Chamberlain informed its members of his continuing belief that Hitler's aims were limited to a final solution of the Sudeten problem. However, there was a slight modification to the policy. It was reported that the French harboured suspicions about Chamberlain's motives in arranging the Berchtesgaden meeting without full consultation. As a result, Chamberlain and Halifax agreed that joint Anglo-French action was required during the next crucial stage towards a peaceful settlement. French leaders were invited to 10 Downing Street.[17] On 18 September, Chamberlain met Daladier in order to persuade him to agree to the orderly transfer of the Sudeten areas to Germany. Daladier told Chamberlain the French would agree to support the Berchtesgaden demands only in return for a British agreement to join the French alliance system in eastern Europe. Chamberlain neatly side-stepped this demand and finally agreed only to the idea of Britain joining a general guarantee of Czechoslovakia.

The major outcome of these talks was the creation of an Anglo-French plan which agreed to the transfer of all Sudeten areas with populations comprising over 50 per cent German speakers. France and Britain were now in agreement to placate German demands. The only obstacle remaining was the attitude of the Czech government. On 18 September, Halifax told the cabinet that if the Czechs did not agree to this plan they would be left to face the Third Reich alone. The cabinet, with the exception of a few doubters, was easily won round once again. By skilful diplomacy, Chamberlain had blended the forcible demands of Hitler with his own desire for peace and had managed some gentle persuasion of the French to produce an agreed Anglo-French policy.[18] On 19 September, the Czech government, which had been kept in the dark, was given a grim ultimatum by Chamberlain: accept the Anglo-French plan or face Hitler alone. Quite bravely, the Czech government attempted to hold out against Hitler's demands and wrangled, with great emotion and dignity, for over two days, before very reluctantly giving in to Anglo-French pressure. On 21 September, Litvinov, the Soviet foreign minister, told the assembly of the League of Nations that the Soviet Union intended to fulfil its obligations towards Czechoslovakia, if France would do the same.[19] But the attitude of the Soviet Union was of little interest to Chamberlain, as he had already overcome most of the chief obstacles to a peaceful solution. France was immobilised, the Franco-Soviet agreement a virtual dead letter and the Czechs had been successfully browbeaten into accepting the Anglo-French plan.

All that now remained was for Chamberlain to return to Germany to tell the good news to Hitler. The Czech crisis seemed to be all over bar the shouting. 'European peace is what I am aiming at,' Chamberlain told reporters on 22 September as he prepared to board his plane to Germany, 'and on this trip I hope to get it'.[20] The second meeting between Chamberlain and Hitler took place later the same day, at the Hotel Dreeden in the picturesque Rhineland town of Godesberg. Chamberlain, accompanied by Ivone Kirkpatrick, a foreign office official who acted as his interpreter, confidently read out the Anglo-French agreement. 'I'm sorry,' Hitler replied after a brief pause, 'but that won't do any more.'[21] He went on to make a series of new demands. He wanted the immediate occupation of Sudeten areas and non-German-speakers who wished to leave would be allowed to take only a single suitcase of belongings with them. He also added certain areas with less than 50 per cent German speakers and raised Polish and Hungarian grievances in other areas of Czechoslovakia.

Chamberlain was flabbergasted, but remained composed. In a very quiet but assertive tone he explained to the Nazi leader how he had already risked his entire political reputation to gain the Anglo-French plan and could not hope to win further support for Nazi troops marching into the Sudetenland. Hitler refused to budge, so the prime minister decided to break off the talks. He returned to the Hotel Petersburg and paced the floor in a tense silence for the rest of the late afternoon. In a final desperate move, Chamberlain wrote a letter to Hitler requesting a detailed outline of German claims, accompanied by a map of the territory to be occupied. The next day, Chamberlain received what became known as 'the Godesberg memorandum'. It simply made concrete what Hitler had demanded verbally on the previous day.

Late in the evening of 23 September, Chamberlain met Hitler once more; he told him the memorandum was little more than 'an ultimatum'. 'No,' replied Hitler, 'Read the top, it says memorandum'. The only concession Chamberlain managed to wring from Hitler during the Godesberg meetings was an agreement to delay the proposed occupation of the Sudeten areas until 1 October 1938. As the meeting broke up, Chamberlain knew the crisis had reached another point of deadlock.

On 24 September, the cabinet met three times in an all-day emergency session to discuss the very harsh and uncompromising Godesberg proposals. Chamberlain told the cabinet he was 'satisfied Herr Hitler would not go back on his word' and was not using the crisis as an excuse to 'crush Czechoslovakia or dominate Europe'. He suggested that as there was little 'substantive difference' between the Anglo-French plan and the Godesberg proposals they should be accepted. Halifax pointed out that it was extremely unlikely the Czechs would accept the Godesberg proposals. With many ministers intensely disturbed about Hitler's new demands, it was decided to discuss the matter further the next day.[22]

On Sunday 25 September, the cabinet met twice, but Halifax, who had had a 'sleepless night', dropped a bombshell by stating he could not support a policy based on the Godesberg proposals. Chamberlain later commented that this came as 'a horrible blow'. Halifax told the cabinet he saw acceptance of the original German demands as the only logical policy to avoid war, but events at Godesberg had convinced him of the 'immorality of yielding to force'. He now saw a 'difference in principle' between the orderly transfer envisaged by the Anglo-French plan and the 'disorderly transfer' outlined at Godesberg. Halifax proposed that Britain should put the facts before the Czechs and if the French decided to fight then Britain should offer full support. Halifax was supported in this view, to greater and lesser degrees, by the majority of the cabinet, but William Morrison (minister of agriculture), Inskip (minister for the co-ordination of defence), Simon and Hoare suggested the Czechs should be 'given the facts' – namely, that they would be crushed if they did not accept the plan – and be allowed to make up their minds. Only three members of the cabinet – Lord Stanhope, Lord Maughan and Kingsley Wood – loyal supporters of

Chamberlain – continued to urge the outright acceptance of the Godesberg proposals. For the first time, Chamberlain, on a key foreign policy issue, was in a minority in the cabinet. Halifax had emerged as an independent political force who placed limits on Chamberlain's actions at a time of national crisis.[23]

The cabinet meeting of 25 September adjourned briefly to allow Chamberlain and Halifax to meet French leaders who had arrived during the day. It soon emerged that the French government could not accept Hitler taking the Sudeten areas by force. Daladier suggested Hitler should either accept the Anglo-French plan or face war. The limit of French weakness had also been reached. However, when Chamberlain asked if the French were prepared to fight a European war, without a promise of British support, Daladier was evasive and only promised that 'Each of us will do his duty'. When Daladier asked what would the British do, Chamberlain suggested all depended on what the Czechs and French would do. No firm commitment by Britain was offered to France at this stage. The Czech government described the Godesberg proposals as a *de facto* ultimatum of the type usually presented to a nation defeated in war and rejected it.

In the resumed cabinet meeting late in the evening of 25 September, Chamberlain reported the views of the French and Czech governments, but outlined another proposal which aimed to keep a last despairing lifeline open for a peaceful settlement. He told the cabinet he would send a final personal letter to Hitler, to be delivered by Sir Horace Wilson, proposing a conference between Germany, Czechoslovakia and other major powers to reach a negotiated settlement. But the majority of the cabinet insisted Wilson should inform Hitler, at the same time, that if he rejected this appeal the Czechs would fight, France would fight and Britain would stand by the French.

These heated cabinet meetings of 24 and 25 September clearly rattled Chamberlain, but only forced him to find some neat way to escape this pressure. What Chamberlain was really up to was skilfully attempting to manoeuvre the cabinet into keeping a lifeline open for continued negotiations. After all, the Wilson mission was making Hitler a completely new offer, namely, to settle the matter peacefully at an international conference. This was Chamberlain's own idea. He ensured the proposed threat to Hitler the cabinet desired was to be uttered only verbally and not contained in the letter the ever faithful Wilson would deliver. This allowed Wilson, no doubt with Chamberlain's permission, the opportunity not to issue the threat and keep negotiations dragging on further.

By now, Halifax had come down firmly against any further pressure being put on Czechoslovakia. According to Oliver Stanley, 'the Foreign Secretary had lost all his illusions about Hitler and now regards him as a criminal lunatic'.[24] This view is reinforced by a foreign office press release of 26 September 1938 which read, 'If in spite of all the efforts made by the Prime Minister a German attack is made upon Czechoslovakia, the immediate result must be that France will be bound to come to her assistance, and Great Britain and Russia will certainly stand by France'. The release of this provocative message before Wilson had met Hitler has been attributed to Rex Leeper, foreign office press secretary. But it turns out to have been the work of Halifax, acting without Chamberlain's permission, who recalled that 'greatly to my surprise, Neville was much put out when the communiqué appeared and reproved me for not having submitted it to him'.[25] Halifax, the foreign office and the majority of the cabinet were now prepared openly to threaten force against Hitler, while Chamberlain still wanted to conciliate and keep negotiations open.

This was why Wilson had been sent by Chamberlain to Germany. On 26 September 1938, Wilson met Hitler for a 'violent hour' of heated conversation. Wilson told him that the Godesberg demands were unacceptable and that a conference of powers was now the best way to solve the crisis. In reply, Hitler said the Czech government should accept the Godesberg memorandum before he would consider a compromise. At this point, Wilson should have issued the strong warning demanded by the cabinet but he did not. In the evening, Chamberlain realised that further delay was impossible and told Wilson to issue the warning on the next day – 'more in sorrow than in anger'. On 27 September, Wilson finally, and reluctantly, informed Hitler that if France went to the aid of Czechoslovakia, Britain would 'feel obliged to support France'. In response, Hitler said that if Czechoslovakia did not accept the Godesberg memorandum then 'in six days we will all be at war'. In a final parting word to Hitler, Wilson promised he would 'try and make those Czechs sensible'.[26]

Even at the eleventh hour, Chamberlain was still prepared to 'snatch at the last tuft of grass on the very verge of the precipice' rather than fight a war over an issue. On the evening of 27 September, most people in Britain expected a European war. In a letter to Beneš, the Czech president, on 28 September, Chamberlain informed him that nothing that any power could do could prevent Germany mounting a massive invasion of Czechoslovakia.[27] On the same day, Chamberlain received a letter from Hitler which promised German troops would occupy only agreed areas and would join all parties in guaranteeing the remaining territory of Czechoslovakia. This was just the lifeline Chamberlain needed. 'I feel certain,' wrote Chamberlain in reply, 'that you can get all the essentials without war and without delay,' and he further promised: 'I am ready to come to Berlin myself at once to discuss arrangements for transfer with you and representatives of the Czech government, together with representatives of France and Italy if you desire. I feel convinced we could reach agreement in a week'.[28] This personal offer by Chamberlain to give Hitler all he wanted was never discussed with the cabinet or with the French and Czech governments. It reinforces the idea that many of the impromptu decisions Chamberlain took during September 1938 amounted to personal diplomacy. In a final desperate move, Chamberlain sent a telegram to Mussolini urging him to place pressure on Hitler to settle the matter at a conference.

All this pressure seems to have persuaded Hitler he could get all he wanted without a war, even though it seems the Nazi leader would probably have preferred to crush Czechoslovakia. On 28 September 1938, Hitler announced he would settle the matter peacefully at a conference to be held at Munich, beginning the next day. When this news was announced in the House of Commons, Churchill said to Chamberlain: 'I congratulate you on your good fortune. You were very lucky.'[29] Chamberlain, tired and under immense strain, felt vindicated. On the evening before departing for Munich, he did not summon the cabinet.

After all this high drama, the Munich conference was something of an anticlimax. Hitler, Chamberlain, Daladier and Mussolini gathered in Munich on 29 September 1938 finally to resolve the Czech crisis. The Munich settlement, signed in the early hours of 30 September, resembled pre-1914 European diplomacy, with four major powers forcing a small nation, without the power to resist, to concede territory to a major power. The agreement deprived Czechoslovakia of its heavily fortified border defences, its rail communications were cut and a great deal of economic power was lost. The fate of the remainder of Czechoslovakia now lay at the discretion of the Nazi regime. It was justified on the principle that national self-determination had been denied to the Sudeten Germans in the first place. The terms of the agreement provided that the German occupation of the Sudetenland should be completed by 10 October 1938; an international commission composed of two German generals and one official each from Britain, Italy and Czechoslovakia was appointed to supervise the operation, and a four-power guarantee for the remainder of Czechoslovakia was promised. In reality, the actual territory gained by Nazi pressure was even more favourable than that set out in the Godesberg memorandum.

But Chamberlain wanted Munich to be viewed by the British public as something more fundamental than a bloodless victory for Hitler. To this end, Chamberlain met the Nazi leader in private to gain his autograph on a very famous piece of paper, which Chamberlain famously read out to reporters and waved enthusiastically above his head at Heston Airport on his triumphant return. The famous 'piece of paper in my pocket' was grandly dubbed the 'Anglo-German declaration'. It promised Britain and Germany would adopt 'the method of consultation' in any future disputes and would 'never go to war with one another again'. Crowds cheered, in relief more than exultation, all along Chamberlain's route from the airport back to Buckingham Palace, where he was to brief King George VI on the incredible turn of events. He was greeted by more cheering crowds outside 10 Downing Street as he arrived home. A few minutes later, Chamberlain was persuaded to step forwards and peer out of the first-floor window. He leaned forwards, waved an arm above his head and said, 'My good friends: this is the second time in our history that there has come back to Downing Street from Germany peace with honour. I believe it is peace for our time.'[30]

### Notes

1 R. A. C. Parker, *Chamberlain and Appeasement: British Policy and the Coming of the Second World War* (London, 1993), p. 123.

2 *Ibid.*, p. 124.

3 CAB 23, cabinet meeting, 12 March 1938.

4   J. W. Bruegel, *Czechoslovakia Before Munich: The German Minority Problem and German and British Appeasement* (Cambridge, 1973), pp. 215–16.

5   Chamberlain's diary, 20 March 1938, quoted in K. Feiling, *The Life of Neville Chamberlain* (London, 1946), pp. 347–8.

6   CAB 27, 'Military Implications of German Aggression Against Czechoslovakia', report by chiefs of staff sub-committee, March 1938.

7   I. Colvin, *The Chamberlain Cabinet* (London, 1971), p. 112.

8   A. Adamthwaite, *The Making of the Second World War* (London, 1977), p. 77.

9   Parker, *Appeasement*, p. 149.

10   *DBFP*, vol. 2, no. 665.

11   R. Lamb, *The Ghosts of Peace, 1935–45* (London, 1987), pp. 2–5.

12   CAB 23, cabinet meeting, 30 August 1938.

13   *The Times*, 7 September 1937.

14   CAB 23, cabinet meeting, 14 September 1938.

15   T. Taylor, *Munich: The Price of Peace* (London, 1979), p. 740.

16   Parker, *Appeasement*, p. 162.

17   CAB 23, cabinet meeting, 17 September 1938.

18   *Ibid.*, 18 September 1938.

19   J. Wheeler-Bennett, *Munich: Prologue to Tragedy* (London, 1948), pp. 105–6, 127, 143.

20   *The Times*, 23 September 1938.

21   P. Schmidt, *Hitler's Interpreter* (London, 1952), pp. 95–7.

22   CAB 23, cabinet meeting, 24 September 1938.

23   *Ibid.*, 25 September 1939.

24   A. Roberts, *The Holy Fox: A Biography of Lord Halifax* (London, 1991), p. 119.

25   *Ibid.*

26   M. Gilbert, 'Horace Wilson: Man of Munich', *History Today* (1982).

27   *DBFP*, vol. 2, no. 570.

28   A. Bryant, *In Search of Peace* (London, 1939), pp. 135–6.

29   Quoted in N. Nicholson (ed.), *Harold Nicolson: Diaries and Letters, Volume 1, 1930–39* (London, 1966), p. 370.

30   Wheeler-Bennett, *Munich*, p. 478.

# 6

# The approach of war,
# October 1938–September 1939

For his energetic efforts to secure the Munich agreement Chamberlain received over 20,000 letters and telegrams of praise, and numerous gifts from people at home and abroad. 'No conqueror returning from victory on the battlefield,' wrote *The Times* on 2 October, 'had come adorned with greater laurels'. A popular record was produced at the time entitled 'God Bless You Mr. Chamberlain', which contained the line: 'We're all mighty proud of you'. Quite clearly, there was an overwhelming sense of relief that war had been averted. This was accompanied by a great deal of criticism. Alfred Duff Cooper, the first lord of the admiralty, resigned from the Chamberlain cabinet. In the famous Munich debate in the Commons, Churchill described the agreement as 'a shameful betrayal'. Although a government motion approving of the Munich agreement was passed by 366 votes to 144, 30 Tories withheld support.[1]

It is important to examine what Chamberlain expected to flow from Munich. It seems he believed that Hitler was anxious for British friendship and wanted to 'take active steps to follow up the Munich agreement by other measures aimed at securing better relations'.[2] It is also equally apparent that Chamberlain had not lost faith in conciliation and diplomacy as the best weapons to prevent war. On 3 October 1938, Chamberlain believed 'we were now in a more hopeful position, and that contacts with the Dictator Powers had opened up the possibility that we might be able to reach some agreement with them which would stop the rearmament race'.[3] On

31 October 1938, Chamberlain told the cabinet: 'Our Foreign policy was one of appeasement,' with the central aim of 'establishing relations with the Dictator Powers which will lead to a settlement in Europe and to a sense of stability'.[4] What Chamberlain wanted, above all, was 'more support for my policy, and not a strengthening of those who don't believe in it'. He was not as harassed by doubts over appeasement as many of his colleagues.[5]

In contrast, Halifax regarded Hitler as 'a criminal lunatic' and confessed, 'There will be no more Munich's'. This pessimism led Halifax to request Chamberlain to create a government of national unity, including Churchill, Eden and Labour and Liberal critics. But Chamberlain thought such a move would 'wreck the policy with which I am identified and would soon make my position intolerable'.[6] In the crucial area of rearmament, Halifax called for a rapid speeding up of the programme. To a very large extent, British policy after Munich increasingly meant more spending on armaments. Halifax ensured that gas masks handed out during the Czech crisis were not handed back, and pressed Chamberlain to introduce a ministry of supply. To Chamberlain, all this was evidence of 'talking and thinking as though Munich had made war more instead of less imminent'.[7]

Yet Hitler offered only disappointment after disappointment to those who thought Munich would lead to improved Anglo-German relations. News from Germany indicated that Hitler regarded Munich as a defeat for Germany. In a speech to the party faithful on 9 October 1938, the Nazi leader launched a violent attack on Churchill, Eden and Duff Cooper. In another speech, at Weimar on 6 November 1938, Hitler made a derogatory reference to 'umbrella carrying British statesmen' (an obvious reference to Chamberlain).[8] There was also a decidedly anti-British tone in the German press. Events in Czechoslovakia added to the growing disquiet over the Munich settlement. It became evident that German military officials were bullying the new Czech government into conceding far more territory than allowed by Munich. Poland was allowed to seize Tecschen and Hungary was awarded a strip of territory in Ruthenia and southern Slovakia beyond what had been granted in the Munich agreement. Germany and Italy were in no hurry to sign a guarantee for the remainder of Czech territory.

Another event in November 1938 placed a further serious question mark over the wisdom of appeasing the Nazi regime. A young

Polish Jew shot dead a German diplomat in Paris on 7 November. This was used as a convenient excuse to unleash a wave of anti-Semitic thuggery throughout Germany: the night of 9–10 November saw Jewish-owned shops, houses and synagogues set on fire and vandalised, and many people were killed. *Kristallnacht*, the 'night of broken glass', sent a shock wave of anger around the world. British public opinion was outraged. Duff Cooper thought that Chamberlain had as much chance of successfully appeasing Hitler as 'Little Lord Fauntleroy would have of concluding a satisfactory deal with Al Capone'.[9]

On 14 November 1938, the cabinet foreign policy committee met to discuss its response to the alarming news from Germany. Halifax believed that although many Germans might desire peace, the same was not true of 'the crazy persons who had managed to secure control of the country'. In such circumstances, Halifax saw 'no useful purpose' in resuming political discussions and urged Chamberlain to correct the false impression that 'we are decadent, spineless and could with impunity be kicked about'. It was finally agreed to put the political appeasement of Hitler on the shelf.[10]

To keep momentum in the policy, Chamberlain pursued friendly relations with Italy. On 2 November 1938, Chamberlain had announced his intention to implement the Anglo-Italian agreement which gave recognition to the Italian occupation of Abyssinia. The motive for opening fresh talks with Mussolini was to use him as a conduit to keep open talks with Germany. 'An hour of talk with Mussolini,' wrote Chamberlain in early November 1938, 'might be extraordinarily valuable in making plans to talk with Germany'.[11] To this end, Chamberlain decided to pay an official visit to Italy in January 1939.

Meanwhile, a flood of rumours came out of Berlin, from British intelligence sources, which indicated that Hitler was mad, unpredictable and unappeasable. These reports included an alleged plan by Hitler to attack the Low Countries; Nazi plans to aid Ukranian nationalism as a pretext for an assault on the Soviet Union; and plans by the Luftwaffe to bomb London in a surprise 'knock-out blow'. By and large, Chamberlain believed these intelligence reports were being used by opponents of Hitler in Germany and by anti-appeasers in the foreign office to manipulate him to change course. Halifax increasingly employed this confidential information in the months after Munich, which indicates that he was also moving in

an anti-appeasement direction; he certainly opposed further political dialogue with the Nazi regime.

It seems that Halifax wanted the prime minister to dampen down
optimism in the policy of appeasement. This view is reinforced by
the events surrounding Chamberlain's speech on 13 December 1938
to the Foreign Press Association. It was a very important speech on
the state of British foreign policy. The prime minister knew it would
receive enormous press attention. In preparing the speech, Chamberlain took advice from Sir Joseph Ball, the Tory press chief at
Downing Street, who prepared notes and drafts for most of the
prime minister's leading foreign affairs speeches in 1938 and 1939.[12]
Only on the day of the speech itself did Chamberlain bother to let
Cadogan, the permanent under-secretary at the foreign office, have a
look at it. After reading it, Cadogan was 'horrified' by its optimistic
tone and he told Halifax to get the prime minister to 'stiffen it up'.
Halifax tried to persuade Chamberlain to insert new passages into
the speech to give it a far stronger tone, but Chamberlain neatly side-
stepped this request by saying he could not change it, because the
speech had already been printed and distributed to guests.

It is useful to examine Chamberlain's speech to the Foreign Press
Association in more detail. Chamberlain claimed only two alternatives were open to deal with the rapidly deteriorating situation in
Europe. The first was to decide that war was inevitable and 'throw
the whole energies of the country into preparation for it'. Chamberlain claimed that those who favoured this course were in 'a small
minority'. The second was to make a 'prolonged and determined
effort to eradicate the possible causes of war' through personal
contact and discussion, while attempting to 'restore the power of
the defence forces'. This was the policy to which Chamberlain was
still committed at the end of 1938.

In fact, Chamberlain used the speech to launch an attack on the
pessimism being expressed by critics of Munich: 'We should rather
remember what was the alternative which the Munich Agreement
averted, namely an attempt to effect a revision of the Treaty of
Versailles by force instead of by discussion'. On Anglo-German
relations, Chamberlain struck an extremely optimistic tone and
remained 'convinced that the wish of our two peoples remains still
as recorded in the Munich declaration, namely, that never again
should we go to war with one another, but we should deal with any
differences between us by the method of consultation'. To give even

further signs of optimism over the policy of appeasing the dictators, he gave notice of his proposed visit to Italy, which he claimed aimed to establish 'a greater mutual confidence to co-operate in one way or another in further steps towards the greater sense of stability and security'. Chamberlain hoped arms would 'never be required' and 'certainly they will not be required for aggressive purposes'.

This extremely optimistic speech was bluntly described by Halifax as a 'bad speech'.[13] 'I had a message from Halifax that he didn't like the speech,' Chamberlain commented a few days later, 'as he thought it laid too much emphasis on appeasement and was not stiff enough to the dictators'.[14] Rab Butler, the parliamentary under-secretary for foreign affairs, suggested that Chamberlain was 'extremely bad' for not showing important speeches on foreign affairs to Halifax and observed: 'this is the type of occurrence which lay behind his parting with Anthony'.[15] More alarmingly, an MI5 officer informed the foreign office that George Steward, a member of the Downing Street press office, was having secret conversations with Dr Fritz Hesse, of the German press agency, despite the earlier cabinet decision to suspend all direct political negotiations.

It seems Chamberlain was still hankering for a means of keeping appeasement alive. In such circumstances, the visit by Chamberlain to Italy in January 1939 assumed greater significance. Chamberlain wanted to use the visit to keep up momentum for appeasement and hoped to persuade Mussolini to advise Hitler not to embark on 'some mad dog act'.[16] But Halifax was much less enthusiastic about the visit and was careful to ensure that Chamberlain was not allowed the sort of freedom to employ impromptu acts of diplomacy which had so characterised events surrounding Munich. Halifax decided to accompany the prime minister to Rome and advised Chamberlain not to offer Mussolini anything tangible unless he agreed to work positively towards a general settlement.[17] He also told Chamberlain to keep a written record of his conversations with Mussolini.

On 11 January 1939, Chamberlain, accompanied by Halifax, reportedly looking like 'two undertakers', arrived in Italy. Mussolini told Chamberlain that Italy desired peace but gave no promise to restrain Hitler. In private, Mussolini said of his British visitors: 'These men are not made of the same stuff as Francis Drake and the other magnificent adventurers who created the Empire.' The Italian government kept the visit in a very low key. 'The British,' recorded

Count Ciano, the Italian foreign minister, in his diary, 'do not want to fight'.[18] Ever the optimist, Chamberlain described the visit as 'truly wonderful', because it had 'strengthened the channels of peace'.[19] The more pessimistic Halifax thought Italy had 'no stamina to face a modern war'.[20] As he left Rome, Chamberlain was reportedly moved to tears by the loud cheering he received from his Italian hosts and journeyed back to London in an optimistic mood.[21]

After Chamberlain returned from Rome, he was confronted with a flood of even gloomier intelligence reports from Germany. Halifax claimed the atmosphere in Europe in early 1939 was one 'in which all things were both possible and impossible, but where there were no rational guidelines'.[22] The most alarming report, presented to the cabinet on 18 January 1939, came from the Secret Intelligence Service (SIS). It predicted that Hitler was planning an imminent attack on Holland. Halifax argued strongly, and was supported by the cabinet, for a British commitment to stand by Holland in the event of a German attack.[23] On 26 January 1939, a meeting took place of the foreign policy committee, with Halifax and Chamberlain in attendance, with the leading army, navy and air force ministers, and the chiefs of staff also present, where it was agreed that a German attack on Holland would be considered a reason to go to war. This peacetime guarantee was not, on Chamberlain's insistence, made known to the public.

In January 1939, the pressure grew on Chamberlain from the increasingly powerful and independent Halifax, supported by a majority of the cabinet, the foreign office and the chiefs of staff, to make a greater public commitment to the defence of western Europe. According to Rab Butler, Halifax was attempting to establish a policy of standing up to Hitler in western Europe and reportedly 'moved the Cabinet, by what at first sight appeared to be rumours, along this path'.[24] The prime minister was unable to resist a policy of taking precautions against a German advance in western Europe. On 6 February 1939, Chamberlain told the Commons that any threat to the vital interests of France would bring forth 'the immediate co-operation of Britain'.[25] This decision was quickly followed by others, including the promise to create an enlarged British expeditionary force and to open staff talks between Britain and France.

As a relief from such pressure, Chamberlain welcomed the return of Henderson to Berlin after a three-month absence through illness.

His presence would provide an antidote to the gloomy intelligence reports. 'My definite impression,' Henderson told the foreign office on 18 February 1939, 'is that Herr Hitler does not contemplate any adventures at the moment and that all the stories and rumours to the contrary are completely without foundation'.[26] All the diplomatic reports from Berlin started to become stubbornly optimistic. Chamberlain was soon striking a similar tone. In late February, Chamberlain, after wandering around his garden, wrote: 'All the information I get seems to point in the direction of peace'.[27]

Chamberlain decided to mount a counter-offensive against the gloom merchants in his own cabinet. In early March, he summoned a number of leading parliamentary correspondents to 10 Downing Street for a press briefing. He told them that 'The foreign situation is less anxious and gives me less concern for possible unpleasant developments than it has done for some time'. He went on to paint a rosy picture of relations between Italy and France, was sanguine about Anglo-German economic talks, and even raised hopes for a disarmament conference before the end of the year.[28]

This extremely optimistic view of the prospects for appeasement was widely reported in the British press. It was to cause outrage at the foreign office. On 10 March, Halifax wrote Chamberlain a letter objecting to the lack of liaison between the foreign office and Downing Street over the press briefing and made the following very firm request: 'I think that when you are going to make a general review of Foreign Affairs it might be helpful and well, if you felt able to let me know in advance that you were going to do it, and give me some idea of what you had in mind to say'.[29] In reply, Chamberlain claimed to be 'horrified' at how his views were reported and promised 'faithfully not to do it again' but Halifax was only 'half convinced'.[30] In fact, on the very same day, Hoare gave a speech, with Chamberlain's blessing, which spoke of Munich heralding the beginning of a 'golden age of appeasement'.

On 15 March 1939, Nazi tanks suddenly entered Prague. The occupation ended the independence of what remained of Czechoslovakia, destroyed the Munich agreement and made it extremely difficult to follow a policy of direct negotiation with Germany. To view Hitler's aims as linked to a revision of legitimate grievances left behind by Versailles seemed foolish. The annexation of an area peopled by non-Germans removed the fig leaf of respectability

surrounding German grievances. It showed that diplomatic agreements signed by Hitler were likely to be of no permanent value. It is
tempting to equate the occupation of Prague with the abandonment
of appeasement and the beginning of the road to inevitable war. The
actual story is far more complex.

It is probably more accurate to suggest that Prague shattered
Chamberlain's illusion concerning the aims of Hitler, but not his
underlying belief that appeasement was still the best means of
solving international conflict. In fact, the immediate public reaction
of Chamberlain to Prague was extremely ambiguous. To the cabinet
on 15 March he said, 'Czechoslovakia had spontaneously fallen
apart'.[31] It was agreed that the government would find a form of
words in order to back out of honouring what amounted to a moral
guarantee to Czechoslovakia implicit in the Munich agreement, but
never formally ratified in the months which followed by Britain,
France, Germany and Italy. It was claimed, not very convincingly,
that when Hitler's troops went in, no legal Czech state existed. In
the Commons, the prime minister deplored the violation of the
Munich agreement and adopted a tone of extreme disappointment,
but could not seem to decide whether Prague was a setback to, or
the actual end of, appeasement. 'Though we may have to suffer
checks and disappointments, from time to time,' said Chamberlain,
'the object that we have in mind is of too great significance to the
happiness of mankind for us lightly to give it up'.[32]

On the next day, the weight of public opinion was so enormous
that no politician could safely ignore it. The overwhelming majority
of national and local newspapers called for a bold and determined
policy to stop Hitler. Even *The Times*, the most consistent supporter
of appeasement among in the national press, suggested that 'German policy no longer seeks the protection of a moral case' and
urged a policy of close co-operation with other nations to resist
Hitler.[33] To most people, war now seemed inevitable. 'As soon as I
had time to think,' Chamberlain wrote in his diary, 'I saw it was
impossible to deal with Hitler after he had thrown his own assurances to the winds'.[34] On 17 March 1939, in a famous speech in
Birmingham, Chamberlain uttered his first real words of warning to
Hitler: 'Is this the end of an old adventure, or the beginning of a
new one? Is this a step in the direction of an attempt to dominate
the world by force?' If this was the case, then Chamberlain pledged
Britain would resist 'to the utmost of its power'. But he added that

he was 'not prepared to engage this country by new unspecified commitments'.[35]

On 18 March, the cabinet met to discuss the policy options. Chamberlain said that if Germany proceeded along a course of world domination, then Britain 'had no alternative, but to meet force with force'. Moreover, he accepted that it was impossible to follow a policy of direct negotiation with the Nazi regime.[36] This is not to say Chamberlain now accepted that appeasement was a failed policy, but he very reluctantly conceded that it was unlikely to work with Hitler and accepted the need for a policy of deterrence, which he termed 'a positive policy for peace'.

Three options dominated post-Prague discussions of British foreign policy. The first was a proposal from the Soviet Union to convene a conference of Britain, France, the Soviet Union, Poland, Rumania and Turkey to find a collective means of resisting further aggression. This was the least popular option. The second was to construct a four-power guarantee against further aggression by Germany consisting of Britain, France, the Soviet Union and Poland. This was widely supported by the cabinet and seemed acceptable to the prime minister. The third, and least popular option at this stage, was to offer Anglo-French guarantees to Poland and Rumania.

But events in Europe were moving so swiftly that British policy makers were forced to improvise a new policy very quickly. On 21 March, Hitler's troops marched into Memel, after threatening the Lithuanian government with aggression. On the same day, the Polish government received a set of German demands, including a request for the return of the free city of Danzig and the amendment of the Polish corridor. Not surprisingly, Poland called on the British government for help. On 24 April, Colonel Beck, the Polish foreign minister, arrived in London and proposed a secret understanding involving Britain, France and Poland, but excluding the Soviet Union. Chamberlain applauded this news, because it fitted nicely with his own private desire to keep the Soviet Union at arm's length and allowed him to pursue a policy of deterrence, without extreme provocation, which he believed a pre-1914-style alliance would have done.[37]

On 30 March 1939, the cabinet was faced with more alarming intelligence reports, which indicated that Germany was ready to strike against Poland. It was Halifax who was the most passionate supporter of an unconditional guarantee of Poland. Yet this impetuous 'blank cheque' to Poland was decided upon in much haste and without any real assessment of the overall strategic situation in eastern Europe or Polish military capacity. The guarantee to Poland, which France joined, officially announced on 31 March, can be seen as the first tangible sign of a new British policy of deterrence, which set a clear limit on Anglo-French toleration of further German expansion. On the other hand, it was an impromptu response to the nightmare scenarios coming out of Germany and was of very little military value to Poland. 'If war occurred tomorrow,' Lloyd George told Chamberlain in the Commons on 3 April 1939, 'you could not send a single battalion to Poland'. However, Chamberlain hoped the guarantee would point 'not towards war, which wins nothing or settles nothing, cures nothing, ends nothing' but would open the way towards 'a more wholesome era, when reason will take place of force'.[38]

Yet Hitler did not share this optimism. The Polish guarantee made little difference to the military plans and dreams of the Nazi leader. In fact, Hitler virtually laughed in the face of the guarantee and warned, quite accurately, 'I'll make them a hell's broth'.[39] On 3 April 1939, Hitler set a firm date for the implementation of Operation White (the German attack on Poland). In that same month he demanded the return of Danzig and ripped up both the 1934 German–Polish agreement and the 1935 Anglo-German naval agreement. On hearing this news, Chamberlain wrote, 'Hitler finds it so easy to tear up treaties and throw overboard assurances, that no one can feel any confidence in new ones'.[40] The actions of Mussolini were soon a second source of misery. On 7 April, Mussolini seized Albania, leaving Chamberlain to confess, 'I am afraid that such faith as I ever had in the assurances of dictators is rapidly being whittled away'.[41]

Further measures by the British government to deter the dictators were quickly enacted. On 13 April, further Anglo-French guarantees were offered to Rumania, Greece and Turkey, but guarantees were turned down by Holland, Switzerland and Denmark. In an attempt to give Hitler further evidence of British resolve, Chamberlain introduced conscription on 21 April for all males aged twenty and twenty-one. Spending limits on the army, navy and air force were abandoned and a ministry of supply to co-ordinate the supply of war materials was established. The dictators responded in kind. On 22 May, Mussolini and Hitler signed a military alliance –

'the Pact of Steel' – which added further to the idea of an inevitable war.

Europe had entered a period which was neither peace nor war. In such circumstances, questions were raised about whether Chamberlain's guarantee system could really stop Hitler. A great majority of politicians argued that any truly viable new security system in eastern Europe must involve the Soviet Union.[42] But Chamberlain gave the impression he was only moving reluctantly forwards under 'the impulsion of the national will' in seeking collaboration with the 'evil Empire'. 'I have a very considerable mistrust of the Soviet Union,' Chamberlain told the cabinet on 5 April 1939, 'and I have no confidence that we should obtain active and constant support from that country'. Indeed, Chamberlain claimed it was 'a pathetic belief' to view 'Russia as the key to our salvation'. He accepted the opening of negotiations with the Soviet Union only with the greatest reluctance.[43] These reservations were shared by Halifax, another lifelong opponent of communism, who believed an alliance would add little to security, arouse the suspicion of allies and aggravate the hostility of potential enemies.

This lack of faith in Soviet military power and dislike of Soviet communism was widespread in British Conservative circles. In military circles, a very low opinion was held of the fighting strength of the numerically vast Red Army which, it was believed, had been exhausted by the blood letting of Stalin's purges. This may explain why the chiefs of staff painted such a negative and highly prejudiced picture in the 'Military Value of the USSR', its first report on the subject in April 1939. In this report, the incredible numerical strength of Soviet forces is outlined, but it is emphasised that this strength is cancelled out by military, administrative and economic weaknesses. The chiefs of staff also suggested 'deep seated hostility to communism and vice versa' would serve to 'nullify many of the military advantages' of any Soviet agreement. The chiefs of staff saw only two advantages to an Anglo-Soviet alliance. First, it would prevent Germany drawing on the Soviet Union's economic resources. Second, it would act as a restraining influence on Japan in the far east.[44] This lukewarm endorsement by the chiefs of staff allowed Chamberlain to convey the impression that the time for a military alliance was not yet ripe.

It was the gravity of the international situation in 1939, combined with the strength of public opinion, which soon changed matters.

But the negotiations between Britain and the Soviet Union from April to August 1939 were slow, complex and ultimately unsuccessful. The process began on 14 April with Britain pressing the Soviet Union to offer its neighbours assistance in the event of an unprovoked attack. On 18 April, the Soviet Union rejected this idea, but proposed a simple three-power military alliance involving Britain, France and the Soviet Union. Many of the small nations of eastern Europe dreaded Soviet assistance as much as they feared Nazi aggression.

Even so, support for a firm Anglo-Soviet alliance gathered momentum. The chiefs of staff were the first to move strongly towards the idea. On 16 May, Lord Chatfield, the minister for the co-ordination of defence, strongly urged the conclusion of an Anglo-Soviet agreement. He also warned that if the Soviet Union stood aside in a European war it might 'secure an advantage from the exhaustion of the western powers' and that if negotiations failed, a Nazi–Soviet agreement was a distinct possibility. To Chamberlain, an Anglo-Soviet agreement meant a return to the pre-1914 alliance system and he expressed surprise at the willingness of chiefs of staff to 'seriously increase our liabilities' and 'increase the probability of war'.[45] Chamberlain preferred to 'extend our guarantees' in eastern Europe rather than sign an Anglo-Soviet military alliance, which he thought would involve 'changing the whole basis of our policy'.[46] On 20 May, Chamberlain told Cadogan he would prefer to resign rather than sign such an agreement and felt 'some members of the Cabinet who were unwilling to agree to an alliance now appear to have swung to the opposite view'.[47] It appears likely that if Chamberlain had been given full cabinet support for his own view, then negotiations for an alliance with the Soviet Union would probably have never been undertaken.[48] In a lengthy memorandum of 22 May, Halifax echoed the prime minister's scepticism by claiming that a military alliance would be seen as a 'definite change of policy', from a defensive to an offensive one.[49]

On 24 May 1939, the cabinet discussed whether to open negotiations for an Anglo-Soviet alliance. The strength of cabinet support was overwhelmingly in favour. Chamberlain conceded that 'In present circumstances, it was impossible to stand out against the conclusion of an agreement,' but he stressed the 'question of presentation was of the utmost importance'. He hoped that any Anglo-Soviet agreement could be hidden under the banner of the

League of Nations. Halifax declared support for an alliance in a similarly negative manner, and seemed most concerned to sign an agreement to prevent a Nazi–Soviet pact. It was the cabinet, egged on by public pressure, which pushed a reluctant Chamberlain and a hesitant Halifax along the path towards opening negotiations with the Soviet Union.[50] By this time, the cabinet was a very powerful force in the consideration of foreign policy. Many of its members were unfriendly towards Chamberlain and determined to ensure there would be no more compromise with Nazi Germany. In a weakened political position, Chamberlain could not conduct policy without the majority consent of his cabinet. After all, a wave of resignations would have probably caused the downfall of his government.[51] Public opinion provided a second powerful restraint on foreign policy. In June 1939, a public opinion poll showed that 84 per cent of the British public favoured an Anglo-French-Soviet military alliance.

In these circumstances, the British government agreed to pursue the Soviet proposal for a military alliance. The British strategy in the negotiations, which dragged on during the summer of 1939, had a number of key elements. Chamberlain did not seem to care less whether an Anglo-Soviet agreement was signed at all, kept placing obstructions in the way of concluding an agreement swiftly and confessed bluntly: 'I am so sceptical of the value of Russian help that I should not feel that our position was greatly worsened if we had to do without them'.[52] The lack of urgency on Chamberlain's part was reinforced by Henderson's view from Berlin that 'it was quite impossible for Germany and the Soviet Union to come together' and by the indifference of Halifax to the negotiations.[53]

It was not until 23 July that the British government agreed to full-blown talks to sign a military agreement. The French, also involved in the talks, ideally wanted a swift agreement but reluctantly followed the British lead. The British mission to the Soviet Union was headed by the virtually unknown Admiral Sir Reginald Aylmer Ranfurly Plunkett-Ernle-Erle-Drax and Sir William Strang from the foreign office. They were advised by Halifax to spin the negotiations out until the October snow began to fall in Poland. They did not depart for Leningrad (by merchant ship) until 5 August and arrived six days later. The actual negotiations proceeded in a very cordial atmosphere but broke down over three issues. First, the British insisted on cloaking the agreement under the League of Nations. The Soviets thought this might lead to no action being taken when the proposal for 'collective action' was put to a vote at Geneva. Second, there was no agreement on deciding the exact circumstances which would trigger joint Soviet, French and British action. Third, Poland, upon consultation, steadfastly refused to allow Soviet troops on its soil in the event of war. The Soviet Union, in a very strong diplomatic position, showed no intention of promising aid to small states threatened by Hitler unless Britain and France gave copper-bottom guarantees they would not back out from meeting the German challenge.

The tardiness of the British government in attempting to conclude an Anglo-Soviet alliance allowed Hitler to offer the Soviet Union an attractive non-aggression pact. The fragmentary Soviet evidence leaves open the question of when Stalin decided to abandon working with Britain and France, and considered coming to terms with Hitler. It seems that the Soviet Union was keeping its diplomatic options open and Stalin was indifferent to the fate of Poland. In December 1938, a trade agreement between the Soviet Union and German authorities had been signed. In May 1939, the pro-League, and Jewish, Litvinov was replaced by the hard-line Molotov as Soviet foreign minister. The friendly tone of the German press towards Stalin is noticeable in the summer of 1939. Yet all these events can be seen as isolated incidents, not part of a long-term Soviet plan for a pact. Indeed, even more examples can be used to build up a scenario of western powers wanting improved relations with Germany at the expense of Soviet security. What was probably more important in persuading Stalin to consider a pact with Hitler was a deep suspicion of Chamberlain's appeasement, especially at Munich, and his dislike of the British decision to guarantee Poland, a nation known to be hostile to the Soviet Union.

In spite of all the various attempts to build up a picture of Stalin cold-bloodedly plotting a Nazi–Soviet pact, the whole argument is extremely unconvincing. It depends on the assumption that the Soviet Union entered negotiations with Britain and France for an alliance under false pretences. It seems much more likely, and more in accordance with the diplomatic evidence, that if Britain and France had sought a straightforward military alliance, and had agreed the details later, then this agreement could have been signed quickly in the weeks after the German attack on Prague. It was British delay and Polish intransigence that were the most significant reasons for failure. After all, the Soviets made a definite offer of an alliance in April 1939. It was a full four months before talks broke down. 'We formed the impression,' Stalin confessed to Churchill in 1942, 'that the British and French governments were not resolved to go to war if Poland were attacked'.[54]

It was only on 17 August 1939 that the Soviets were actually informed of Hitler's desire for a pact. By this stage, it was clear Poland would not allow Soviet troops on its soil. It was only on 19 August, when talks with Britain and France ceased, that Stalin accepted the German offer, and not until 21 August did Stalin agree to let Ribbentrop fly to Moscow to conclude the agreement. The Nazi–Soviet pact was finally signed on 23 August 1939. It offered Stalin far more security, in the short term, from Nazi aggression than a military alliance with western democracies he did not trust. Marshal Voroshilov, a leading figure in the Anglo-French-Soviet negotiations, claimed the primary reason the talks had failed was that the British and French governments 'dragged out the military discussions too long'.[55]

Hitler was convinced the Nazi–Soviet pact would lead swiftly to the isolation of Poland. The first response of Halifax to the pact was extremely calm. In his view, British policy had 'always discounted Russia, so materially the position is not really changed'.[56] The British promise to Poland was now to be put to the test. On 22 August 1939, Chamberlain told the cabinet, 'It is unthinkable that we should not carry out our obligations to Poland'.[57] He sent Hitler an unequivocal letter, approved by the cabinet, which stated that Britain intended to stand by Poland. On 24 August, Chamberlain, in expectation of war, gained parliamentary agreement to pass the Emergency Powers Act.[58] The following day, a formal Anglo-Polish military alliance was signed, to reinforce the British resolve not to abandon Poland.

This display of firmness clearly shocked Hitler, because he decided to postpone the attack on Poland, which had been set for dawn on 26 August. In a carefully calculated move, Hitler sent a letter to Chamberlain on 25 August 1939, in which he demanded the Danzig and Polish corridor questions be settled immediately. In return for a settlement, Hitler offered a non-aggression pact to Britain and promised to guarantee the British empire and to sign a treaty of disarmament. This offer aroused some discussion among British ministers. So too did the peace efforts of Birger Dahlerus, a

Swedish businessman who acted as a peace envoy for the 'moderate' Goering in the final days before war. On 26 August 1939, Dahlerus met Halifax at 10 Downing Street (he was sneaked in through the back door) and urged the foreign secretary to make a cordial plea to Hitler in order to calm his wrath. It seems Dahlerus was probably sincere, but was being used by the German government to give the impression that Germany was genuinely seeking a peaceful solution to the German–Polish dispute and thus leaving a door open for Chamberlain to set up a new Munich-style settlement.

With Hitler seemingly in a fix, a great deal of discussion went on within the British government over the next two days about how to respond to his proposals. Very few wanted to give Hitler a free hand over Poland, though Wilson, Butler and Henderson were all very optimistic about the chances of peace and favoured some sort of positive response. They were accused by Oliver Harvey of 'working like beavers for a Polish Munich'.[59] Chamberlain was anxious 'to bring things to a head' with Hitler and would accept a peaceful settlement only if it was compatible with Polish independence and entered into freely by the Polish government.[60]

The reply to Hitler went through several drafts, until it was finally agreed by the whole cabinet on 28 August. In the letter, Chamberlain suggested direct Polish–German talks to settle the issue peacefully, but would not 'acquiesce in a settlement which put in jeopardy the independence of the state to whom they had given their guarantee'.[61] In response, Hitler demanded a Polish emissary 'with full powers' go to Berlin on 30 August 1939, but the Polish government refused. The nearest Chamberlain came to placing any pressure on the Poles to negotiate with Hitler was a telegram sent on 30 August, which advised the Polish government to request Nazi terms for a settlement. But no pressure was placed by the British government on Poland to concede territory to Germany at any time from the offer of the guarantee to the outbreak of war.

At dawn on 1 September 1939, Hitler sent fifty-seven army divisions, heavily supported by tanks and aircraft, across the Polish border in a lightning *Blitzkrieg* attack. On the same day, Chamberlain told the cabinet, 'Our conscience was clear and there could be no question where our duty lay'. A telegram was sent to Hitler warning of the possibility of war unless he withdrew his troops from Poland.[62] On the same evening, Chamberlain told the Commons,

'Eighteen months ago in this House I prayed that the responsibility might not fall on me to ask this country to accept the awful arbitration of war. I fear I may not be able to avoid that responsibility'.[63] It might be thought that this speech would have ended with an immediate declaration of war. But the actual announcement did not come until 11.15 a.m. on 3 September. The decision not to go to war immediately was due to two factors. First, the Italian government proposed a conference to 'revise the clauses of the Treaty of Versailles'. Chamberlain and Halifax were prepared to delay the announcement of war to see if Hitler might accept this proposal. Second, the French government wanted to delay the announcement of war until 5 September in order to give the Italians a chance to pull Hitler back from war and to enable the effective mobilisation of the French army.[64]

On 2 September 1939, the cabinet, which did not meet until 4.15 p.m., was in an extremely difficult mood. The cabinet wanted the prime minister to announce war at midnight and to inform the Commons of this as soon as possible. But Chamberlain closed the meeting by suggesting the French government had to agree to a midnight declaration beforehand. The cabinet agreed to this, but did not agree to any further attempt to negotiate at a conference with Hitler.[65] Yet Halifax, supported by Chamberlain, ignored the cabinet and frantically urged Count Ciano, by telephone, to put further pressure on Berlin to withdraw troops from Poland and settle the matter at a conference. At the same time, Halifax was also trying to get the French government to finalise the details for the timing of the declaration of war, but the French would not agree to a midnight deadline. All this further delay left the worst possible impression on the cabinet and the overwhelming majority of MPs.

It was not until 7.15 p.m. that Chamberlain walked into the Commons to make what everyone thought was to be a declaration of war. Chamberlain told MPs of the Italian proposal for a conference and appeared to endorse the proposal, provided Germany would agree to withdraw its troops from Poland. There was no mention of a declaration of war nor an ultimatum, but only a further delay. The reaction of the Commons to this news was passionate, outraged and bitter. Halifax had reportedly 'never seen the Prime Minister so disturbed' and he expected the government to fall the next day unless an ultimatum was sent to Germany.[66] Shortly after this deeply humiliating episode in the Commons,

Simon told Chamberlain that the majority of the cabinet wanted an ultimatum sent straightaway. Meanwhile, Halifax was on the telephone to Bonnet, the French foreign minister, to inform him that Britain would have to send Germany a firm deadline for German withdrawal or war would begin. The final deadline of noon on Sunday 3 September 1939 was issued late on the previous evening. News also filtered through from Italy that the proposed conference was a non-starter. Hitler had no intention of withdrawing his troops from Poland.

Shortly before midnight, on the very eventful day of 2 September, the cabinet met for a second time. Chamberlain told its members that 'it was impossible to hold the position' after his mauling in the Commons. It was quickly agreed to issue an ultimatum which would be delivered by Henderson to the German government in Berlin at 9.00 a.m. on 3 September 1939. It stated that unless Hitler made a firm promise to withdraw his troops from Poland by 11.00 a.m. then Britain would declare war.[67] At 11.15 a.m. Neville Chamberlain went on radio to announce, in a low, sorrowful and dignified voice, 'Britain is at war with Germany', and to confess 'everything I have worked for, everything that I hoped for, everything I believed in during my public life, has crashed in ruins'.[68]

### Notes

1   R. A. C. Parker, *Chamberlain and Appeasement: British Policy and the Coming of the Second World War* (London, 1993), p. 324.

2   CAB 23, cabinet meeting, 31 October 1938.

3   *The Times*, 4 October 1938.

4   CAB 23, cabinet meeting, 31 October 1939.

5   Parker, *Appeasement*, pp. 182–5.

6   *Ibid.*, p. 185.

7   A. Roberts, *The Holy Fox: A Biography of Lord Halifax* (London, 1991), p. 127.

8   Parker, *Appeasement*, p. 188.

9   *Ibid.*, p. 131.

10   CAB 27, meeting of the foreign policy committee, 14 November 1938.

11   Chamberlain's diary, 6 November 1938, quoted in K. Feiling, *The Life of Neville Chamberlain* (London, 1946), p. 389.

**12** Conservative Party archive (Bodleian Library, Oxford) (hereafter CPA), foreign affairs files, 1937–40, Chamberlain to Ball, 3 February 1937.

**13** CPA, Neville Chamberlain, speech, 13 December 1938.

**14** Roberts, *Halifax*, p. 132.

**15** *Ibid.*, p. 133.

**16** Parker, *Appeasement*, p. 192.

**17** CAB 23, cabinet meeting, 21 December 1938.

**18** M. Muggeridge (ed.), *Ciano's Diplomatic Papers* (Oxford, 1948), pp. 9–10.

**19** J. Charmley, *Chamberlain and the Lost Peace* (London, 1989), pp. 187–8.

**20** Roberts, *Halifax*, p. 138.

**21** M. Cowling, *The Impact of Hitler. British Politics and British Policy 1933–1940* (London, 1975), p. 382.

**22** CAB 27, foreign policy committee, 25 January 1939.

**23** CAB 23, cabinet meeting, 18 January 1939.

**24** R. A. Butler, *The Art of the Possible* (London, 1971), p. 177.

**25** *The Times*, 7 February 1939.

**26** Charmley, *Chamberlain*, p. 160.

**27** Feiling, *Chamberlain*, p. 396.

**28** *Ibid.*

**29** *Ibid.*, pp. 396–7.

**30** Roberts, *Halifax*, pp. 141–2.

**31** CAB 23, cabinet meeting, 15 March 1939.

**32** *The Times*, 16 March 1939.

**33** *Ibid.*

**34** Chamberlain's diary, 19 March 1939, quoted in Feiling, *Chamberlain*, p. 401.

**35** *The Times*, 18 March 1939.

**36** CAB 23, cabinet meeting, 18 March 1939.

**37** Parker, *Appeasement*, p. 210.

**38** *The Times*, 19 March 1939.

**39** W. Carr, *Arms, Autarchy and Aggression* (London, 1968), p. 109.

**40** Feiling, *Chamberlain*, p. 407.

**41** *Ibid.*, p. 404.

**42** CAB 23, cabinet meeting, 30 March 1939.

**43** CAB 23, cabinet meeting, 5 April 1939.

**44** CAB 27, 'The Military Value of the USSR', report by the chiefs of staff sub-committee, presented to the foreign policy committee, April 1939.

**45** CAB 27, foreign policy committee, 16 May 1939.

**46** Parker, *Appeasement*, p. 228.

**47** Roberts, *Halifax*, p. 158.

**48** D. Dilks (ed.), *The Diaries of Sir Alexander Cadogan, 1938–45* (London, 1971), p. 182.

**49**   CAB 24, memorandum by Lord Halifax on advantages and disadvantages of an Anglo-Soviet alliance, 22 May 1939.

**50**   CAB 23, cabinet meeting, 24 May 1939.

**51**   Cowling, *Hitler*, p. 342.

**52**   Parker, *Appeasement*, p. 236.

**53**   *Ibid.*, p. 239.

**54**   W. S. Churchill, *The Gathering Storm* (London, 1962, 2nd edn), p. 347.

**55**   *Ibid.*, p. 348.

**56**   Roberts, *Halifax*, p. 167.

**57**   CAB 23, cabinet meeting 22 August 1939.

**58**   Charmley, *Chamberlain*, p. 201.

**59**   *Ibid.*, p. 202.

**60**   Chamberlain's diary, 10 September 1939, quoted in Feiling, *Chamberlain*, p. 417.

**61**   Parker, *Appeasement*, p. 333.

**62**   CAB 23, cabinet meeting, 1 September 1939.

**63**   Feiling, *Chamberlain*, p. 415.

**64**   *Ibid.*, p. 416.

**65**   CAB 23, cabinet meeting, 2 September 1939.

**66**   Parker, *Appeasement*, p. 241.

**67**   CAB 23, cabinet meeting, 2 September 1939.

**68**   Parker, *Appeasement*, p. 1.

# Part II
# Appeasement and British society
# 1918–1939

# 7

# Appeasers and anti-appeasers

The supporters of appeasement came from diverse groups – the Conservative Party, the Church of England and a number of right-wing extreme elements. The only significant group on the centre left to support appeasement under Chamberlain were pacifists. The feeling that the treaty of Versailles was unjust was widespread. Few Tories favoured direct British military involvement in European problems. Sir Arnold Wilson, a Tory MP, was not alone in calling for a return to a policy of isolation from European problems, supported by armaments but uncommitted to upholding collective security or taking part in any alliance system.[1]

There was very strong Conservative opposition to the formation of an Anglo-French alliance. It was widely thought that French belligerence towards Germany was a major cause of European tension. The only other possible candidate for an anti-German alliance was the Soviet Union, but the Stalinist regime was regarded by Tories in a less favourable light than Germany. Sir Edward Grigg, Tory MP, claimed that 'most Conservatives prefer the German system to the Russian because it is nationalistic in spirit and does not seek to unbalance the unity of other nations by dividing them on class lines'.[2] Mussolini's fascist regime was greatly admired by some. 'I am confident,' claimed Sir Austen Chamberlain, the previous Tory foreign secretary, 'that Mussolini is a patriot and a sincere man; I trust his word when given, and I think we might easily go far before finding an Italian, with whom it would be easier for the British government to work'.[3]

The League of Nations was never as popular with Conservatives as it was with members of the other two major political parties. Most Tories looked at European issues through the narrow prism of British self-interest and doubted whether collective security could deter military aggression. As Leopold Amery, Tory MP, put it, 'If we were the victims of unprovoked aggression today, we might as well call on the man in the moon for help as make a direct appeal to the League'.[4] Many Tories saw the policy of appeasement as an attractive alternative to support for the League.

By and large, there was very little opposition within the Conservative Party, especially before Munich, to the idea of removing the legitimate grievances of Nazi Germany. However, before Chamberlain became prime minister, the official party line was to support the 'appeasement of Europe' within the framework of the League of Nations. The most passionate supporters of appeasement in the Tory Party were those who wanted to place Anglo-German understanding at the forefront of British policy.

Lord Mount Temple was a keen supporter of the appeasement of Nazi Germany. Mount Temple was an ex-cabinet minister, a solid representative of the Tory aristocracy, a lifelong anti-communist and a great believer in the usefulness of pressure group activity to influence changes in party policy. In the Edwardian period, Mount Temple (then plain Wilfred Ashley, MP) was a leading figure in the Navy League, and founded the Anti Socialist Union. During the First World War, he set up the No More Waste Committee, which opposed the growth of state power. After 1918, Mount Temple helped set up the British Legion, organised several annual meetings of British and German war veterans and was an active member of the Anglo-German Association, a pressure group of businessmen set up before 1914, which encouraged close commercial links between the two countries.

In line with most Tory appeasers, Mount Temple believed Versailles was extremely unjust and he saw no reason to alter this view because Germany was ruled after 1933 by Hitler. Indeed, the Tory peer welcomed the Nazi revolution in 1933, which he claimed marked the birth of German nationhood and helped to destroy communist ideas which threatened to 'tear Germany apart'. Mount Temple thought Hitler had produced a 'national re-awakening' with the essentially liberal aim of uniting all German-speaking people, including those in Austria and Czechoslovakia, in one strong nation state which could act as a bulwark against the spread of communism, provide stability in central Europe and become an important trading partner for British business.[5] To this end, Mount Temple helped found yet another pressure group, the Anglo-German Fellowship, in 1935, which spread the gospel of the likely economic benefits for British business of close friendship with Nazi Germany. 'The friendly feelings of the English people towards Germany,' Mount Temple told an audience of German businessmen, 'are stronger than you imagine, and our public opinion is convinced that a final and clear understanding between our two peoples must be attained so that the peace and stability of the world can be truly established'.[6]

Another leading Tory appeaser was Lord Londonderry, who believed British policy under Baldwin consisted of slavish subservience towards France and urged close Anglo-German friendship as well as forming close personal links with leading Nazi figures. Ribbentrop, while German ambassador in London, regarded Londonderry as one of the most appreciative people in Britain of the Nazi regime. In the mid-1930s, Londonderry could not understand why the Baldwin government 'could not make common ground in some form or other with Germany in opposition to communism'.[7]

The desire to appease Nazi Germany became something of a fashion within British high society. The most famous meeting places were Londonderry House, and Cliveden, the beautiful Buckinghamshire retreat of Viscount Waldorf Astor, proprietor of the *Observer* and husband of Nancy Astor, the celebrated pro-appeasement Tory MP. Much has been written about the weekend parties and the influence of the so-called 'Cliveden set'. In retrospect, Cliveden has generally been dismissed as a side show of upper-class eccentrics with no great influence on British policy. This probably underestimates the importance of networking within British upper-class society during the 1930s. Many leading Tory appeasers were regulars at the weekend parties there and shared a number of attitudes, including: a desire for a more active policy of appeasement in which Anglo-German relations played a much more central role; a strong feeling that the foreign office – especially Vansittart – was a major barrier to closer Anglo-German relations; a deep hostility to communism; very little enthusiasm for the League of Nations; and a penchant for believing Hitler's aims were limited to a revision of the treaty of Versailles. Key figures in the Cliveden set – such as

Geoffrey Dawson, editor of *The Times*, Lady Astor, J. L. Garvin, editor of the *Observer*, Lord Halifax, Lord Lothian, Lord Mount Temple and Lord Londonderry – had the ear of many leading figures in the national government and all desired a programme to improve Anglo-German relations. They should not be completely dismissed as a background influence.

Such appeasers saw a visit to Nazi Germany as the most important method to counteract negative views of Hitler's regime. Geoffrey Dawson pioneered the use of a special envoy (Lord Lothian) who regularly visited Germany to meet leading Nazi figures. Lothian listened to the 'German point of view' while there and reported his views in *The Times* in order to influence public opinion back home. After one such visit, he reassuringly informed *Times* readers that 'Hitler has said explicitly to me, as he has also said publicly, that what Germany wants is equality, not war, that she is prepared to absolutely renounce war'.[8] Lothian often portrayed Hitler's foreign policy aims in an extremely favourable light in the British press and, along with other appeasers, sought to turn the appeasement of Nazi Germany into a respectable pastime.

It was part of the mentality of appeasement to believe steadfastly that personal and informal contact with leading Nazis was a vital means of encouraging cordial Anglo-German relations. Appeasers who visited Germany discussed Nazi philosophy with leading figures, attended the vast Nazi rallies at Nuremberg and wrote books, pamphlets and articles in the press generally favourable to appeasing Hitler on their return.

It seems Hitler greatly enjoyed meeting these often gullible British visitors. Josef Goebbels, minister of propaganda, quite openly used such visits to promote a favourable image of Nazism abroad. Sir Arnold Wilson accepted an invitation from the Nazi regime to visit Germany and gave a German radio audience his impressions:

> The country is bristling with new ideas and new methods. I was impressed by the energy and the skill of many hands directed towards a single task. I see less of a spirit of rivalry between nations, more of a comradeship within the nation. Less of preparations for external war, more of a desire to attain internal unity. I came to Germany as a student. I have found fresh hope and renewed confidence.[9]

On his return, Wilson claimed 'There was no Great Power with which we were less likely to become involved in war than Germany'.[10] Sir Thomas Moore, another Tory MP, also paid frequent visits and returned with similar optimistic accounts of the likely success of appeasement. 'If I may judge from my personal experience of Herr Hitler,' wrote Moore, 'peace and justice are the cornerstones of his policy'.[11]

These visits helped to promote the idea that the Nazis were sensible, charming, honest and sincere people, once you got to know them a little better. The only way really to get to know them well was through face-to-face contact, preferably in an informal setting. After meeting Hitler, ran the argument of British visitors to Germany, you would find the Nazi leader was not a fanatic but a statesman who might be willing to take part in a general settlement of European affairs. These visits helped to give Hitler a human face and amounted to public relations without the facts. The nasty side of life inside Nazi Germany was largely glossed over, explained away or mostly ignored.

This obviously helped the appeasement of Hitler to become respectable in the most surprising areas of British society. The policy even received the blessing of the leading figures in the Church of England. Most bishops also believed Versailles was unjust towards Germany and in need of revision. Cosmo Lang, archbishop of Canterbury, frequently urged a peaceful solution to international problems and enthusiastically supported Chamberlain's energetic efforts to find a peaceful solution to the Czech crisis. In February 1938, an editorial in the *Church Times* stated 'Czechoslovakia would be better off all around if it lost its German minority'.[12] After the signing of the Munich agreement, Lang gave a sermon in Westminster Abbey which portrayed Chamberlain as a national saviour who had prevented a second world war. However, *Kristallnacht* forced most Church of England bishops to have second thoughts about the morality of appeasing Hitler and support for the policy drained away completely after Prague.[13]

Another respectable group who supported appeasement were members of the pacifist movement. Inter-war Britain was a golden age for dedicated followers of pacifism. Numerous pacifist societies flourished – the Peace Pledge Union (PPU), the No More War Committee and the Peace Society. One estimate suggests over fifty pacifist groups existed in the 1930s. The growth of pacifism reflected a widespread public mood which suggested war was useless, wasteful, costly and should be opposed. In October 1934, Canon Richard ('Dick') Sheppard, the most well known pacifist, sent a famous 'peace letter' to all British national newspapers which called on those who opposed war to send him a postcard giving a pledge to 'renounce war'. Quite incredibly, 80,000 people replied and the result was the formation of the PPU. By 1939, the PPU had 130,000 members, 1,150 different groups nation-wide and its own newspaper, *Peace News*, with a circulation of 22,000. The PPU organised meetings, demonstrations and lectures, and produced pamphlets, books and documentary films to spread the gospel of peace. Dick Sheppard died in October 1937 and assumed the mantle of a martyr for peace.

The threat posed by Nazi Germany to world peace in the late 1930s became a central issue of discussion within the peace movement. Few PPU members had any false illusions about the brutal nature of Nazism, but the desire to avoid war meant pacifists often explained away, and sometimes even endorsed, many of Hitler's acts of aggression. Much PPU propaganda from 1936 to 1939 suggested Germany's long-term problems could be solved only by a revision of Versailles, accompanied by colonial and economic concessions. *Peace News* contains a great deal of pro-German, if not outright pro-Nazi, sympathy. During the Czech crisis, *Peace News* was one of the most enthusiastic supporters of Chamberlain's policy and carried a series of articles with one constant theme – the Sudeten Germans were an oppressed minority and Hitler had a strong moral case in pressing their claims. The leadership of the PPU also offered strong support for the Munich agreement. In October 1938, Stuart Morris, chairman of the PPU, not only pointed to the great sacrifice the Czechs had just made, but called on other countries to get ready to make similar sacrifices in the near future in the 'cause of peace'. After Hitler's march into Prague, *Peace News* was still willing to 'see the German point of view'.[14]

However, Prague caused some PPU supporters to question the morality of an extreme pacifist position when faced with an obvious aggressor. 'Occasionally,' claimed Rose Macaulay, a PPU sceptic, 'when reading some of the letters in *Peace News*, I (and others) half think we have got hold of the *Blackshirt* [the official newspaper of the British Union of Fascists] by mistake'.[15] Nevertheless, *Peace News* went on offering sympathy with German claims during the summer of 1939 and the PPU leadership went on urging for the policy of appeasement to be continued. On 11 August 1939, Morris was interviewed by a reporter from the *News Chronicle* and suggested that Chamberlain should have been prepared to 'give away much more to Hitler if any serious appeasement of German grievances was to be achieved'.[16] These remarks produced a deluge of public hostility which forced Morris, in a damage-limitation exercise, to write a letter to *News Chronicle* not only claiming he was misquoted in the interview, but also taking pains to stress that the PPU did not support peace 'at the expense of the national sovereignty of small nations'.[17] However, in their hatred of war, PPU members went on urging the appeasement of the dictators right up to the outbreak of war.

However, appeasement attracted many less than respectable supporters, in particular fringe groups on the extreme right. The most well known group in this category was the British Union of Fascists (BUF), led by Sir Oswald Mosley, the ex-Labour cabinet minister. The BUF was a child of the great depression. In 1932, the year in which he established the BUF, Mosley published *Greater Britain*, which called for a one-party state with industry under state control. Mosley's version of fascism aped European versions and never attracted mass support. Membership of the BUF came primarily from some right-wing eccentrics in high society, younger members of the middle class and white-collar workers. It peaked at 50,000 in 1934, but had fallen to 22,000 by 1939. Wherever the BUF went, violence usually followed close behind and was the major reason the party failed to attract mass support.[18]

The most important turning point in the fortunes of the BUF was a meeting held at Olympia, London, in June 1934, attended by 15,000 blackshirts, who proceeded to beat up a group of anti-fascist gatecrashers. These violent scenes, which were roundly condemned by *The Times* as a 'disgusting display of force' and by most mainstream political leaders, led to a dramatic fall in membership. After 1936 the BUF became more stridently pro-Nazi and anti-Semitic and changed its name to the British Union of Fascists and National Socialists (British Union). Marches by the BUF through Jewish districts of east London and cities in the Midlands and the north provoked violent street fights and induced the national government to introduce the Public Order Act in 1936, which gave the police extensive new powers to ban demonstrations and prohibited the use of uniforms by political parties.

On international affairs, the BUF had – for such a violent organisation – a decidedly anti-war outlook, designed to appeal to former soldiers. 'Our generation does not want war,' wrote a young BUF activist, 'we march for peace, as you marched in war. You fought for us and we cannot betray you'.[19] Another feature of BUF speeches and writings was a call for a return to 'splendid isolation' from European affairs. Mosley wanted Britain to keep out of all quarrels in Europe, concentrate on the empire and deal harshly with what he called 'the socialist enemy within'.

By and large, the BUF gave support to Chamberlain's appeasement, especially during the Czech crisis of 1938, primarily because most BUF members thought the policy favoured Hitler's aims, not out of any real affection for the prime minister. A Nazi-dominated Europe, with Britain left alone to concentrate on domestic politics and the preservation of its empire, was a place where Mosley and most BUF activists would have been quite happy to live. BUF members were the most enthusiastic fellow travellers with Nazism. Many had real sympathy with the foreign policy aims of the fascist dictators.[20] In March 1939, Mosley actually denounced Chamberlain for abandoning appeasement and offering a guarantee to Poland. In September 1939, Mosley was even calling for Chamberlain to organise 'another Munich' over Poland. In May 1940, Mosley was seen by Churchill as an 'enemy of the state' and put in prison, along with other leading figures in the BUF.

Other small right-wing pressure groups also supported appeasement. One of the most notable was the Link, established by Admiral Sir Barry Domvile in July 1937 to 'foster mutual understanding' between Britain and Germany.[21] Its leadership included a few eccentric Tory peers, the most notable being Lord Resedale, some minor academics and clergy and a number of cranky ex-colonels and ex-admirals. The rank and file members of the Link were largely drawn from *petit bourgeois* white-collar workers. Local branches of the Link were established all over the country and membership peaked at 4,300 in July 1939. The Link was a stridently pro-Nazi, anti-Semitic organisation, but its members also offered enthusiastic support to Chamberlain. A major feature of Link propaganda was to claim that Nazi Germany had received a bad press in Britain, and that groups, usually depicted as being 'Jews' or 'communist' inspired, had attempted to wreck Chamberlain's efforts for peace. Prague produced no real drop in support for the Link. 'I see no cause in what has happened,' wrote Sir Raymond Beazley, a leading figure in the Link, 'for increased tension between Britain and Germany'.[22] By the summer of 1939, however, the Link was regarded, even by the home secretary, as 'an instrument of pro-Nazi propaganda', and its most fervent activists went on advocating appeasement up until the outbreak of the Second World War.

Most of the groups described above supported Chamberlain's variety of appeasement very strongly. But there were important differences between them. The leading appeasers in the Tory Party wanted the alleviation of German grievances left behind by the treaty of Versailles and cordial Anglo-German friendship. Most were short-sighted and blinkered patriots and nearly all lost complete faith in the policy because of Hitler's actions, especially after the occupation of Prague. Mount Temple would support appeasement no further when news came of the anti-Semitic thuggery of *Kristallnacht*. Sir Arnold Wilson claimed Hitler could not be trusted again after Prague, and when war broke out he immediately volunteered, at the age of fifty-five, to serve as an RAF pilot. He was killed while on a bombing mission over Germany in May 1940.[23] Lady Astor and nearly all the Cliveden set were also convinced appeasement was futile once Hitler ripped up the Munich agreement. Without the establishment oxygen that had made it respectable, appeasement suddenly became a marginal and secretive pastime. It was only among members of the BUF and, perhaps, a few eccentrics on the right that real sympathy existed for a Nazi-dominated Europe. As for pacifists, they often ended up apologising for aggression even though most had no sympathy with the militarism Hitler's regime encouraged.

The critics of appeasement have attracted much less attention, but included a much wider spectrum of political opinion, including a majority of the Labour and Liberal Parties, a minority group of Tories and several left-wing groups and factions. The Labour Party was not opposed to the idea of the appeasement of legitimate grievances left behind by Versailles; before 1933, it had been seen as 'pro-German' and in favour of a revision of Versailles, but the Labour Party was opposed to the appeasement of Nazi Germany. The two cornerstones of Labour's outlook on international problems in the inter-war years were: support for the League – which was viewed by the Labour Party as the key means by which war was going to be prevented; and a strong conviction that increased arms spending would lead to war. In October 1933, the Labour Party conference voted unanimously to take no part in any future war and to resist war with the full force of the Labour movement. But Clement Attlee confessed in 1934 that 'The party has really not made up its mind whether to support extreme disarmament, isolation from European affairs, or to uphold collective security'.[24] In an effort to clarify Labour foreign policy, a pamphlet was produced entitled *For Socialism and Peace*, which was approved by the 1934 Labour Party conference. It promised that a future Labour government would: organise peace through the League; remove the causes of war; enact a 'Peace Act' which would make it impossible for a British government to use force as an instrument of national policy; disarm drastically; and ensure all international disputes were settled by 'peaceful means'.[25]

However, the rise of Hitler posed problems for Labour's peace crusade, given the pro-German stance of the Party before 1933. This was resolved by most Labour MPs, who suggested it was one thing to appease a democratic and disarmed Germany under moderate leadership, as the Labour Party had done before 1933, but quite another matter to appease the totalitarian, armed and nationalistic dictatorship of Adolf Hitler, which was viewed as immoral and futile.[26] By and large, the Labour Party blamed the slide towards Nazism in Germany on the failure to grant economic and colonial concessions to democratic Germany before Hitler took office.

With this opportunity lost, the Labour Party did not see Nazi Germany as a suitable case for appeasement. Most Labour MPs and trade unionists expressed alarm concerning the Nazi threat. In 1933, criticism from Labour MPs of Hitler's regime concentrated on domestic issues, such as the brutal suppression of trade unions, democracy, socialist parties and the free press.[27] However, the idea of building up arms to meet the Nazi threat initially found few supporters. In March 1935, for example, when the national government published the defence white paper which began the process of rearmament, Attlee claimed that the proposals were at variance with the spirit of the League. The reaction of the Labour Party to the German march into the Rhineland was equally ambiguous. Hugh Dalton, a Labour front-bench spokesman, told the Commons:

Public opinion does, I think, draw a distinction between the actions of Signor Mussolini in resorting to aggression, and the actions of Herr Hitler, which as much as we regard as reprehensible, have taken place within the frontiers of Germany.[28]

Many groups on the left of the Labour Party defied the leadership and criticised the League. The most significant critic was the outspoken Sir Stafford Cripps, who had supporters in the Socialist League. Cripps viewed the League of Nations as a club of 'capitalist imperialists' and considered the best means to resist the Hitler peril was to form a popular front of opponents of fascism and an alliance with the Soviet Union. But the latter demand was overwhelmingly rejected by the Labour Party at its 1937 conference and the Socialist League was expelled. After Munich, Cripps urged the Labour Party to make common cause with all opponents of Chamberlain's policy. This was also rejected by the moderate leadership of the party and Cripps was expelled for consistently refusing to toe the party line in May 1939.

It was the Spanish civil war and the heated debate it produced within the Labour Party which mark the real starting point of passionate opposition within the party to the whole idea of appeasing the fascist dictators. The crisis in Spain touched a nerve in the Labour movement. However, the first reaction of the Labour Party to the Spanish civil war, put forward at the 1936 conference, was to offer qualified support for the policy of non-intervention. Yet when it became clear that Hitler and Mussolini were giving direct military aid to Franco and his supporters, there was a sharp shift in attitudes. At the 1937 conference, it was agreed the party would agitate against non-intervention and advocate support for military action to halt fascism. The bombing of Guernica in April 1937 by the Luftwaffe provoked bitter outrage against the 'ruthless butchery' of the Fascist dictators.

By the time Chamberlain took office, the Labour Party had become extremely hostile to the whole idea of appeasing dictators. As Harold Laski, a Labour MP, recalled: 'The Labour Party stood four square against the policy of appeasement'.[29] In the view of Clement Attlee, the Labour leader, Chamberlain's appeasement was a futile attempt to pacify an obvious aggressor by satisfying specific demands without 'any guarantee such demands would cease in future or pave the way to any real and lasting peace.' Another

Labour MP saw it as a disreputable attempt, 'to appease the aggressor by the sacrifice of weaker states'.[30] Many in the Labour Party also felt that appeasers of Chamberlain's type were deluded in thinking Hitler was actually appeasable. 'I have believed from the first day Hitler came to office,' said Ernest Bevin in February 1938, 'that he intended right from that moment, and when he was strong enough, to wage war in the world'. By and large, the Labour Party felt it was 'impossible' to make lasting peace in Europe by satisfying the desires of Hitler at the expense of small nations.

As the tension in Europe mounted, the Labour Party slowly, and with some reservations, dropped its opposition to rearmament. In the spring of 1938, Attlee was criticising Chamberlain for his half-hearted attempt to improve air defence and in May 1938 the Labour Party called for a government inquiry to investigate the inadequacy of air rearmament. While Chamberlain was prime minister, the Labour Party constantly put difficult questions to him at question time and frequently sought parliamentary debates on foreign policy. From February to July 1938 alone, Chamberlain and Halifax had to deal with no less than 1,400 questions on foreign affairs and took part in no less than twenty-four debates on the subject.[31]

It was the Czech crisis of 1938 which revealed the depth of the gulf between Chamberlain and the Labour Party over appeasement. A large number of Labour MPs hurled a volley of abuse at Chamberlain for putting intolerable pressure on the Czechs. On 21 September 1938, the Labour Party and the TUC issued a joint statement which described the Anglo-French plan to cede the Sudetenland to Germany as a 'shameful surrender'. Attlee was so incensed by what he saw as 'the betrayal of the Czechs' that he arranged a private meeting with Chamberlain in which he asked for parliament to be recalled. Numerous Labour MPs attended public meetings and demonstrations which pledged to 'Stand Up for the Czechs'. A typical example was a speech by Emanuel Shinwell, MP, who pledged Labour's strong support for the 'defenceless Czechs' and denounced Chamberlain's policy as mere 'capitulation to Hitler's demands'.[32]

The Labour Party denounced Chamberlain for abandoning the Czechs at Munich. Hugh Dalton, a Labour front-bench spokesman, suggested the piece of paper Chamberlain flourished to reporters on his return from Germany was 'torn from the pages of *Mein Kampf*'.

Colonel Wedgwood, a Labour MP, claimed Chamberlain had 'purchased peace at the price of chains and slavery'. For Attlee, Munich was 'one of the gravest diplomatic defeats that this country and France have ever sustained' which left the Czechs abandoned and Britain and France isolated with 'all our potential allies gone'.[33]

However, there were flaws in Labour's approach to the Nazi threat. The Labour Party was not prepared to support the introduction of conscription and opposed increased spending to create a vast continental-style army to support France.

Quite clearly, Chamberlain's conduct of policy during the Czech crisis created sour feelings and mistrust between the two major British political parties. The Labour Party did not trust Chamberlain. They always believed he was willing to compromise with Hitler and Mussolini and wanted 'peace at any price'. On the day that Hitler's tanks motored through the streets of Prague in March 1939, Labour's anger with Chamberlain scaled new heights. Even when Chamberlain announced the guarantee to Poland, Attlee said he had 'no real trust in the Government to actually meet its obligations'.[34] In April 1939, when Chamberlain announced the introduction of conscription, Attlee denounced the move as 'useless and divisive' and likely to be followed by industrial conscription designed to weaken the power of the trade unions.

Few Labour MPs could believe the architect of Munich was serious in his drive to 'stop Hitler'. Deep-seated Labour suspicion of Chamberlain's underlying motives spilled out again over the negotiations for an Anglo-Soviet alliance. By this time, the Labour Party saw an alliance with the Soviet Union as essential if war stood any chance of being avoided. On 3 April 1939, for example, Dalton told Chamberlain bluntly either to gain an Anglo-Soviet agreement or 'get out'.[35] It seemed to most Labour MPs that Chamberlain was not serious about signing an Anglo-Soviet agreement and the leisurely pace of the negotiations was denounced in speeches by leading Labour figures. In August 1939, news of the Nazi–Soviet pact, although greeted with horror, within the Labour Party was largely blamed on Chamberlain's poor political judgement.

After the German attack on Poland on 1 September 1939, many Labour MPs suspected Chamberlain was eagerly planning another Munich-style settlement. Arthur Greenwood, deputising for Attlee, informed the Commons that 'aggression must cease now' and warned that 'Poland will not be allowed to go to the grave with those nations that were hanged by the appeasers'.[36] The delay in declaring war led to just about the most bitter opposition attack ever seen against a government in the Commons. When war was finally declared, the Labour Party refused to join a coalition government as long as Neville Chamberlain remained prime minister.

There was also a significant minority of opposition to Chamberlain's conduct of policy within the Conservative Party. The most famous Tory critic was Winston Churchill – a consistent opponent of appeasing Nazi Germany. In the 1930s Churchill was a discredited figure, viewed by the majority of Conservative MPs as a self-seeking individualist who lacked sound judgement, but he was still a powerful figure in the House of Commons, and his confidential contacts inside the navy, army and air force often made him a thorn in the side of the Chamberlain government in defence debates. In Chamberlain's view, it was Churchill's 'restless ambition that keeps him incessantly criticising any administration of which he is not a member'.[37] Only two Tory MPs, Brendan Bracken, an eccentric Irish firebrand, and Duncan Sandys, Churchill's son-in-law, offered anything like consistent support to Churchill.

On the day Hitler came to power, Churchill exclaimed 'Thank God for the French Army', and he consistently urged increased spending on defence, especially adequate air defence.[38] It is probably correct to view Churchill as an unreconstructed supporter of the balance-of-power principle, which often made him sound like yesterday's man. To counteract this impression, Churchill cloaked support for old-fashioned alliances in the rhetoric of the covenant of the League of Nations. Thus, 'Arms and the Covenant' became Churchill's alternative policy to deal with the Nazi threat and this allowed him to court centre and left-wing groups. In 1936, Churchill became involved in the Anti Nazi Association, led by Walter Citrine, the trade union leader, and was also a leading figure in Focus, a group closely associated with the League of Nations Union (see below). It is tempting to conclude that Churchill struck more of a chord with critics of appeasement outside the Tory Party, rather than within it.[39] For Churchill, Munich was 'the blackest page in British history' and only the 'first sip of a bitter cup which will be proffered to us year by year unless by a supreme recovery of moral health and martial vigour, we arise again and take our stand for freedom as in the olden time'. After Prague, Churchill was a passionate advocate of an Anglo-Soviet alliance.

Leopold Amery, a disgruntled backbencher from the imperialist right, represents a second and more ambiguous strand of Tory criticism of Chamberlain. Amery was a dedicated supporter of the British empire, a fervent anti-communist and an advocate of conscription, and wanted Britain to 'avoid Continental entanglements'. Indeed, Amery regarded Chamberlain's scepticism of the League of Nations as 'a breath of fresh air' and had no real objection to Germany gaining peaceful economic hegemony over central and eastern Europe. What Amery objected to about Chamberlain's policy was the idea of using the former German colonies as a bargaining chip in any new Anglo-German understanding. A number of right-wing imperialist Tories shared similar views. Robert Boothby, often portrayed as a Churchill supporter, claimed in his memoirs he was a member of an 'Amery group' of perhaps ten MPs who never worked closely with Churchill and came strongly to oppose Chamberlain.[40]

It is worth looking more closely at Amery's public and private views on appeasement. Amery urged cabinet ministers during the Czech crisis to reject the forcible hand-over of the Sudetenland to Hitler and described the Munich agreement as 'surrender in the face of the blatant use of force'. On the other hand, Amery confessed in his diary, only days later, 'I have never objected to German hegemony in central Europe'; he also suggested a settlement of European problems between Germany, Italy, Britain and France was preferable to 'closer collaboration with Soviet communism'.[41] In November 1938, Amery supported a motion with 227 other Tory MPs which pledged 'unqualified support' to Chamberlain's foreign policy.[42] It was only after the invasion of Prague that Amery became much more openly critical of Chamberlain's policy.

The most influential critic of Chamberlain's policy within the Tory Party was undoubtedly Sir Anthony Eden and after his resignation a definite 'Eden group' of about twenty-five MPs emerged. Apart from Duff Cooper, the ex-cabinet minister who resigned after Munich, the group consisted of mainly young or rebellious MPs – dubbed 'the Glamour Boys' – most notably Harold Macmillan, a future prime minister but a notorious and rather left-wing Tory rebel, Richard Law, son of the former Tory leader, and Ronald Cartland, brother of the famous romantic novelist. In his memoirs, Eden suggests 'about thirty' out of nearly 400 national government MPs supported his views on foreign policy.[43]

The 'Eden group' offered restrained criticism of Chamberlain's handling of the Czech crisis and over twenty-five of Eden's supporters abstained at the end of the Munich debate. Harold Nicolson, a firm Eden supporter, claimed Chamberlain's appeasement of Nazi Germany amounted to 'We give and they take'. But it was by no means an easy task to oppose the prime minister on foreign policy. Indeed, Chamberlain asked Conservative central office to warn the rebel MPs of the possible consequences of continued criticism. This led many local Conservative associations to meet rebel MPs and point out that de-selection would be the price of continued criticism. In parliament, government whips issued similar warnings. This probably helped keep criticism of Chamberlain's policy at a much lower level than might have been the case had Tory MPs been allowed a completely free hand. On the other hand, one historian claims open Tory criticism of Chamberlain's appeasement was so low it can be seen as 'a mirage, the more it is studied, the less substantial it appears'.[44]

The Liberal Party, although in decline, can also be regarded as yet another critic of Chamberlain's appeasement. In 1931, most of the Liberal Party, apart from Lloyd George and his few supporters, joined the national government. They were divided into two groups: the Simonite Liberals, led by Sir John Simon, who eventually became indistinguishable from Conservatives, and the Samuelite Liberals, led by Herbert Samuel, who remained committed to the ideals of free trade and who left the national government when imperial preference was introduced in 1932. The Liberal vote fell from over 5 million in 1931 to 1.5 million in 1935, and a mere twenty Liberal MPs sat in the Commons in the late 1930s, led by Sir Archibald Sinclair.

The dominant theme of the Liberal Party's attitude to foreign affairs was passionate support for the League of Nations. In 1937, Sinclair claimed Liberal foreign policy combined support for the covenant with the possession of adequate armaments to ensure the principles of collective security could be upheld by force if necessary. However, the party opposed the formation of an anti-fascist alliance between Britain, France and the Soviet Union until 1939. Liberals also initially supported non-intervention in the Spanish civil war but soon changed their minds. In 1938, the Liberals joined Labour in attacking Chamberlain's abandonment of support for the League of Nations.

A key Liberal pressure group on foreign policy was the League of Nations Union, led by Sir Robert Cecil. In 1931 the League of Nations Union boasted 400,000 members. Nearly every politician felt it expedient to express support for the organisation, but Liberal supporters were the true believers. Members spoke of abolishing war by negotiation and disarmament and claimed to be supported by the 'full weight of public opinion'. In 1935, the League of Nations Union helped organise the famous 'peace ballot'. Sir Austen Chamberlain thought it made political sense for Tories to join the League of Nations Union, even though he admitted it was 'full of the worst cranks he had ever known'.[45] Cecil believed most of the Conservative Party was anti-League and by 1938 reckoned Chamberlain had allowed the League to disintegrate. After Hitler's march into Prague, most Liberals favoured an Anglo-Soviet alliance and the formation an all-party coalition government led by Winston Churchill.

David Lloyd George ultimately shared these views but followed a largely independent line on foreign policy. Lloyd George had long been a keen advocate of the revision of the Versailles treaty he had helped create. He visited Hitler in 1936 and described him as a 'great figure'. He urged Britain to seek an Anglo-German settlement in which Hitler pledged to guarantee the frontiers in the west in return for sympathetic treatment of his grievances in eastern Europe. As late as the spring of 1937, Lloyd George was still expressing a great deal of sympathy for German grievances. But he soon changed his mind. He greatly mistrusted Chamberlain's political judgement and became a leading critic of his effort for peace. As the Czech crisis developed, Lloyd George's views grew closer to those of Churchill and after Prague he became a leading advocate for an Anglo-Soviet alliance.

Quite clearly, Chamberlain's appeasement had opponents from across the political spectrum. By and large, most critics, except those on the communist fringe and in the Socialist League, favoured support of the League of Nations, and the upholding of the principles of collective security. What the critics could not agree about was the level of military support required to deal with the fascist threat. The Labour and Liberal Parties supported the invoking of collective security, while Churchill favoured a grand anti-fascist alliance, cloaked under the banner of the League. It was only after Prague that the critics of appeasement came to favour an

Anglo-Soviet agreement. However, the Labour Party opposed conscription and only supported rearmament directed at air and naval power. It was only Churchill who had a fully thought out alternative military strategy, but he was largely an independent force.

What the critics of appeasement highlighted was a difference between the appeasement of legitimate grievances and the appeasement of the desires of a well armed and brutal dictator. The critics of appeasement were part of a mounting public dislike of the fascist dictators, which grew alongside Chamberlain's drive to preserve peace. The critics grew as Hitler proved unappeasable. It is probably worth adding that many of the leading figures in the Churchill coalition during the Second World War were also the leading critics of Chamberlain's policy. If the appeasers contributed to a political environment in which appeasement became a viable policy, then its critics helped to create doubts about the likely success of appeasement, and ultimately helped shift public attitudes to support for war. The tremendous unity against Nazi Germany during the Second World War owes far more to the critics of appeasement than to its supporters.

### Notes

1  R. A. C. Parker, *Chamberlain and Appeasement: British Policy and the Coming of the Second World War* (London, 1993), p. 317.

2  Sir E. Grigg, *Britain Looks at Germany* (London, 1938), p. 14.

3  C. Petrie, *The Life and Letters of Sir Austen Chamberlain*, vol. II (London, 1940), pp. 295–6.

4  *Hansard*, 11 March 1935, col. 100.

5  *The Times*, 26 February 1938.

6  Broadlands papers (Lord Mount Temple papers) (Hartley Library, University of Southampton) (hereafter BP) 81/1, speech in Berlin, 11 January 1936.

7  R. Gott and M. Gilbert, *The Appeasers* (London, 1966), p. 28.

8  *The Times*, 1 February 1935.

9  Times archive (London) (hereafter TA), transcript of radio broadcast by Sir Arnold Wilson, 16 May 1934.

10  Gott and Gilbert, *Appeasers*, p. 31.

11  *Ibid*.

12  F. R. Gannon, *The British Press and Germany, 1936–1939* (London, 1971), p. 178.

**13** For a more detailed examination of the position of the Church of England, see A. Wilkinson, *Dissent or Conform? War, Peace and the English Churches 1900–1945* (London, 1986).

**14** *Peace News*, 7 April 1939.

**15** *Ibid.*, 19 May 1939.

**16** *News Chronicle*, 11 August 1939.

**17** *Ibid.*, 13 August 1939.

**18** For a stimulating discussion see J. Stevenson, 'Conservatism and the Failure of Fascism in Interwar Britain', in M. Blinkhorn (ed.), *Fascists and Conservatives* (London, 1990), pp. 264–82.

**19** *The Blackshirt*, 8 August 1936.

**20** S. Cullen, 'The Development of the Idea and Policy of the British Union of Fascists 1932–1940', *Journal of Contemporary History* (1987), p. 129.

**21** Sir B. Domvile, *From Admiral to Cabin Boy* (London, 1947), pp. 64–5.

**22** *Anglo German Review*, April 1939.

**23** M. Cowling, *The Impact of Hitler. British Politics and British Policy 1933–1940* (London, 1975), p. 358.

**24** K. Harris, *Attlee* (London, 1982), p. 117.

**25** C. L. Mowat, *Britain Between the Wars* (London, 1955), p. 550.

**26** *Labour*, September 1933.

**27** *Report of the 35th Annual Conference of the Labour Party* (London, 1935), p. 178.

**28** Quoted in R. R. James, *Anthony Eden* (London, 1987), p. 117.

**29** H. Laski, *The War and the Future* (London, 1940), p. 3.

**30** *Hansard*, 21 October 1937, col. 76.

**31** *Ibid.*, 26 July 1938, col. 3033.

**32** *The Times*, 26 September 1938.

**33** *Hansard*, 3 October 1938, col. 52.

**34** *Ibid.*, 6 December 1938, col. 1038.

**35** *The Times*, 4 April 1939.

**36** *Ibid.*, 30 August 1939.

**37** J. Charmley, *Chamberlain and the Lost Peace* (London, 1989), p. 53.

**38** Parker, *Appeasement*, p. 320.

**39** *Hansard*, 5 October 1938, col. 370.

**40** R. Boothby, *I Fight to Live* (London, 1947), p. 164.

**41** N. Thompson, *The Anti-Appeasers: Conservative Opposition to Appeasement in the 1930s* (Oxford, 1971), p. 181.

**42** *The Times*, 22 November 1938.

**43** Earl of Avon, *Facing the Dictators* (London, 1962), p. 598.

**44** Thompson, *Anti-Appeasers*, p. 2.

**45** Cowling, *Hitler*, p. 21.

# 8

# The mass media, public opinion and appeasement

Many studies of appeasement assume the policy enjoyed widespread pubic support.[1] Most leading figures involved in the making of British policy during the 1930s held a similar belief. Yet the influence of the elusive force known as public opinion on British foreign policy has been curiously neglected. This chapter provides a wide survey of attitudes in the mass media and public opinion towards appeasement and shows the high level of news management, media manipulation, pressure and complicity which helped to restrict public debate.

The public was told about international events by the mass media. The dominant media in the 1930s were the press, radio (or wireless as it was popularly called) and the cinema. During the 1930s the media assumed their modern importance in the lives of the British people. In 1937, there were 1,577 newspapers and 3,119 weekly periodicals. Sales of national daily newspapers were 9.9 million and Sunday papers sold 15.7 million every week. Virtually every family in Britain, regardless of class, took a national newspaper. Headlines in the popular press grew larger and photographs and cartoons added to the visual presentation of news. The quality press used a more sober style, with less use of pictures and cartoons and more extensive reporting of world events. In addition, numerous local newspapers enjoyed healthy readerships. A national opinion poll conducted in 1938 found newspapers were the major information source used by the public to formulate opinions on foreign affairs, followed by friends, the radio and the cinema.[2]

The press faced competition from two new forms of mass entertainment during the inter-war years. The first was radio, confined to one single outlet: the British Broadcasting Corporation (BBC), founded in 1922. Radio was the major form of home entertainment. In 1938, 8.95 million households owned a radio licence.[3] BBC radio was heavily regulated, censored and restricted by the British government. News and current affairs programmes were not broadcast, except in exceptional circumstances, before 6 p.m. On Sunday, no programmes were aired before 12.30 p.m. Sir John Reith, the BBC director general, accepted government interference in foreign affairs reports and programming on current affairs. The views of opponents of government policy were hardly aired at all. A major reason for the BBC being keen to avoid controversy was its dependence on the licence fee, raised annually by the government.

Another relatively new form of mass communication was the cinema (or 'the pictures'), which had existed before 1918 but which expanded rapidly in the early 1930s. Films were originally silent, but after 1927 sound was added. In 1934, there were 4,305 cinemas in England, Wales and Scotland.[4] One estimate indicates that 23 million people visited the picture houses every week. Cinema was an extremely powerful medium, greatly enjoyed by the working classes, who liked feature films, made predominantly in Hollywood. But all cinemas also showed newsreels, which presented individual news and current affairs stories, accompanied by an upbeat commentary with a musical background, in the breaks between the main feature film and the second feature (known as the 'B' movie). In the 1930s five companies produced them – British-Gaumont, Pathe and Movietone, all British owned, and Paramount and Universal, owned by US subsidiaries. Over 500 individual newsreels were produced every year. The cinema was tightly controlled by the British Board of Film Censors and local councils. The content of newsreels was further restricted by self-censorship employed by the editors of the newsreel companies, who met regularly to decide how to cover touchy subjects. Only Paramount gave any coverage at all to critics of British foreign policy. Newsreels therefore presented a highly sanitised view of foreign policy. Chamberlain was presented as a peacemaker with good intentions, supported by a patriotic, happy and united British public.[5]

It is worth looking at the views presented by the mass media towards appeasement in greater detail. The press presented a wide variety of views. By far the most influential national newspaper during the inter-war years was *The Times*, known as the 'voice of the British government' in foreign capitals.[6] It was said that the editor of *The Times* was one of the four most powerful figures in British public life, along with the king, the prime minister and the archbishop of Canterbury. In 1939, its circulation was 204,491, but its select readership included the great and the good of British public life. In the 1930s, the paper was controlled by J. J. Astor and edited by Geoffrey Dawson, a gregarious Yorkshireman, educated at Eton and Balliol College, Oxford, who enjoyed a special relationship with most of the leading figures in the national government.

The role played by *The Times* in supporting appeasement has aroused controversy.[7] The most serious charge levelled against it revolves around the issue of whether the editorial team based at Printing House Square, London, systematically cut and censored articles by its Berlin correspondent, Norman Ebbut, to suit the needs of British diplomacy. The main defence against these charges comes in biographies of Dawson and Barrington-Ward, his deputy.[8] In fact, all the leading supporters of appeasement on *The Times* denied that Ebbut's articles were altered or distorted to fit an active policy of appeasement. G. R. Pearson, a chief foreign sub-editor, who dealt with Ebbut's dispatches, claimed, 'I am sure there was never an occasion when the editor intervened to alter a message from Ebbut so as to give a false picture of the situation. That would be tinkering with the facts, and it was not done. Ebbut's stuff was not modified.'[9]

*The Times* prided itself on the breadth and depth of its coverage of foreign affairs. It employed a vast team of foreign correspondents in every capital. In many ways, *The Times* had much better sources of information from abroad than the government. It was an unwritten rule never to change the views reported by a foreign correspondent.[10] Norman Ebbut was the leading *Times* correspondent in Germany from 1927 to 1937, ably assisted by Douglas Reed, his deputy. Ebbut's wide knowledge of German affairs was highly respected by fellow journalists in Berlin. In 1933, he was elected president of the Foreign Correspondents Association, a post which gave him great pleasure.[11] William Shirer, the noted US journalist, described Ebbut as 'by far the best-informed foreign correspondent in Germany during the 1930s'.[12]

However, Ebbut was completely dissatisfied with the mild image portrayed of Nazi Germany, not only in *The Times* but in most of the

British press.[13] It is equally clear that the Nazis did not like Ebbut. In February 1933, the propaganda ministry warned Ebbut his articles were 'critical and annoying' and urged him to take 'a more positive attitude' to Hitler now he was chancellor.[14] But Ebbut had no intention of following the news management of the regime. 'Certain things must be said,' Ebbut told a foreign news editor, 'carefully, but unmistakably about the regime for my own self respect'.[15]

It proved difficult for Ebbut to have Nazi Germany reported exactly in the way he wanted. The pressure came first from the Nazi regime, which threatened journalists with expulsion if they reported details of rearmament plans, anti-Semitism or life in the concentration camps. The verification of a controversial story was also difficult, because for a foreign correspondent to reveal a source was to place that person in danger. Thus, reports by foreign journalists in Germany could not reveal the whole truth. Ebbut's task was made doubly difficult by an editorial team in London which came to support closer Anglo-German relations.

'There is nothing I want less than to be a scaremonger,' Ebbut told Ralph Deakin, foreign news editor for *The Times* in November 1934, 'but there are nasty possibilities and it seems to me it would do no harm for them to be put fairly plainly to our public'.[16] But Ebbut found his own desire to report the truth about Nazi Germany soon conflicted with the editorial priorities of the paper. In November 1934, for example, Ebbut was complaining that twelve recent articles from Berlin were cut by *Times* sub-editors in such a manner 'as to leave the original distorted'.[17] One of Ebbut's most frequent complaints was of whole paragraphs in articles being 'torn from their context giving a distorted effect to the whole message'. By the end of 1934, Ebbut found he was being increasingly directed from London to cover certain stories. In December 1934, for example, Ebbut complained: 'Leading articles are now being requested, setting a dangerous precedent, as it tends to give a disproportionate prominence to matters which do not deserve it'.[18] Ebbut became increasingly dissatisfied with his treatment by the sub-editors in London and often complained about this to Dawson, who usually gave a soothing reassurance, such as 'I will tell the sub-editors you are to be the best judge of what you can and cannot say, of how your messages can be most discreetly framed'.[19]

In spite of this, the direction of Ebbut from London continued. In January 1935, Deakin made it clear the editorial team did not want

Ebbut to cover the League of Nations plebiscite on the return of the Saar to Nazi Germany.[20] On another occasion, Reed had informed the *Times* editors about startling new information concerning the Reichstag fire, but he was told: 'Let the Reichstag fire story drop. We have no belief in the story and there is little interest in it here'.[21] Within a matter of weeks, Ebbut was informed: 'It's time Reed was transferred to another area. Regard this as strictly confidential'.[22] Ebbut also found his own articles being increasingly restricted in subject matter, style and content. 'I sent you a request not to exceed a column on any story,' wrote Deakin, 'but you sent a column and a half of comment for which we could find no place'.[23] Shirer recorded Ebbut's dissatisfaction during this period in his diary: 'Ebbut has complained to me several times in private that *The Times* does not print all he sends, and does not want to hear too much of the bad side of nazi Germany'.[24]

Ebbut was aware that the desire to appease Germany was growing stronger at *The Times* and as it did the independence of journalists who were not happy about this state of affairs was jeopardised. Reed complained that as the European crisis grew intense his own frequent warnings about the German military threat were consistently ignored, and he was 'moved off the news maps of Europe'. During the Czech crisis, Reed asked to go to Prague; his request was not only refused but he was told bluntly to 'go to Belgrade'.[25] Reed resigned from *The Times* in October 1938, shortly after the signing of the Munich agreement.

There were many other journalists on *The Times* who also recalled critics of appeasement being given a hard time during the late 1930s. Colin Coote described those who dealt with reports from Germany on the paper as a 'carefully selected cabal' who ignored criticism of the Nazi regime in an atmosphere which was 'quite horrible' and even worse when Barrington-Ward was deputising for Dawson as editor.[26] A. L. Kennedy resigned as a *Times* reporter in 1937, convinced German intentions were wholly aggressive and feeling this view would not be published.[27] A. L. Barker also left in 1937, convinced the paper was determined to support appeasement and would not tolerate opposition to this editorial line.[28]

As for Ebbut, he was expelled from Germany in August 1937. The 'official' history of *The Times* reckons Ebbut was expelled because the Nazis feared his capacity for investigative journalism more than they valued the soothing editorials of Dawson. Horst

Michael, Ebbut's secret German contact, felt Ebbut's dismissal was linked to the Nazis' psychological preparation of German public opinion for war. This involved removing journalists who might try to unhinge the careful news management of the regime. This view is reinforced by the expulsion of Karl Robson of the *News Chronicle* in the same year. The German press claimed Ebbut had been 'spreading lies and distortions about the regime' for a long time and would have been expelled earlier but for the desire of Germany to 'maintain good press relations with Britain'.[29]

When Ebbut left Germany for the last time on 17 August 1937, fifty foreign correspondents braved the wrath of the Nazis to bid him farewell.[30] The great strain on Ebbut took a toll on his health and on his return to Britain he never again worked as a journalist, never wrote his memoirs and died in 1968.

Ebbut's relationship with the *Times* editors is really a microcosm of appeasement. Appeasers on *The Times* cut, directed and distorted Ebbut's reports and moved the highly talented investigative journalist Douglas Reed well away from the centre of European affairs. The Nazis wanted Ebbut and Reed to send out of Germany a sanitised view of the regime, and the *Times* editors, by cutting and distorting the words of its Berlin correspondents, ensured coverage of Nazi Germany was carefully manipulated, increasingly to suit the needs of the policy of appeasement.

The views of the remainder of the British press were not so rigidly supportive of appeasement. The *Daily Express*, owned by Lord Beaverbrook, also proprietor of the *Sunday Express* and the London *Evening Standard*, claimed to have the world's largest daily sale at 2.3 million copies. The *Express* was the most widely read popular newspaper during the 1930s, with a readership encompassing every income group except the very poorest members of the working class. Arthur Christiansen, the editor, claimed the role of a popular newspaper was 'to make the news exciting even when it is dull'.[31]

In the early 1930s the *Express* gave very favourable coverage to the Nazi regime. Sefton Delmer, the Berlin correspondent, was a favourite of Hitler.[32] In fact, Delmer became so intimate with leading Nazis that he was suspected of being on their payroll, a charge he denied in several later libel cases.[33] Delmer was interested in finding 'exclusive' stories on Hitler and the Nazis. He portrayed Hitler as a messianic leader risen from the people, who aimed to create a 'new Germany' from the ashes of what he termed 'communist violence and democratic instability'. In August 1931, Delmer invited Hitler to write an article on the British financial crisis, but the Nazi leader declined on the grounds that 'British public opinion might find it presumptuous of me to put forward views which in conformity with my knowledge and my conscience can only be a criticism of British political measures'.[34]

The close relationship Delmer enjoyed with Hitler often paid dividends. He was the first journalist to be given an interview with the Nazi leader when he was appointed chancellor. He was personally invited by a Nazi press chief to the scene of the Reichstag fire. However, when Delmer gave warts-and-all coverage of Nazi brutality on the 'night of the long knives', 30 June 1934, his cosy relationship quickly ended and he was expelled. With Delmer gone, the *Express* was more critical of the domestic policy of the regime, but its editorial line remained fully in support of appeasement. 'There Will be No War' was the slogan the paper ran on the front page on numerous occasions during the 1930s. The *Express* welcomed the Munich agreement, but the Nazi take-over in Czechoslovakia led it to claim that appeasement was based on a 'childlike faith' in Hitler's good intentions, which had proved groundless.[35]

The *Daily Mail*, owned by Lord Rothermere, enjoyed a circulation of 1.6 million and its readership came predominantly from the middle class. The *Mail* adopted a very sympathetic attitude towards Nazi Germany and even supported the BUF up until the Olympia meeting. George Ward Price, the Berlin correspondent, portrayed Nazi Germany in glowing terms and described Hitler as 'a sincere man of peace'. Hitler described him as the only British journalist who ever consistently reported his regime without prejudice. The *Mail* was an enthusiastic supporter of appeasement but also urged rearmament. It offered glowing praise for Chamberlain's efforts in securing the Munich agreement, but after Prague did a sudden about face and urged Chamberlain to prepare the nation for war.[36]

The *Daily Telegraph* was a quality newspaper with a distinctly pro-Conservative bias. Its circulation rose from over 226,000 in 1933 to over 763,000 in 1939. Its readership was predominantly drawn from the upper middle classes. The *Telegraph* was not opposed to the appeasement of legitimate grievances but was very critical of appeasing Hitler. Arthur Mann, the Berlin correspondent, never had any difficulty getting very critical articles of Hitler and the Nazis published. During the Czech crisis of 1938, Hoare, the home secretary, informed Arthur Watson, the *Telegraph* editor, that Chamberlain was angry about the critical coverage of his policy in the paper, but the warning was politely ignored. The *Telegraph* never urged Britain to fight a war to save Czechoslovakia in 1938 but was deeply critical of what it saw as the 'sacrifice' of that small nation.[37] The *Telegraph* wrote of Munich: 'It was Mr Disraeli who said that England's two great assets in the world were her fleet and her good name. Today we must console ourselves that we still have our fleet'.[38] The *Telegraph* viewed Prague as 'a monstrous outrage' which had reduced Munich to a 'complete mockery and left appeasement dead and buried'.[39]

The *Observer* was a quality Sunday newspaper, owned by William Waldorf Astor and edited by J. L. Garvin, a leading figure in the Cliveden set. Its circulation of 214,000 came predominantly from the professional middle classes. The *Observer* offered enthusiastic support for the policy of appeasement and constantly suggested that Hitler wanted a peaceful and negotiated settlement of German grievances. Garvin believed Chamberlain was 'a thousand times right' to save peace at Munich, but he also thought the Czech crisis had revealed Britain's military weakness and he urged a new surge of spending on arms.[40] Prague was shocking to Garvin, who described it as 'the most shameful page in the annals of Europe', and he changed the editorial line from appeasement to a very strident anti-Nazi stance.[41]

The *News Chronicle*, owned by the Cadbury family, was a popular and lightweight newspaper, with a circulation of 1,320,000, drawn mainly from the lower middle class. The *Chronicle*, now defunct, can be regarded as a very bitter critic of Chamberlain's drive for appeasement. Ribbentrop, then German ambassador in London, complained to the foreign office about the *Chronicle*'s 'mischief making' coverage of Nazi Germany. In 1937 Karl Robson, the Berlin correspondent of the *Chronicle*, was expelled from Germany because of his critical reporting. The *Chronicle* claimed that the Munich agreement had put the Czechs at 'the mercy of the Nazis',[42] and after Prague claimed that Chamberlain had operated under the title 'appeasement' – a policy which sacrificed small nations and severely dented Britain's moral standing in the world for no obvious gain.[43]

The *Manchester Guardian* enjoyed a circulation of 45,000, primarily composed of educated middle-class intellectuals with a social conscience. The *Guardian* denounced Versailles and supported the League of Nations. It was not certain Hitler should be offered concessions denied to democratic Germany. F. A. Voigt, the Berlin correspondent, was a bitter critic of the Nazi regime and came to believe Hitler's aims were wholly aggressive. The *Guardian* described Munich as an 'intolerable price to pay for peace' and urged Chamberlain to strengthen Britain's relations with the United States and the Soviet Union, instead of 'keeping in with dictators no matter what the price'.[44] The *Guardian* claimed the invasion of Czechoslovakia left Chamberlain's policy exposed as 'a dream fantasy'.[45]

The *Daily Herald* was the only major popular daily national newspaper to offer consistent support to the Labour Party during the 1930s. It was viewed as a working person's newspaper and most of its readers came from the lowest-income groups. The *Herald* saw the Czech problem as a 'Hitler crisis' that 'should be settled peacefully' and viewed Munich with a sense of relief, but this quickly gave way to unreserved condemnation. The *Herald* claimed Chamberlain's Munich diplomacy had neglected principles of international law, order and morality.[46] Prague was viewed by the *Herald* as an act of 'naked aggression' which could only be stopped by a 'determined policy of co-operation' between Britain, France, the Soviet Union and the United States.[47]

The local press expressed an equally wide variety of views. The *Glasgow Herald* reckoned Munich was a 'diktat' and urged Chamberlain to pursue rearmament with renewed vigour.[48] The Cardiff *Western Mail* could not understand the 'foolish and quite inexcusable disparagement of the Prime Minister's splendid achievement in securing the Munich agreement'[49] but its editor suggested after Prague that any further talk of appeasement would be 'a greater folly than reading a tract to a Bengal Tiger'.[50] The *Yorkshire Observer* praised Chamberlain for giving Europe 'one more chance for peace' at Munich,[51] but accepted it was only 'a scrap of paper' after Prague.[52] The Liverpool *Daily Post* described Hitler's actions towards Czechoslovakia as 'mean and sadistic' and urged Chamberlain to support collective security to 'save the world from disaster'.[53] The Leeds *Weekly Citizen* claimed after Prague: 'We have been brought to this pass by a Government which was formed to defend democracy and collective security and which has spent its energies destroying both'.[54]

The leading weekly periodicals displayed similarly diverse views. The *New Statesman*, with a circulation of 30,000 per week, was the most influential. Its editorial line strongly opposed Nazi Germany but expressed a hatred of war, rejected rearmament and saw Versailles as unjust. However, the *New Statesman* reckoned offering appeasement to Hitler was fraught with moral difficulties and likely to bring on a German–Soviet war. It cautiously welcomed Munich, but after Prague admitted appeasement was not feasible, given the obvious aggressive designs of the Nazi regime.

The *Spectator*, with a circulation of 25,000, was a centre-right publication which offered firm support to Chamberlain. It disliked communism, opposed war and constantly stressed that Hitler's foreign policy aims were restricted to a revision of legitimate grievances left behind by Versailles. The *Spectator* suggested Chamberlain had no alternative but to sign the Munich agreement. However, Prague forced it to abandon its support for appeasement and accept that Hitler had been driving for 'continental hegemony' dressed up in the language of legitimate grievances all along.

The *Economist*, with a circulation of 12,000, was a Liberal periodical and was very stridently anti-Nazi. A constant theme of the editorial line was that strategic weakness lay at the heart of Britain's weak diplomatic stance. The *Economist* was very critical of Chamberlain's appeasement, which was defined as 'throwing the weak to the wolves in the hope this would satisfy the appetite of the wolves'. It urged the creation of a power bloc against Germany and suggested British policy should move closer to the United States and the Soviet Union.

*Tribune*, with a circulation of 25,000, was a socialist periodical which opposed the appeasement of Nazi Germany and rearmament, but did urge the formation of a popular front to uphold the principles of collective security. *Tribune* described Chamberlain's policy as the 'appeasement of Hitler's aims in eastern Europe at the expense of small nations' and it believed this policy would enable Hitler to build up power for the destruction of the Soviet Union. It described Munich as a 'sell out' to Hitler and after Prague denounced Chamberlain as a 'guilty man'.[55]

It seems that Hitler was deeply unhappy with the way his foreign policy was portrayed in the British press. 'Hitler was unreasonably sensitive to press criticism,' recalled Neville Henderson, the British ambassador in Berlin, 'and it did not help me in my diplomatic task if Hitler's back was constantly being rubbed up the wrong way by press criticism'.[56] After 1937, Hitler's dislike of British press coverage of Nazi Germany intensified. As a result, pressure mounted on foreign journalists who produced critical reports. In speeches by Hitler, attacks on the British press were a frequent theme: 'The British government wishes to limit armaments and ban bombing. I once proposed this myself. But at the same time I also suggested it was still more important to prevent the poisoning of public opinion in the press'.[57] When Hitler met Halifax in November 1937 he told him bluntly that 'nine tenths of all international tension was due to the licentious press of the democratic nations'. In reply, Halifax gave an assurance to the Nazi leader that 'His Majesty's government would do everything in their power to influence our press to avoid unnecessary offence'.[58] It is known that Halifax did make some effort to persuade the press to avoid giving offence to the Nazi regime. He met the proprietors of newspapers known to be critical of the Nazis, including Lord Southwood, who controlled the *Daily Herald*, and Sir Walter Layton, head of the *News Chronicle*, and asked them to treat coverage of Nazi Germany with restraint. Halifax also asked the general manager of the London *Evening Standard* if he would press David Low, the cartoonist, to tone down his wickedly brilliant cartoons of leading Nazi figures.

By and large, the Chamberlain government tried to persuade editors to operate an informal self-censorship. Hoare made some effort to urge restraint on the press during the Czech crisis. Editors of leading national newspapers were asked to support Chamberlain's efforts to gain a peaceful settlement and to avoid critical comment. Yet the freedom enjoyed by the press ensured that total government control was never feasible and critical comment continued to appear.

Government pressure to restrict criticism of appeasement on BBC radio was far more successful. Radio coverage of foreign policy during the inter-war years was severely restricted through a combination of discreet pressure, self-censorship and guidance from Downing Street and the foreign office. It was believed the BBC was regarded abroad as an official government organisation and needed to operate with great caution. As a result, BBC coverage of international events hardly ever offered critical comments and severely limited the opportunities for opponents to criticise government policy.

In February 1938, the BBC was told by the foreign office 'to say nothing of Germany and Italy' when reporting Eden's resignation. In March 1938, Halifax approached the BBC and asked it to take account of the 'extreme sensitiveness of Hitler and Mussolini' when reporting news about them. Lord Reith did not resist this pressure and reportedly told Ribbentrop to inform Hitler that the BBC was not anti-Nazi. A great deal of government pressure on the BBC was reserved for critics of Chamberlain's policy. In early 1938, Josiah Wedgwood, the Labour MP, refused to delete critical comments on Hitler and Mussolini from a talk show called 'The Way of Peace' and found the broadcast promptly cancelled.

Pressure on the BBC from the Chamberlain government's media machine grew extremely strong during the Czech crisis. In July 1938, Harold Nicolson, a leading anti-appeaser, started a series of programmes called 'The Past Week', but this ran into trouble with the foreign office because Nicolson started including weekly developments on the Czech crisis. As a result, the foreign office gained agreement from the BBC to vet Nicolson's scripts before each broadcast. On 5 September 1938, the foreign office asked Nicolson not to discuss the Czech crisis at all on 'The Past Week'. After much heated discussion, a reluctant and angry Nicolson changed his script and ended up talking not about the Czech crisis but about a rise in the price of milk. In the same period, two talks by Vernon Bartlett on 'Children's Hour' were cancelled on advice from the foreign office.[59]

In fact, BBC radio listeners knew hardly anything about what took place in the meetings between Hitler and Chamberlain. The lack of discussion of the Czech crisis on the BBC led the *Listener* to comment:

This week as never before during the whole history of broadcasting the people of this country have listened in for news and information. Two speeches stand out. They are the recorded statements of Mr. Chamberlain before leaving for Germany and on his return.... But what else are we being given? Certainly less than we might reasonably have expected ... five minutes in the street, or in the Tube, listening to people talking are sufficient to show that the majority are extremely vague about the issues involved in Czechoslovakia.[60]

Little wonder Chamberlain could tell BBC radio listeners on 27 September 1938 'How horrible, fantastic, incredible it is, that we should be trying on gas masks here because of a quarrel in a far away country between people of whom we know nothing'.[61] Yet listeners were told a great deal about Chamberlain's triumphant return from Munich. The BBC presented live radio commentary of his arrival and a BBC reporter estimated the crowd outside 10 Downing Street at 5,000. What he failed to mention was that 16,000 people were demonstrating at the same time in Trafalgar Square, less than a mile away, against the agreement. The BBC also reported news of Chamberlain receiving tremendous fan mail and presents from well-wishers after Munich. But Mass Observation noted that at one single protest meeting against Munich, 800 letters alone were written and posted to 10 Downing Street.[62]

The cinema newsreels gave an equally sanitised presentation of events. Chamberlain displayed a remarkably modern skill in presenting his peace mission for the newsreels with eye-catching photo opportunities and brief sound bites. The typically upbeat newsreel commentary presented Chamberlain as a noble politician on a 'mission for peace'. In September 1938, a British-Gaumont newsreel described Chamberlain as 'Our great statesman, who has brought to politics the common-sense point of view of the ordinary man in the street and on whose same judgement we place our hopes of peace and happiness'. The only newsreel which ran counter to the carefully constructed image of Chamberlain as the sincere peacemaker was produced by Paramount, a US-owned company, and appeared on 22 September 1938. It included interviews with three critics of Chamberlain's policy. But the foreign office immediately contacted the owner of the parent company in the United States and the newsreel was withdrawn. Uncomfortable facts were not allowed to interfere with the powerful propaganda images of Chamberlain as the 'dove of peace'. Chamberlain's return from Munich was the major cinema newsreel event of the inter-war period. It was at Heston Airport that Chamberlain flourished the famous piece of paper above his head, in a classic gesture designed by Chamberlain to leave the newsreel cameramen and press photographers with a powerful image of peace. This was propaganda without the facts. It was typical of the careful news management employed by Chamberlain and the British government throughout the crisis. No indication was given of the pressure placed on Czechoslovakia to secure the agreement and few insights were offered into the warlike personality Hitler had so obviously displayed in his meetings with the prime minister.

It is more difficult to assess accurately the views of ordinary members of the public towards appeasement. However, public opinion polls were used in the late 1930s. These were pioneered by Dr George Gallup, who applied market research techniques to politics. When his Gallup organisation correctly predicted the outcome of the 1936 US presidential election by compiling a carefully selected representative sample of the electorate, the technique became popular. By 1937, polls were taken frequently in Britain and they offer an opportunity to assess public opinion.

Evidence from British opinion polls shows the most favoured foreign policy in the late 1930s was not appeasement but support for the League of Nations and collective security. In July 1937, 71 per cent of the British public favoured support for the League of Nations as the best method to keep the peace. In December 1937, 72 per cent still expressed support for the League. These polls were undertaken by the British Institute of Public Opinion, a British subsidiary of Gallup, which undertook monthly surveys of opinion on key issues. One survey conducted in February 1938 showed 71 per cent of those polled thought Eden was right to resign. Another poll in March 1938 asked, 'Do you support Mr. Chamberlain's foreign policy?' and found 58 per cent said no, 26 per cent said yes and 16 per cent expressed no opinion at all.[63]

Another very interesting exercise in evaluating public opinion towards foreign policy was conducted by Mass Observation. However, the techniques used by Mass Observation differed greatly from those of the opinion pollsters. They employed a national panel of 2,000 volunteers who not only collected views from a wide selection of people, but also observed ordinary people at work, in the pub, at home and at the cinema. Mass Observation undertook a detailed study of the Czech crisis in 1938. The majority of people interviewed had little knowledge of the issues and most put this down to two factors. One was the high level of government secrecy surrounding the negotiations and the other was a difficulty in comprehending the wide variety of contradictory solutions offered by the newspapers.[64]

In August 1938, Mass Observation undertook a national survey on whether the Czech crisis would lead to war. This found 36 per cent thought war likely, 46 per cent thought it unlikely, while 14 per cent thought there was a fifty–fifty chance, with 4 per cent holding no view. Most middle-class people interviewed thought there would be no war, while most of the working class felt war was a real possibility. On 15 September 1938, a national survey asked the rather bland question 'Do you think Chamberlain flying to see Hitler will help peace?' This showed 70 per cent thinking 'it was a good thing', 10 per cent viewing it as 'a bad thing' and 20 per cent undecided.

Yet when news emerged of the harsh terms imposed on Czecho-slovakia at Godesberg, a national poll found 44 per cent of the public 'indignant', with only 18 per cent 'pro-Chamberlain' and a mere 6 per cent believing there would be no war. Yet such was the high level of public ignorance that 32 per cent held no firm view at all. It seems that without the facts, the public was easily misled about the real prospects for peace. It is equally difficult to imagine Chamberlain's conduct of the Czech crisis would have been so popular had the public been allowed full scrutiny of the facts and an open debate of the issues in all areas of the mass media.

A national opinion poll taken shortly after Munich showed 51 per cent 'satisfied' with Chamberlain's actions, but 39 per cent were 'not satisfied'. Another poll taken in the same period showed that 86 per cent of the public did not believe Hitler's claim about having 'no more territorial ambitions in Europe'. It also seems Hitler was a deeply unpopular figure among the vast majority of the British public. Mass Observation noted that when newsreels concerning the Czech crisis appeared, the majority of the audiences booed very loudly whenever they saw Hitler. The same was true even of children. In October 1938, for example, a wide-ranging survey was undertaken among the 150,000 youngsters who attended the Satur-day morning 'Mickey Mouse Club', organised by the Odeon cinema chain. This found that 88 per cent of children showed a strong dislike of Hitler and Mussolini whenever they appeared on screen and 53 per cent of them booed and hissed very loudly whenever they saw either dictator.[65]

In November 1938, when the British public heard news of Nazi brutality on *Kristallnacht*, a national opinion poll showed 73 per cent thought Nazi ill-treatment of the Jews was a major obstacle to

Anglo-German understanding, with only 15 per cent in disagreement and 12 per cent 'don't knows'. It seems very likely that if the government had opposed concessions to Hitler and chose to portray his designs as aggressive then public opinion would have supported a policy designed to 'stop Hitler' well before Prague. News management during the Munich crisis simply postponed the inevitable day when Hitler's openly aggressive designs could no longer be hidden. In March 1939, the British-Gaumont newsreel commentator said over pictures of German tanks rumbling through the streets of Prague, 'Once again the rattle of a German army on the march echoes throughout Europe.... At Munich, the Fuhrer gave his word that he wanted no more land in Europe. These pictures show you what his words are worth'.

The growth of the mass media during the inter-war years made the public increasingly more aware of major foreign events. At the same time, the power of the mass media to influence public opinion led the government to think more carefully about how it wanted these events covered. The relative freedom enjoyed by the press was not extended to radio and newsreels. After 1918, mass democracy had arrived and public opinion did become an important factor in the minds of politicians.

The BBC and the newsreels allowed themselves to be used as witting agents of the government propaganda machine during the Czech crisis. Open public debate on foreign policy was largely confined to sections of the press, public meetings, street demonstrations and private conversations. The British public were given in the newsreels photo opportunities and on radio sound bites and few facts. This careful news management served to keep a small majority in favour of the Munich agreement. But the euphoria quickly died away and was replaced by a large amount of anger and discontent. Electoral evidence in the months after Munich tends to reinforce this view. In the by-elections which followed Munich, in October and November 1938, foreign policy played a dominant role and the national government suffered a substantial fall in its vote. The Tories actually lost two safe seats, at Dartford and Bridgwater. The Labour Party, which opposed Munich, saw its support rise substantially, even though a year earlier the *Economist* had remarked, 'For some time now it has become evident that the Labour Party is making no headway in the country'.[66] It seems that opposition to Chamberlain's conduct of foreign policy was the major factor which produced this unusually sharp fall in the Conservative vote in the by-elections which followed Munich. The immediate feeling of relief which followed Munich was soon replaced by anger and bitterness. The major change in public opinion towards appeasing Hitler, which is often seen to begin with the invasion of Prague, was actually being kept under wraps by a news management of events. Public hostility towards Hitler and Nazi Germany was already extremely powerful. Perhaps a poster outside a cinema in the days after Munich summed up the state of British public opinion quite well. It read, 'Chamberlain the Peacemaker: For One Week Only'.

### Notes

1  See, for example, R. A. C. Parker, *Chamberlain and Appeasement: British Policy and the Coming of the Second World War* (London, 1993), p. 1.

2  T. Harrison and C. Madge, *Britain by Mass Observation* (London, 1986), p. 30.

3  D. H. Butler and S. Freeman, *British Political Facts* (London, 1968), pp. 212–14.

4  S. Rowson. 'A Statistical Survey of the Cinema Industry in Great Britain', *Journal of the Royal Historical Society* (1936).

5  See N. Pronay, 'British Newsreels in the 1930s. 1. Audience and Producers', *History* (1971).

6  B. Inglis, 'The Influence of the Times', *Historical Studies* (1971).

7  See: *The History of the Times*, vol. IV, part 2 (London, 1952); F. Williams, *The Press, Parliament and the People* (London, 1964); S. Koss, *The Rise and Fall of the Political Press in Britain. Vol. II: The Twentieth Century* (London, 1984); F. McDonough, 'The Times, Norman Ebbut and the Nazis, 1927–1937', *Journal of Contemporary History* (1992).

8  See: F. R. Gannon, *The British Press and Nazi Germany, 1936–1939* (London, 1971); D. MacLachlin, *In the Chair: Barrington-Ward of the Times, 1927–1948* (London, 1972); J. E. Wrench, *Geoffrey Dawson and our Times* (London, 1955).

9  Gannon, *Press*, p. 125.

10  *Ibid.*, p. 124.

11  *The Times*, 19 October 1968.

12  W. Shirer, *Berlin Dairy* (London, 1941), p. 33.

13  TA, report by Ebbut to the British Board of Deputies of British Jews, May 1932.

14  Manchester Guardian archive (John Rylands Library, Manchester), Werth to Crozier, 10 February 1933.

15  TA, Ebbut to Deakin, April 1933.

16  TA, Ebbut to Deakin, 16 November 1934.

17  TA, Ebbut to Deakin, 11 November 1934.

18  TA, Ebbut to Deakin, 18 November 1934.

19  TA, Dawson to Ebbut, 20 December 1934.

20  TA, Deakin to Ebbut, 2 January 1935.

21  TA, foreign news editor to Reed, 8 January 1935 (telegram). On 27 February 1933, the Reichstag went up in flames in mysterious circumstances. The Nazis blamed the fire on a young Dutch communist, van der Lubbe, and it seems he may have been responsible. However, in the early 1930s many people outside Germany believed the fire was engineered by Hitler as a pretext to suppress communism.

22  TA, Deakin to Ebbut, 30 January 1935.

23  TA, Deakin to Ebbut, 4 April 1935.

24  Shirer, *Diary*, p. 42.

25  TA, Reed to Dawson, 16 March 1938, Reed to Dawson, 10 October 1938.

26  C. Coote, *Editorial* (London, 1964), p. 170.

27  TA, Kennedy to Dawson, 17 October 1937.

28  MacLachlin, *In the Chair*, p. 115.

29  TA, European Press Association report, 10 September 1937.

30  Shirer, *Diary*, p. 68.

31  A. Christiansen, *Headlines All My Life* (London, 1957), p. 144.

32  E. Hanfstangl, *Hitler: Missing Years* (London, 1957), p. 180.

33  J. C. Harsh, *Patterns of Conquest* (London, 1942), p. 241.

34  Facsimile of letter by Hitler reproduced in S. Delmer, *Trail Sinister* (London, 1961).

35  *Daily Express*, 16 March 1939.

36  *Daily Mail*, 17 March 1939.

37  *Daily Telegraph*, 29 September 1938.

38  *Ibid.*, 4 October 1938.

39  *Ibid.*, 16 March 1939.

40  *Observer*, 18 December 1938.

41  *Ibid.*, 19 March 1939.

42  *News Chronicle*, 1 October 1938.

43  *Ibid.*, 16 March 1939.

44  *Manchester Guardian*, 3 and 7 October 1938.

45  *Ibid.*, 16 March 1939.

46  *Daily Herald*, 3–7 October 1939.

47  *Ibid.*, 16 March 1939.

48  *Glasgow Herald*, 1 October 1938.

49  Cardiff *Western Mail*, 3 October 1938.

50  *Ibid.*, 16 March 1939.

**51**   *Yorkshire Observer*, 29 September 1938.

**52**   *Ibid.*, 16 March 1939.

**53**   Liverpool *Daily Post*, 16 March 1939.

**54**   Leeds *Weekly Citizen*, 16 March 1939

**55**   For a detailed examination of the entire weekly and periodical press see B. Morris, *The Roots of Appeasement: The British Weekly Press and Nazi Germany during the 1930s* (London, 1991).

**56**   N. Henderson, *Failure of a Mission* (London, 1940), p. 135.

**57**   *Volkischer Beobachter*, 21 February 1938.

**58**   Foreign office, general correspondence (PRO, London) (hereafter FO 371), account by Lord Halifax of a visit to Germany, 17–21 November 1937.

**59**   See A. Adamthwaite, 'The British Government and the Media 1937–1938', *Journal of Contemporary History* (1983).

**60**   *Ibid.*

**61**   *The Times*, 28 September 1938.

**62**   Harrison and Madge, *Mass Observation*, p. 50.

**63**   R. J. Wybrow, *Britain Speaks Out, 1937–1987: A Social History as Seen Through Gallup* (London, 1989).

**64**   Harrison and Madge, *Mass Observation*, p. 50.

**65**   *Today's Cinema*, 2 November 1938.

**66**   *Economist*, 9 October 1937.

# 9

# Economic appeasement

No full understanding of appeasement can ignore the importance of economic factors. The British desire for peace was quite clearly linked to its role as a major trading nation with world-wide economic and imperial interests. A second world war was widely viewed as likely to erode British economic power. Chamberlain always believed a political settlement of German grievances was important for British economic interests.[1] As early as 1919, British economic experts believed the recovery of Germany was vital to the restoration of British trade.[2] It was not only among economic experts that such views found favour. All the major parties, many business people and most on the left believed mistrust between nations stemmed from economic conflicts.

Yet the subject of economic appeasement has all too often been relegated to secondary importance, behind political factors.[3] Economic appeasement is extremely complex and involves assessing economic influences both inside and outside government circles. The records of government economic activity are extensive, but those for Anglo-German industrial and commercial interests are often patchy. There are few opportunities to examine British and German business groups discussing economic relations in detail. Another major difficulty is that politicians and business groups operated in separate spheres and were often divided over aims and objectives. By its very nature, a private enterprise, or even a business pressure group, has a much narrower focus of interest than a modern democratic government. The major motive of business, the profit motive, is narrower than that of government, which juggles and arbitrates over a wide range of interests within society. Yet the difficulties involved in assessing the importance of economic relations in the unfolding of British policy must not be allowed to lessen their importance. British policy makers were acutely aware of the relationship between economic resources and foreign policy and business groups were aware of the need for cordial relations for the benefit of trade.

The most active economic appeasers were business and financial groups with interests in Anglo-German trade and finance. British business groups regarded Versailles as detrimental to the triangle of trade which existed before 1914 between Germany, Britain and the empire. In 1914, several subsidiaries of prominent German firms in the electrical, chemical and pharmaceutical industries existed in Britain, and Germany was the leading European market for British goods. However, all German investments in Britain were sequestrated in 1919 and German investment was virtually curtailed because of the terms of Versailles. There was a similar decline in British exports to, and investment in, Germany. Significantly, all efforts by the German government to re-acquire German assets seized as a result of Versailles were rejected by the British government.

From 1918 to 1932, the financial relations between Britain and Germany were dominated by reparations payments and the loan arrangements to Germany under the Dawes and Young plans. In these circumstances, the personal initiative of Anglo-German business groups became an extremely important mechanism for improving economic relations. Montagu Norman, governor of the Bank of England, disliked the high-handed attitude of the French over the reparations issue, which he described as 'incompatible with loyalty to the League'. He also believed British economic well-being was inter-linked with the health of the German economy.[4] Indeed, Norman became very closely associated with Dr Hjalmar Schacht, president of the Reichsbank, made efforts to improve German currency stability and negotiated extensive short-term loans for German business during the 1920s.[5]

Extensive conversations also took place between prominent members of British and German industry, with the object of improving trade relations. One group which engaged in this informal economic diplomacy was the Anglo-German Association, under the leadership of Lord Reading, a Liberal peer. The Association sponsored meetings between German and British business and conducted cordial dinners at which business links between the two countries were cemented.[6] It was this informal contact between British and German business which helped in the negotiation of a number of significant trading and shipping agreements, most notably the Anglo-German shipping contract (1919) and the Anglo-German trading agreement (1924). In addition, the British iron and steel industries continued their long and fruitful trading links with German producers. Billets and semi-finished Bessemer steel were derived largely from Germany and Belgium, and became more important after 1918 because British production of Bessemer steel almost ceased. Many German business groups visited Britain with the desire of creating a mutually advantageous trading environment between the two countries.[7]

These informal channels between British and German business and industrial groups lay at the heart of efforts towards economic appeasement. This view is reinforced by examining the views of the leaders of British and German business expressed at the largest Anglo-German economic conference of the 1920s. This was held at Broadlands, Hampshire, the former home of Lord Palmerston, in October 1926, and was clearly an outgrowth of the improved Anglo-German relations which followed the Locarno agreement.

The Broadlands conference was organised by three well known Conservative figures: Patrick Hannon, MP, Sir Robert Horne, MP, and Wilfred Ashley, MP (later Lord Mount Temple). No official support for the Broadlands meeting was given by the prime minister, the foreign secretary or the foreign office.[8] The very fact that the conference was taking place at all, in a blaze of publicity, aroused deep criticism from the French and the Italian governments.[9] Sir Austen Chamberlain, the foreign secretary, was 'deeply unhappy' over the decision of three Tories to arrange a major conference on Anglo-German economic relations without foreign office approval. However, Hannon told Ashley that the prime minister and the foreign secretary had been fully briefed about the conference and that although 'there was no great enthusiasm' for it within the foreign office, there was no attempt to prevent it and no objection to the general idea of improving Anglo-German trade relations.[10] At the opening of the conference, Ashley informed delegates of the wish of the government not to be publicly associated with it, even though approving of its general aim of improving Anglo-German relations.[11]

The list of delegates at Broadlands read like a *Who's Who* in British and German business during the inter-war period. The Germans included: Dr Duisberg, chairman of the Federation of German Industry, Dr Gorge, board member oi Krupps, Dr Cuno, former German chancellor, Herr Karl von Weinberg, a member of the board of I. G. Farben, Herr Wasserman, of Deutsche Bank, Dr Kastl, managing director of the Federation of German Industry, and representatives of the German textile, railway and steel industries. The British delegates, drawn from heavy industry, were equally eminent and included: Sir Max Muspratt, president of the Federation of British Industry (FBI), H. Bond, president of the Iron and Steel Confederation, Sir William Larke, representing the National Federation of Iron and Steel Manufacturers, Sir Archibald Kass, president of the Engineering Employers' Federation, Sir Euan Williams, president of the Coal Federation, and Sir Robert Horne, a Conservative MP. A major banking figure, F. C. Goodenough, chairman of Barclays Bank, a major figure from the shipping world, Sir Thomas Royden, and two important representatives from new modern industries, Sir Hugo Hirst, the chairman of General Electric, and Sir Edward Manville, the chairman of Daimler, were also in attendance.[12]

The British press took a keen interest in the Broadlands conference, which they dubbed 'The Industrial Locarno'.[13] The *Daily Mail* claimed that 'much ill informed speculation' had surrounded the Broadlands meeting, which, it added, 'has no connection with the proposed League of Nations economic conference'.[14] The *Observer* saw the meeting as a direct result of the improved Anglo-German relations brought about by Locarno, and stressed it was an important first stage towards 'an economic Locarno'.[15] However, the press was not allowed entry to the meeting, and reporters could only speculate about what was discussed. The *Sunday Times* reporter, on information from a secret contact at the meeting, claimed an extraordinarily interesting exchange of information took place at the conference, which delegates agreed would do an 'immense amount of good' for Anglo-German economic relations.[16]

A secret report of the meeting has survived which sheds important light on the state of Anglo-German economic relations before the onset of the economic depression and the rise of Hitler. It appears the central motive of British delegates from the iron and steel industry was to elicit German support for British entry into the newly formed European iron and steel cartel, consisting of Germany, France, Belgium, the Saar and Luxembourg. Indeed, iron and steel delegates held a special session at the conference at which German delegates promised to support British entry into the European cartel arrangements.

In fact, much of the discussion at Broadlands centred on the formation of Anglo-German cartels and monopolistic arrangements. This was especially true of the representatives of traditional export-oriented staple industries, including iron, steel, shipbuilding, engineering, coal and textiles, which were in decline as a result of the general downturn in world trade which had followed the First World War. In these industries, a major rationalisation programme was already under way and export opportunities were shrinking. The only means of regaining former industrial glories for these industries were tariffs, government help, amalgamation and cartel arrangements with overseas competitors.

It was market-sharing and cartel arrangements with German business which most attracted the representatives of British industry. Robert Horne suggested the system of cartels had brought great benefits to German industry and he believed British participation in such cartels was a vital means of thwarting US penetration of European markets. Dr Duisberg told the conference there was a desire in many European countries to exclude Britain from their cartels, but he added this view was not shared by the majority of German industrialists, who welcomed British participation in cartel arrangements. Indeed, German delegates emphasised the benefits that monopoly production and cartel arrangements would bring to Anglo-German trade.

The idea of greater monopoly control over the iron and steel industry was attractive to Mr H. Bond. He told German delegates that he would consult the iron and steel industry about moves towards greater amalgamation and international co-operation. A British delegate representing the wool industry was also keen on the formation of an international cartel. The representatives of German dye manufacturers offered to give away secrets in exchange for a guaranteed 50 per cent share of the world market. Sir Max Muspratt commented that international cartels in the chemicals industry already worked effectively and that he was exploring the possibility of expanding such arrangements in other areas of industry. The representatives of the textile industry in Britain and Germany promised to exchange statistics and information but expressed less enthusiasm towards monopoly agreements. Hugo Hirst suggested that new developments in the electrical trade would provide a sound basis for future collaboration. Under Hirst's plan, agreements would be reached between British and German manufacturers whereby the home market would be protected for the domestic producer, Germany would gain access to colonial markets and bilateral Anglo-German agreements on trade would be signed to control common markets. Goodenough informed German delegates that the City of London would provide finance at low interest rates to Germany, which could be used to purchase raw materials from the empire.

There was less enthusiasm from British delegates for developing trade with the Soviet Union. They showed hardly any interest at all in this idea and suggested Germany was in a far better position to exploit the Soviet market. Goodenough warned German delegates that the main competition to the development of German trade with the Soviet Union would come from the United States.

The discussion of cartel arrangements in the coal industry was postponed owing to the 1926 British coal strike. Dr Cuno reported that good relations already existed between British and German shipping interests, and recorded that the shipping contract between Britain and Germany of 1919 was still working very effectively. However, Manville reported that no agreement between British and German car manufacturers could be contemplated.

By and large, the leaders of British and German industry saw the planning and the co-ordination of Anglo-German production, cartel arrangements, market-sharing agreements and bilateral trade agreements as the key economic weapons to prevent antagonism between the two countries. Indeed, the whole tone of the Broadlands discussions was one of mutual economic self-interest; it was a search for ways of both improving co-operation between British and German industry and promoting increased credit arrangements to improve Germany's purchasing power in the British market and the empire.

Many of the ideas discussed at Broadlands were later adopted. There was certainly a greater drive by British industry to engage in cartelisation and market-sharing agreements. Under Sir William Larke's guidance, the iron and steel industry was transformed into a cartel – the British Iron and Steel Federation. However, Britain did not gain entry to the European iron and steel cartel until 1934. It was Larke who led the negotiations for British entry and was aided by a promise from the national government to lower duties on goods from the European cartel from 50 per cent to 20 per cent. As a result of joining the iron and steel cartel, Britain received export quotas in continental markets. Many other industries also moved towards amalgamation. In 1926, Imperial Chemical Industries (ICI) was formed by a merger of companies in mining, explosives and electrical industries, and a world market in chemicals and explosives was negotiated with I. G. Farben and the French company du Pont. In 1928, the consolidation of the electrical industry was completed through the creation of Associated Electrical Industries. In 1929, Cable and Wireless, an amalgamation of all telegraph and radio communication companies in the British empire, was created. By these means, the free market gave way to the idea of the organised market.

In the 1930s, British business became involved in further economic diplomacy with foreign companies. Most of these moves were designed to limit competition and arrange cartel agreements in industries as diverse as steel, electronics, telecommunications equipment, oil, chemicals, tubes, rails, tin plate, ship plate, railway rolling stock, wire rods and explosives. The drive towards cartelisation during the inter-wars years became extremely popular.[17] These agreements primarily resulted from the desolate nature of world trade and were motivated by economic self-interest and the survival instinct of industrialists in the midst of rapid economic change.

There was also a greater willingness of British banks to provide short-term loans and credit facilities to Germany. In the late 1920s, several different types of loans and credit facilities were provided to Germany. In July 1931, a leading Treasury official admitted, 'great assets of ours' were tied up in Germany.[18] The most important were the short-term credits issued to German industry, banks and commerce to finance Anglo-German trade. However, most of these bank credits were frozen under standstill arrangements agreed in London in July and September 1931, which ensured at least interest payments were made on existing loans. These agreements helped to save Germany in 1931 from a complete banking and currency collapse. Yet when the Bank of England asked the Treasury to guarantee new credit to Germany of $100 million in July 1931, it was told this was out of the question. In November 1931, British bankers asked the national government to suspend reparation payments to ease the pressure on Germany and enable it to meet interest payments on its existing loans. When reparations were suspended in 1932, an embargo was placed by the national government on the provision of further loans to Germany, much to the annoyance of British bankers. After Hitler came to power, the major aim of British bankers was to ensure that existing debts were paid. Montagu Norman is often regarded as a pillar of appeasement, but it seems he primarily wanted to maintain the provision of credit to major German banks in order to enable payments in Anglo-German trade to be honoured and interest on former debts to be repaid.

The dream of an 'industrial Locarno' was greatly damaged by the onset of economic depression. The FBI, the leading industrial pressure group, became more concerned to develop imperial rather than European trade. In 1932, Chamberlain, as chancellor of the exchequer, hardly helped matters by introducing high tariffs on manufactured imports, through the Import Duties Act, and signing the Ottawa agreement, which established a system of import quotas from within the empire. Soon after the introduction of the tariff the sterling area was formed by a group of countries heavily dependent on the British market, including Denmark, Sweden, Norway, Finland, Latvia, Lithuania and Estonia in Europe, the British empire, excluding Canada, and Argentina. The Treasury believed the combination of the tariff and the sterling area would give Britain major bargaining powers in international economic negotiations.[19]

The German government responded to these measures by raising tariffs on British goods, which undoubtedly proved detrimental to the German economy. From 1932 to 1939, there was a very marked increase in the proportion of British imports from the British empire and a sharp decrease in imports from European countries. The massive surplus in trade Germany had previously enjoyed with Britain evaporated. For example, in 1931, Germany enjoyed a trade balance of £32.2 million with Britain, but this had fallen to a mere £3.7 million in 1935 and never rose above £8 million for the remainder of the 1930s.[20]

Many British economic experts believed that the advent of the Nazi regime in 1933 was the consequence of the reparations imposed at Versailles, which reduced Germany's purchasing power and contributed to its economic collapse. There was also a powerful minority in the foreign office and the Treasury who still believed, despite the introduction of protectionism, that multilateral trade was a powerful force for peace. From 1933 to 1937, the economic appeasement of Germany became a serious topic of discussion within the national government. Some sympathy for Germany's economic plight was expressed within the economic section of the foreign office, which had been established in 1931.

But the obstacles to cordial Anglo-German economic relations at the government level were very powerful. High tariffs and tight exchange and financial controls introduced by the British and German governments in the early 1930s hampered the development of close economic co-operation and political efforts to relax Anglo-German economic tension from 1933 to 1936 were small scale, primarily designed to aid German payments to British traders and bankers. The most important were the 1933 coal agreement, which aided Anglo-German trade, the Anglo-German transfer agreement of July 1934, which gave German traders considerable freedom to use sterling credits to purchase goods in Britain and the empire, and the Anglo-German payments agreement of 1934, which was supported by the granting of a credit of £750,000 to the German central bank. The last measure was designed to ensure German companies honoured trade payments and was offered as a carrot to encourage the Nazi regime not to liquidate all outstanding debts to British financial institutions.[21] However, Montagu Norman, who had played the leading role in negotiating the payments agreement, gained an assurance from Chamberlain that the provision of a new line of credit to Germany would remain a secret from the public. This suited Chamberlain, as the official line of the government after 1933 was to oppose the provision of any new loans to Germany.[22] Unlike most of Germany's foreign creditors, who had liquidated debts as a result of the standstill agreements of 1932, British creditors kept hold of them, but did not press for full payment from 1933 to 1939.

There was division within the national government about whether an active policy of economic appeasement should be pursued. One group in favour was the economic section of the foreign office, headed by Frank Ashton-Gwatkin and supported by Frederick Leith Ross. They produced a series of reports which favoured efforts to ease the economic pressure on Germany. For Ashton-Gwatkin, economic appeasement was one important means of encouraging Nazi Germany to pull away from measures of economic self-sufficiency and increased spending on armaments. The best means of easing the economic pressure on Germany, according to him, was to relax the tariff, which he believed had 'slammed the door in Germany's face' and had encouraged Hitler to increase arms spending and seek new markets in eastern Europe.

Economic appeasers at the foreign office saw the gradual removal of tariffs and quotas on German exports as essential. Another key reason why they favoured closer Anglo-German economic co-operation was that they believed it would help to prevent close economic collaboration between the Soviet Union and Nazi Germany, which might in turn lead to improved Nazi–Soviet political collaboration.[23]

There was a further tendency among economic appeasers in the foreign office. This was to view Hitler's militarism as an escape from economic problems. The antidote to this was to encourage 'moderates' in the German government, of whom Schacht, the economic minister, was the most favoured figure in guiding Germany along the path of co-operation and interdependence. In the view of Frederick Leith Ross, trans-national economic co-operation between British and German business would place a limitation on extremists in the Nazi regime who wanted to develop policies of self-sufficiency, rearmament and aggression.[24] However, economic appeasers at the foreign office did not want British economic interests to come under political direction, and they felt trade and business negotiations should continue to be conducted by business interest groups using existing methods of economic diplomacy.

But there was opposition from the Treasury and from Board of Trade officials to foreign office ideas concerning economic appease-ment, especially the lowering of tariffs. British foreign policy tended to reject an economic solution of the German problem. The op-ponents of economic appeasement, even at the foreign office, most notably Sir Robert Vansittart and Sir Anthony Eden while he was foreign secretary, were much more powerful. They both opposed a programme of economic aid to Germany as a high-risk strategy which might not aid German 'moderates' but help to boost the military capacity of the regime to wage war. They preferred to keep Germany economically 'lean'.[25] Vansittart believed that all outstanding political problems with Germany had to be settled before economic concessions could be offered. Until then, he believed Nazi Germany should be allowed to 'stew in the juice of her economic difficulties'. The tendency to support a political approach to the German problem remained dominant. In September 1936, Neville Chamberlain regarded the idea of Britain taking the initiative to improve the commercial, monetary and financial situation in Germany as 'dangerous' but he added that it was 'equally dangerous to leave them struggling in the present state of economic constriction'.[26]

The dominance of the political approach to appeasement tended to weaken the impact of economic appeasement within government. This meant that the major economic appeasers of Nazi Germany remained mostly unknown figures beavering away outside government and away from the public gaze. In this respect, the activities of the Anglo-German Fellowship (AGF), founded in 1935 by Lord Mount Temple, one of the leading figures at the 1926 Broadlands conference, merits close scrutiny. The AGF was established as a 'non-political organisation' to promote understanding between England and Germany. However, the membership lists of the AGF show it was predominantly a pressure group of British businessmen, many of whom had financial and trading interests in Germany. Membership was not supposed to imply approval of National Socialism, as the AGF was designed as a forum for a frank exchange of views between like-minded people in Britain and Germany with the aim of promoting economic and political unity.

The council of the AGF included Lord Eltishley, a Tory peer, a number of Tory MPs, including Sir Thomas Moore and Sir Asheton Pownall, and leading figures in business, commerce and industry. One membership list of the AGF shows three directors of the Bank of England, over fifty Tory MPs and peers and countless representatives of British companies (including Unilever, Dunlop and Pilkington) and small and large export industries, ranging from the British Steel Export Association, the Sugar Machinery Manufacturers Association, toy manufacturers and telephone companies to producers of milk cans, typewriters, cod liver oil, leather gloves, fur coats, paper and rope. A closely related Anglo-German society of industrialists – the Deutsch Englische Gesellschaft (DEG) – funded by the Nazi regime was set up and similarly encouraged the development of close Anglo-German business links.

According to *News Review*, the AGF was a pressure group of 'British big business'.[27] It organised informal dinners, cultural events and exchange visits and arranged informal meetings between leading British and German 'moderate' business people. At these meetings, the formation of cartels and mutual trading agreements were discussed and important business deals struck. The AGF was financed by individual and corporate donations from business and industry. Its members favoured greater efforts by the British government to encourage Anglo-German trade. The AGF proved a useful forum for the informal development of economic appeasement.

Another key objective of the AGF was to influence government and public opinion to put the economic benefits of close Anglo-German relations more to the forefront of British foreign policy. 'Public opinion in Britain is a very powerful force,' Lord Mount Temple told a meeting of the DEG in Berlin in January 1936, 'and no government can afford to ignore it'.[28] However, the desire of the AGF to promote good relations was motivated by economic self-interest, which resulted in its members turning a blind eye to the darker side of the Nazi regime. Most AGF members were businessmen who wanted to continue profitable trade relations with Germany. As Simon Haxey, a member of the AGF, observed: 'At meetings of the AGF leading Nazis advanced the merits of Germany's economic interests and foreign policy'.[29] The AGF served to make the economic appeasement of Nazi Germany respectable and suggested political appeasement would meet with similar success.

To influence public opinion, the AGF set up the *Anglo-German Review*, a monthly magazine, which had a highly selective and partial view of the Nazi regime. The *Anglo-German Review* stressed the close dynastic, religious, racial and economic bonds between the British and German peoples. In one article, Frederick the Great, Hitler's great hero, was depicted as a British hero during the Seven Years' War. In other articles, Anglo-German collaboration in the Napoleonic Wars was held up as a shining example of what the two nations could achieve in harmony.[30] By and large, articles in the *Anglo-German Review* stressed the 'peace-loving' desires of Hitler and the German people and the mutual economic benefits cordial relations would bring. Members of the AGF went on supporting the appeasement of Nazi Germany and carried on its economic contact even after the invasion of Prague largely because of its dominant desire to continue to do business with Germany.

A second champion of economic appeasement in the 1930s was Sir William Larke, director of the Iron and Steel Federation and a leading figure in the FBI. Larke is a very significant figure in Anglo-German economic diplomacy during the inter-war years. He was a key figure at Broadlands, was heavily involved in British entry into the European iron and steel cartel in 1934 and offered advice and guidance to other British business groups which also established cartel arrangements with German companies during the 1930s.

By the summer of 1937, many members of British business had come to believe greater export growth to countries outside the sterling area was essential for further economic development. To this end, Larke gained agreement from the FBI to lead a new drive by business to encourage 'negotiations between British industry and their opposite numbers in Germany', with the central aim of expanding cartels and market-sharing arrangements.[31] To aid this new drive of economic diplomacy towards Germany, the FBI wanted the inducement from the British government of further tariff increases, to be used as a bargaining chip in negotiations. The Board of Trade rejected further tariff increases but was prepared to support 'arrangements between individual industries' in order to enable an increase in export trade.[32]

The FBI was soon in talks with German industry to explore opportunities for close Anglo-German economic co-operation. In June 1937, many sessions at the International Chamber of Commerce in Berlin witnessed a number of cordial speeches from British and German delegates on the possibility of economic collaboration. There was also a sharp increase in business dinners in Germany arranged by the AGF.

It was from 1937 to 1939 that the drive for Anglo-German economic understanding reached its height. This is not to suggest economic appeasement achieved dominance within government. In November 1937, for example, Chamberlain still thought economic appeasement would 'have to wait until the general political settlement is at last in sight,' and he further lamented that 'Politics in international relations govern actions at the expense of economics, and often of reason'.[33]

During 1938, Anglo-German industrial and trade discussions noticeably increased. In July 1938, for example, Leith Ross successfully re-negotiated the Anglo-German payments agreement, and gained a German guarantee to buy British exports in return for the provision of credits. At the signing of the agreement in Berlin, Leith Ross said the commercial relations of the two countries should continue on 'the most friendly basis' and promised the British government would 'make every endeavour to take such steps as may be found possible to increase mutual trade and improve trade relations'.[34]

But it was only when the search for a political settlement grew more doubtful, especially after Munich, that economic appeasement finally received some belated backing from the Chamberlain government. This resembled a last-ditch effort to keep channels of communication open with Nazi Germany and fits more into a framework of short-term expediency, a last desperate effort to place pressure on German 'moderates' to act as a restraining influence on Nazi 'extremists', rather than a coherent policy.

After Munich, it is clear that Chamberlain did place some pressure on business to engage in economic diplomacy with Nazi Germany. In November 1938, the Board of Trade advised the FBI to open negotiations with the Reichsgruppe Industrie (RI), its German equivalent, with the aim of making preliminary arrangements for the signing of a new Anglo-German trade agreement and to put individual industries in touch with German business. A German trade delegation to London stressed it wanted a reduction in the British tariff, but Guy Locock, FBI director, suggested a large number of British firms were utterly opposed to this idea and were prepared to enter into industrial agreements with German firms only to restrict Anglo-German competition in third markets and to form more cartels. It was finally agreed between the FBI and the Board of Trade that a trade delegation would be sent to Germany in December 1938 to open discussions and the FBI would also encourage its members to open discussions.

In January 1939, the Board of Trade helped negotiate an Anglo-German coal cartel and shortly afterwards Oliver Stanley, president of the Board of Trade, and Robert Hudson, a Board of Trade official, were invited to Berlin to discuss economic concessions. In February 1939, the Duke of Saxe-Coburg, speaking at a dinner of the AGF, seemingly with the approval of Hitler, referred to the 'friendly' relations between the two countries and 'the very good progress being made in Anglo-German trade negotiations'.[35] For

Chamberlain, these views seemed like evidence of a desire by Hitler to improve Anglo-German economic relations. In February 1939, Ashton-Gwatkin also visited Germany for an exchange of views with the German government on the possibility of exploring economic appeasement further.[36]

Meanwhile, the FBI and the RI agreed to hold a major Anglo-German industrial convention in Dusseldorf in March 1939. The hopes of a new 'industrial Locarno', so evident at Broadlands, extinguished by the economic depression, were briefly ignited at a time when the political discussions between Britain and Germany had fallen into abeyance. In preparation for the Dusseldorf meeting, an FBI meeting, chaired by Sir William Larke, was held in London in early March with the aim of briefing industrialists on the likely content of forthcoming discussions in Germany.

This meeting was attended by the representatives of more than forty British firms and trade associations, from a wide variety of predominantly consumer-oriented industries. At the meeting, Guy Locock told delegates that the British government was placing pressure on the FBI to encourage industry to enter into Anglo-German trade, market-sharing and cartel agreements and he urged delegates not to give in to such pressure unless any Anglo-German agreement was in their own business interests.[37] A few days later, as the British industrial delegation prepared to depart for Dusseldorf, Sir Walter Runciman, lord president, called them to a meeting and told them: 'Gentleman, the peace of Europe is in your hands'.[38]

The Dusseldorf convention was the first major Anglo-German conference to enjoy the full and enthusiastic support of the British government. It opened on the fateful morning of 15 March 1939, just as German tanks were rumbling through the streets of Prague. Political reality had overtaken the search for economic collaboration. The British government called off the proposed trade visit of Stanley and Hudson. 'It is a curious coincidence,' Lockock told a friend, 'that this political trouble should have occurred just at this moment, but with my experience of missions, it is always the unexpected which turns up'. The FBI decided to go ahead with the Dusseldorf convention, on the grounds that 'political difficulties have nothing to do with industrialists'.[39] After two days of discussions, the FBI and RI issued a joint declaration which agreed to start immediate negotiations between British and German firms to sign agreements to end 'destructive competition' and replace it with as 'complete co-operation as possible throughout the industrial structure of their respective countries'. In addition, the FBI and RI agreed to set up a special committee composed of British and German representatives to lay the foundations upon which industries could begin negotiations to their mutual advantage.[40] At the time, a great many Anglo-German bilateral trading and cartel agreements were already in place but a further fifty industrial groups expressed a willingness to enter negotiations with their German counterparts at Dusseldorf. On the eve of the Second World War, there were 133 separate agreements between British and German business groups, a great many signed in 1938 and 1939.[41]

Although the occupation of Prague did not end Anglo-German trade co-operation, it did place some restrictions on it. On 30 March 1939, a FBI meeting took place in London chaired by Larke and attended by delegates from over fifty British firms. The delegates were told by Larke that where international agreements already existed between British and German firms they should be honoured; in cases where British and German firms had been negotiating agreements for a considerable time, FBI members were advised to exercise their own discretion as to whether they should continue; but in cases where British industry still needed to open fresh negotiations with their German counterparts, FBI members were advised 'to mark time' until 'public opinion on this side had to some extent died down'. However, representatives from many industries expressed deep dissatisfaction with the whole process of opening negotiations for bilateral agreements with Germany in the first place. A number of delegates believed that 'negotiations had been more or less forced upon them from government circles as an alternative to increased protectionism in the UK market'. It seems that most FBI members wanted an increased tariff far more urgently than they desired new arrangements with German business. Significantly, the number of firms wishing to enter fresh negotiations had fallen from fifty to twenty in the two weeks following the occupation of Prague.[42]

The Dusseldorf convention proved to be the last high-profile effort towards economic appeasement, although Anglo-German business contacts continued up until the outbreak of war. The last acts of economic appeasement on the part of Chamberlain amounted to 'private whispers' in the ears of German 'moderates'. On four separate occasions in June and July 1939, Sir Horace

Wilson, Chamberlain's chief diplomatic adviser, held discussions with Dr Helmut Wohltat, a close associate of Goering – supposedly one of the remaining so-called German 'moderates' – in London. In these conversations, Wilson emphasised the willingness of Britain to co-operate with Germany in the economic sphere by allowing easier access to British markets, through joint industrial planning schemes and possible colonial concessions, provided Hitler took steps to restore political stability.[43] Robert Hudson, apparently acting on his own initiative, also met Wohltat, on 20 July 1939, and suggested that the British government would be prepared to offer Germany 'a big loan' in return for political guarantees and disarmament agreements.[44] To the dismay of Chamberlain, Hudson gave an interview to the *Daily Express* under the headline: 'I Planned the Peace Loan to Germany'.[45] This caused great embarrassment to the prime minister, who believed the incident revealed it was impossible for him publicly to 'enter into conversations with the Germans on any subject'.

Yet a number of other secret, and equally futile, conversations continued with leading Nazis during the summer of 1939. Lord Kemsley, a press baron, met Hitler in July 1939 and was told that 'Germany was not after money'. Finally, when Neville Henderson told the foreign office that economic help might still preserve peace, he was told bluntly by Ashton-Gwatkin, a previous keen advocate of economic appeasement, 'Let us stop talking nonsense about economic help. The Germans have evolved a system, which by ignoring economic rules, is leading to economic deterioration and perhaps disaster'.[46]

The story of efforts towards economic appeasement from 1918 to 1939 sheds important new light on the differences in approach between government and business to the German problem. One of the most consistent aims of business in its economic relations with Germany was to form market-sharing and cartel arrangements. The aim of the banks was to provide loans during the Locarno period and then preserve payments on them during the Nazi period. British business started to mirror the German love of protectionism and the creation of an organised market. The underlying motive for British business was pure economic self-interest. After 1931, British business was reluctant to sacrifice the benefits of the tariff to provide economic aid to stimulate the German economy. It is tempting to speculate whether British business would have engaged in such a frenetic amount of Anglo-German collaboration between 1937 and 1939 in the absence of pressure from the government. Business appeasement of Germany was motivated by a desire for profitable trade and a belief that political difficulties had nothing to do with the business community. Business people wanted peace in order to aid profitable trade and were willing to turn a blind eye to the extremism of Nazism.

The approach of the British government to economic appeasement was more complex and was influenced by a much broader range of political factors. Unquestionably, economic appeasement was viewed by government as subordinate to the solution of political grievances and it only gave any real encouragement as a sort of crisis strategy, when the political settlement looked to be heading for the rocks. It seems reasonable to conclude that the government was not willing to undertake a specific economic solution to the German problem to the detriment of the broader political framework or of its economic reliance on protectionism.

## Notes

1  C. A. McDonald, 'Economic Appeasement and the German "Moderates" 1937–1939', *Past and Present* (1972), p. 105.

2  J. L.Garvin, *The Economic Foundations of the Peace* (London, 1919).

3  Of course, German historians have shown great interest in the topic, most notably Wendt, who views economic appeasement as a dominant theme of British policy towards Nazi Germany, but this finding is rejected by Schmidt, who suggests that the drive for a political solution overshadowed economic appeasement. See also S. Newton, 'The Anglo-German Connection and the Political Economy of Appeasement', *Diplomacy and Statecraft* (1991).

4  Austen Chamberlain papers (University of Birmingham) (hereafter AC), 55/389, Norman to Chamberlain, 4 February 1928.

5  R. H. Meyer, *Bankers' Diplomacy: Monetary Stabilisation in the Twenties* (London, 1970), p. 14.

6  Lord Reading was Jewish. When Hitler came to power in 1933, the Anglo-German Association, largely supported by Liberal-minded business people, disbanded in protest, and when the Anglo-German Fellowship was formed, Reading attacked the organisation.

7  BP 81/2, 'Report of Conference between English and German Industrialists', Broadlands, 8–11 October 1926.

8  *Daily Express*, 9 October 1926.

**9**  BP 81/2, Hannon to Ashley, 18 October 1926.

**10**  *Ibid.*

**11**  BP 81/2, 'Report of Conference between English and German Industrialists', Broadlands, 8–11 October 1926.

**12**  *Ibid.*

**13**  *Daily Express*, 11 October 1926.

**14**  *Daily Mail*, 11 October 1926.

**15**  *Observer*, 10 October 1926.

**16**  *Sunday Times*, 10 October 1926.

**17**  S. Newton, 'Appeasement as an Industrial Strategy 1938–41', *Contemporary Record* (1995).

**18**  H. James, 'Financial Flows Across Frontiers During the Interwar Depression', *Economic History Review* (1992), p. 601.

**19**  I. Drummond, *The Floating Pound and the Sterling Area 1931–1939* (Cambridge, 1981).

**20**  N. Forbes, 'London Banks, the German Standstill Agreements and "Economic Appeasement" in the 1930s', *Economic History Review* (1987), p. 579.

**21**  NC 18/1/83, November 1934.

**22**  T 160/544/13999/01, Norman to Leith Ross, November 1934.

**23**  M. Gilbert, *The Roots of Appeasement* (London, 1966), pp. 151–8.

**24**  FO 371, 18497, F. Ashton-Gwatkin, 'Economic Survey II: The Post War Period', 1937.

**25**  Earl of Avon, *Facing the Dictators* (London, 1962), p. 480.

**26**  FO 371, 20475, Chamberlain to Ashton-Gwatkin, 2 September 1936.

**27**  *News Review*, 23 January 1936.

**28**  BP 81/1, file relating to the Anglo-German Fellowship, 1935–38.

**29**  R. Griffiths, *Fellow Travellers of the Right: British Enthusiasts for Nazi Germany 1933–1939* (London, 1980), p. 185.

**30**  *Anglo-German Review*, November 1936.

**31**  Modern Records Centre (FBI papers) (University of Warwick) (hereafter MRC) FBI/C/2/1937, grand council minutes, 13 January 1937.

**32**  FO 371, 23986, W1049/173/50, Board of Trade memorandum, 1938.

**33**  Gilbert, *Appeasement*, p. 157.

**34**  *The Board of Trade Journal*, 7 July 1938, pp. 15–16.

**35**  R. A. C. Parker, *Chamberlain and Appeasement: British Policy and the Coming of the Second World War* (London, 1993), pp. 195–6.

**36**  Foreign office private papers series (PRO, London) (hereafter FO 800), 315, H/XV/126, Chamberlain to Henderson, 19 February 1939.

**37**  MRC, D/8138, Anglo-German industrial convention, 'Sir William Larke's Meeting', 1 March 1939.

**38**  Quoted in R. F. Holland, 'The Federation of British Industry and the International Economy', *Economic History Review* (1981), p. 298.

**39** MRC, FBI/S/Walker/14, Lockock to Walker, 15 March 1939.

**40** MRC, FBI/C/D8323, 'Joint Declaration by the Reichsgruppe Industrie and the Federation of British Industry on the Results of the Convention held at Dusseldorf, March 15th. and 16th., 1939', 16 March 1939.

**41** Newton, 'Appeasement', p. 496.

**42** MRC, FBI/Ger/Comp., 'Meeting on Anglo-German Trade Discussions, held at 21 Tothill Street, London, March 30th. 1939'.

**43** *DBFP*, vol. 6, no. 354, memorandum by Sir Horace Wilson, 19 July 1939.

**44** *Ibid.*, no. 370, memorandum by Robert Hudson, 20 July 1939.

**45** *Daily Express*, 24 July 1939.

**46** J. Charmley, *Chamberlain and the Lost Peace* (London, 1989), p. 193.

# 10

# Conclusion

The quite remarkable attempt by the exceptionally strong-willed and obstinate Neville Chamberlain to prevent war will always be controversial. Few individuals have experienced such a sharp reversal of fortunes in life than Chamberlain did from the triumph of Munich to the humiliation of Prague. Few historical figures have been so retrospectively condemned and so contemporarily praised. Only days before he died on 9 November 1940, Chamberlain confessed, 'I regret nothing'.[1]

The original 'guilty men' thesis portrayed Chamberlain and appeasement as a combination of calculated deception, amoral principles, flawed judgement, diplomatic ineptitude and poor military planning. Those who passed historical judgements in the immediate post-war years tended to support this negative view. The very notion of Chamberlain being a competent and effective leader and appeasement a logical and sensible policy was hardly considered.

However, time is a great healer when it comes to historical reputations. In 1965, the shrewd D. C. Watt was already suggesting that a revisionist school which rejected earlier negative views had started to develop.[2] After the official documents were opened for public scrutiny in 1967, the revisionists soon gained the high ground. It has now become commonplace to view Neville Chamberlain not as a weak and ineffective leader but as a complex and able politician with a clear-sighted approach to a foreign policy, based on detailed military and economic advice.[3]

In many ways, the use of the term 'Chamberlain's policy' throughout this book has been a convenient historical shorthand. The foreign policy Chamberlain followed grew out of a set of key assumptions which underpinned British foreign policy during the entire inter-war period. The most important assumption was that another war would be disastrous for Britain, and to prevent it was an all-consuming aim. It is clear that a majority of the cabinet, most of the Tory Party and even the foreign office never seriously favoured a determined policy of stopping Hitler by the use of military force until 1939.

However, it would be completely wrong to believe the appeasement of Hitler was ever as popular as, or exactly the same thing as, appeasing disarmed and democratic Germany before 1933. Appeasement was originally not a policy of fear but a policy of hope, underpinned by strength. The appeasement of Hitler was a project always fraught with great difficulty and under Chamberlain resembled a form of crisis management. In this context, it is probably correct to suggest the version of appeasement which developed from 1937 onwards was infected with a mood of fear and was accompanied by an awareness of military weakness. It was aimed at a German regime which no longer accepted military inferiority and was a high-risk strategy.

Even so, some elements of continuity in the aims of appeasement before and after 1933 require emphasis. Appeasement always favoured diplomacy over arms, conciliation over confrontation and compromise over force. Before and after 1933, there were equally few people within the British government who stridently pushed for a concerted effort to turn the League of Nations into a peace-keeping organisation with real military muscle. No one seriously contemplated creating a vast continental-style army to deter Hitler and there were very few advocates of military alliances. Even Vansittart, the leading hawk in the foreign office, argued in 1937 that British policy should attempt to continue with conciliation and compromise while Britain was regaining its military strength. It is probably worth adding that no one within the British government really believed British rearmament could act as a deterrent to Hitler in the foreseeable future. The choices in foreign policy had narrowed, because of these prevailing assumptions, into support either for a diplomacy which marked time while rearmament continued and which kept the dictators guessing at arm's length, or for a diplomacy which attempted to open a dialogue with them in order to bring their unilateral acts into some kind of negotiated framework and hopefully lead to a reduction in arms spending.

In this context, it is difficult to maintain that Neville Chamberlain was following a completely new set of foreign policy aims as prime minister from 1937 to 1939, or to argue that his particular brand of appeasement diverged markedly from the underlying assumptions of British policy. By wanting the dictators to give up acts of unilateral treaty revision and by wishing them to participate in a negotiated settlement of all outstanding European problems, he was in clear continuity with the political objectives of his predecessors. It appears likely that Chamberlain wanted to steer Hitler, to limit his aims, to get him out of his uniform, to put away the jackboots, buy a pin-stripped suit and a trusty umbrella and become an ordinary German statesman.

From 1918 to 1937, British policy was not linked to some noble search for morality but was wedded to the defence of British interests and to the preservation of British independent power. This meant policy was always based on a rational judgement of what was best for the British national interest. For the whole period, the prevention of war remained the most vital interest. In fact, it would be easy to conclude that Chamberlain's appeasement, in terms of its aims, was a more frenetic and vigorous expression of a set of shared assumptions about British foreign policy.

It must be also be appreciated that Chamberlain was pursuing a policy which he described as 'to seek peace and to ensure it; to use what influence we can command to induce other nations to settle their grievances by peaceful and not by forceful means'.[4] In the view of Sir Horace Wilson, a figure close to Chamberlain, 'Our policy was never designed just to postpone war, or enable us to enter war more unified. The aim of our appeasement was to avoid war altogether, for all time'.[5]

However, under Chamberlain the prevailing desire to prevent war took on the form of a dogmatic and obstinate belief system. The very idea of standing up to Hitler was viewed almost as an act of heresy when put forward by critics who, Chamberlain claimed, 'differed from me because they were ignorant, it is only fair to add wilfully ignorant in many cases'.[6] What Chamberlain brought to British foreign policy was a firmer and clearer belief that a bold effort of conciliation and compromise with Germany, Italy and

Japan was required if war was to be averted and a new era of peaceful co-existence was to begin. This fundamental desire to avoid open confrontation with the dictators and to avoid alliances determined Chamberlain's decisions on foreign policy and led to fatal errors of judgement.

It cannot be denied that Chamberlain was willing to compromise in the 'peaceful evolution' of German grievances left behind by Versailles. It seems highly likely that he wished his policy would lead to a new European order of friendly capitalist powers, excluding the Soviet Union, and he never saw it as immoral to seek agreement with dictators. Chamberlain was also implacably opposed to a return to the pre-1914 alliance system and was determined not to go down the road to the sort of ideological cold war which developed after 1945.

This is not to say that Chamberlain wanted to give Hitler a free hand in eastern Europe, nor to suggest he wanted a Nazi–Soviet war. However, it would be incorrect to believe that Chamberlain had any real objection to the peaceful economic domination of eastern Europe by Germany. If Nazi Germany had truly wished to change its spots, and Hitler had proved willing to become a 'good European', then Munich could have provided a springboard for Hitler to work with Chamberlain to fashion a complete revision of Versailles.

What really distinguished Chamberlain from the cool and detached foreign office was his optimistic belief that Hitler could be persuaded to pursue his aims by peaceful means in collaboration with the other major European capitalist powers. In this context, it is important to stress that Chamberlain was not the typical upper-class Conservative; he was something of an outsider among the Tory grandees, the men in the grey suits, the London gentleman's clubs and especially the high-minded officials in the foreign office. Neville Chamberlain was a businessman in politics, who came from the provinces, never attended university and entered politics at a very late age. The advice of high-minded Oxbridge types at the foreign office telling him his judgement was faulty irked him and made him more determined to prove such people wrong. In essence, Chamberlain believed the methods used by the foreign office were too cautious, slow and theoretical to aid a dynamic drive for appeasement.

In place of advice from the foreign office, Chamberlain wanted to follow his own views, to create his own 'inner circle' of advisers and to give a personal lead and direction to foreign policy. The informal and impromptu methods Chamberlain used have a special significance because they were an essential part of his conduct of foreign policy. Many of these informal methods were borrowed from business and from supporters of the appeasement of Nazi Germany in British society. They included visiting Germany to meet leading Nazis, the use of personal envoys and secret contacts, speeches at informal dinners and the manipulation of the media, all of which were used by Chamberlain to oil the wheels of his diplomacy. It seems that he believed these unconventional methods stood a far better chance of aiding the improvement of Anglo-German relations than the use of the formal diplomatic channels of the foreign office. These informal activities were not symptoms of a clandestine or sinister plot to search for peace at any price but were an integral part of the policy itself. It was not the underlying aims of Chamberlain's policy which were new but the strength of his own beliefs and the informal and personal methods he developed to carry it out.

Chamberlain's overall aim of seeking peace was generally shared with his cabinet colleagues at the outset. As Hoare quite favourably put it, 'If nine times out of ten he had his way, it was because it was also the Cabinet's way'.[7] After Munich, the cabinet increasingly began to stop Chamberlain getting all his own way and was able to ensure the Godesberg memorandum was rejected, spending restrictions were removed from the arms programme, a firm commitment was offered to France and negotiations with the Soviet Union were opened.

It was the foreign office which most often questioned Chamberlain's judgement. Chamberlain's conflicts with Eden nearly always followed incidents in which he had decided to use one of his own informal, personal methods to pursue foreign policy, or had acted without consulting him. It seems the fundamental difference between Chamberlain and Eden was that while the former wanted to concentrate all the efforts of British policy on reducing its number of potential enemies, to the exclusion of other possibilities, the latter wanted to extend the number of potential allies and to remain open to opportunities which could provide further insurance against the possible failure of appeasement. The brief episodes of conflict between Chamberlain and Halifax usually centred around Chamberlain engaging in unilateral acts designed to keep up momentum in the policy of appeasement. It is important to note, however, that when the Anglo-Soviet alliance was proposed in the summer of 1939, Chamberlain and Halifax came back into harmony, as both felt that an Anglo-Soviet alliance was more likely to bring about war rather than prevent it.

In essence, Chamberlain's policy of appeasement as it operated from 1937 to 1939 resembles a political and diplomatic crisis strategy led by a clear-sighted but obstinate prime minister who saw war as a real possibility and tried desperately to prevent it. The idea of a general European settlement, briefly ignited at the time of Munich, never showed any signs of materialising. Hitler and Mussolini continued on the path of unilateral action, frequent surprises and threats of violence, and committed acts which simply escalated tension even further.

The military strategy which Chamberlain favoured centred around a long war of self-defence. The rearmament programme gave very little additional security to any of Britain's potential allies. Eastern Europe could not be defended without the Soviet Union. There was no serious consideration of whether the French army could hold, virtually alone, the western front against Germany. It was contradictory to believe, as Chamberlain did, both that the French army was weak and poorly led and that it could hold a German army he thought was strong, without substantial support. Chamberlain kept rearmament before Munich concentrated exclusively on air defence and naval power. 'As I watch the figures mounting,' Chamberlain said in a speech in Birmingham in January 1937, 'as I reflect on the growing cost of this vast panoply when we have completed it, I cannot help being impressed by the incredible folly of civilisation'.[8] Thus, the reluctance to engage in all-out rearmament actually justified a conciliatory policy. The decision to keep rearmament under tight Treasury control was Chamberlain's, although it was supported by the cabinet and often justified by the chiefs of staff. This flawed strategy was altered only when the diplomacy started to fail. It was finally changed by the pressure of events – not choice. It seems incorrect to suggest that Chamberlain was all along 'buying time' for an inevitable struggle with Hitler. This was Chamberlain's own self-justification for the policy, but it does not adequately fit the facts. The way Chamberlain conducted the 'phoney war' from September 1939 to May 1940 tends to suggest he had wished to avoid war if at all possible and, if it came, to carry it on with defensive and insular military preparations, in the hope that Hitler might still turn to peace or be replaced by moderates.

It is equally clear that Chamberlain's passionate desire to avert war was linked to a belief that war was likely to damage Britain's world-wide trading and imperial interests. In fact, he viewed German militarism as a product of a faulty economic strategy which placed guns before butter. In this context, the economic aspects of appeasement also require explanation. It would seem that Chamberlain never developed an integrated policy of economic appeasement towards Germany to supplement his passionate efforts to gain a political settlement. Economic appeasement always remained subordinate to political appeasement. It was given support by Chamberlain only as a last-ditch crisis strategy when the political talks had ground to a halt. It is tempting to speculate whether British business would have supported even these last informal efforts in the absence of political pressure. It could be suggested that Chamberlain's own adherence to protectionism had actually 'slammed the door in Germany's face' at the height of the economic depression and remained a severe impediment to the development of improved Anglo-German relations. It is perhaps significant that Chamberlain was never prepared to gamble any large sums of British money on the idea that Hitler was essentially 'a good European'.

Neither can it be convincingly accepted that Chamberlain's policy of appeasement enjoyed widespread and sustained public support. A high level of news management and media manipulation was employed by the Chamberlain government, especially on BBC radio and the cinema newsreels. This was specifically designed to encourage the idea that appeasement of Hitler was popular. This was largely a myth. BBC radio and the newsreels told the public largely what the government wanted it to hear and never gave critics any opportunity to engage in an open debate on foreign policy. In the press, a wide variety of views were offered. Only *The Times* can be said to have firmly supported the policy of appeasement. There were many bitter critics of Chamberlain's policy in the Labour and Liberal Parties and even among a minority in the Tory Party. The evidence from opinion polls shows that appeasing Hitler was not a popular policy. Most British people – even small children – booed whenever they saw Hitler in cinema newsreels and over 86 per cent of the public at the time of Munich did not believe the Sudetenland was really Hitler's 'last territorial demand in Europe'. In fact, the very policy that Chamberlain moved away from as prime minister, namely support for the League of Nations, was by far the most popular policy among the British public. It is difficult to believe that a policy of 'standing up to Hitler' would not have been as popular, or probably much more popular, than the one which Chamberlain followed. One opinion poll in 1939, for example, showed that 84 per cent of the British public supported an Anglo-Soviet alliance, while the highest opinion poll rating in support of the Munich agreement was only 51 per cent.

Yet Chamberlain went on believing, even on his deathbed, that, 'there is nothing more or anything different, that I could have done, and that would have been more successful'.[9] Of course, there are some historians who believe a solid anti-fascist alliance, supported by an all-out drive for rearmament, may have prevented war and others who believe a continuation of appeasement might have achieved a complete revision of the treaty of Versailles without war, and maybe even have encouraged Hitler, though this is highly improbable, to have given up his territorial desires.

However, history is not really the study of these hypothetical 'might have beens', but an exercise in interpreting and explaining why certain things did happen in the way they did. Political judgements played a deeply significant role in the errors in foreign policy during the inter-war years, but all the errors cannot be blamed on Chamberlain alone. The desire within British government and society to avoid war, predominantly to preserve economic and imperial interests, was woven into the fabric of British foreign policy. It proved difficult for any politician to take a leap of faith away from it. Yet this widely felt desire to avoid war resembled in Chamberlain a fundamentalist creed. It was supported by a diplomatic strategy which never succeeded in reducing the number of possible enemies, nor increased the number of allies, nor made adequate preparations to help France survive a German assault. Appeasement under Chamberlain was a bold endeavour to find out at the eleventh hour whether Hitler was, as so many supporters of appeasement believed, out for a revision of the treaty of Versailles or whether, as the critics believed, he aimed at European domination. It failed because Chamberlain took too long to decide on the answer to that question; even when he knew the answer, he kept on trying to believe it was not true. Chamberlain was not a guilty man for believing peace was preferable to war, nor was he cowardly, or stupid, or any more sinister than any of those placed in charge of British foreign policy during the inter-war years. Yet appeasement was a policy which was self-interested and defensive. It was also based on flawed judgements, namely that it could succeed with Hitler and that alliances would not act as a deterrent. Neville Chamberlain's fatal misjudgements were simply the final and most potent symbol of all the errors and miscalculations made by those in charge of British policy during the whole period 1918 to 1939. Perhaps Chamberlain's most fatal error was to believe 'if at first you don't succeed, try, try again'.[10] By trying to get Hitler to turn to peace, he was chasing an unlikely dream.

### Notes

1   K. Feiling, *The Life of Neville Chamberlain* (London, 1946), p. 456.

2   D. C. Watt, 'Appeasement: The Rise of a Revisionist School?', *Political Quarterly* (1965).

3   D. Dilks, '"We Must Hope for the Best and Prepare for the Worst": The Prime Minister, the Cabinet and Hitler's Germany, 1937–1939', *Proceedings of the British Academy* (1987).

4   *The Times*, 30 January 1937.

5   M. Gilbert, 'Horace Wilson: Man of Munich?', *History Today* (1982), p. 7.

6   Feiling, *Chamberlain*, p. 456.

7   Viscount Templewood (Sir Samuel Hoare), *Nine Troubled Years* (London, 1954), p. 375.

8   *The Times*, 30 January 1937.

9   R. A. C. Parker, *Chamberlain and Appeasement: British Policy and the Coming of the Second World War* (London, 1993), p. 1.

10   Chamberlain claimed on his trip to Munich that this proverb had appealed to him since he was a child.

# Selected documents

## Document 1

The following is an extract from the famous 1919 Fontainebleau memorandum, in which David Lloyd George offers an assessment of the likely success of the Paris peace settlement.

Source: M. Gilbert, *The Roots of Appeasement* (London, 1966), appendix 1, pp. 189–90.

When nations are exhausted by wars in which they put forth all their strength and which leave them tired, bleeding and broken, it is not difficult to patch up a peace that may last until the generation which experienced the horrors of war has passed away. Pictures of heroism and triumph only tempt those who know nothing of the suffering and terrors of war. It is therefore comparatively easy to patch up a peace which will last for 30 years.

What is difficult, however, is to draw up a peace which will not provoke a fresh struggle.... You may strip Germany of her colonies, reduce her armaments to a mere police force and her navy to that of a fifth rate power, all the same, in the end, if she feels that she has been unjustly treated in the peace of 1919, she will find means of exacting retribution from her conquerors.

... For these reasons I am, therefore, strongly averse to transferring more Germans from German rule to the rule of some other nation than can possibly be helped. I cannot conceive any greater cause of future war than that the German people, who have certainly proved themselves one of the most vigorous and powerful races in the world should be surrounded by a number of small states, many of them consisting of people who have never previously set up a stable government for themselves, but each of them containing large masses of Germans clamouring for reunion with their native land.

## Document 2

Germany had been Britain's major trading partner in Europe before the First World War. Many British and German business people made informal efforts to improve economic relations during the inter-war years. A major initiative was a conference of industrialists held at Broadlands, Hampshire, in October 1926. The following document is from the opening address at the conference given by Sir Robert Horne, a Conservative MP.

Source: BP 81/2, 'Report of Conference between English and German Industrialists', 8–11 October 1926.

During the past four years conversations have taken place between prominent members of German and British industry with the object of creating a better understanding in the trade relations between British and German industry and preventing the acute competition which became more and more intense in world markets to the detriment of both countries.

British deputation's [*sic*] have visited Germany, and in their investigation of German economic conditions realised that with the rise of German economic power it would be imperative to establish some measure of co-operation which would obviate inevitable injury to the industrial life of both countries.

## Document 3

In 1926, a number of discussions were undertaken within the British government about the best means of reconciling the German government to the new European order. In the following document, Sir Austen Chamberlain, the foreign secretary, offers his view of the 'German problem'.

Source: Committee of imperial defence, minutes and reports (PRO, London) (hereafter CAB 2), 195th meeting, 1926.

I have to keep my eyes fixed on a date like 1960 or 1970, when Germany will be in a position, through one cause or another, to attack again if she wants to, and by that time there must have grown up in Germany a new generation who, whatever their feelings of resentment about the Treaty of Versailles, of the pain at the situation which the Treaty brought upon Germany, will yet say, after all, things must have an end; at this moment we have too much to lose and the risks of trying fortune again are too great to undertake a quarrel.... But if you are to have any chance of getting that kind of generation in Germany in 1960 or 1970 you must begin the work of pacification tomorrow.

## Document 4

The arrival of Adolf Hitler in power in Germany in January 1933 raised concerns about his likely intentions in the field of foreign affairs. In February 1934, Sir Anthony Eden, then lord privy seal, visited Nazi Germany. In the following document Eden gives his first impressions of Adolf Hitler.

Source: Stanley Baldwin papers (Cambridge University Library), vol. 122, fol. 31, Eden to Baldwin, 21 February 1933.

We had our first interview with Hitler yesterday afternoon. We were given a grand salute on arrival by a fine SS guard (illegal), armed to the teeth (illegal). Having thus condoned breaches of the Treaty of Versailles we march through the passages greeted by salutes from everyone, even the typists! More like GHQ in war time than any-thing else.... Hitler came forward to greet us. He is a surprise. In conversation quiet, almost shy with a pleasant smile. Without doubt the man has charm ... he likes to talk about war, seems friendly to anyone who was in it, on whatever side.

## Document 5

The announcement in March 1935 by Hitler of his plans for rearma-ment raised some alarm. Sir John Simon, the foreign secretary, decided to visit Berlin a few weeks later. In the following document, Simon explains the major aims of British policy towards Adolf Hitler.

Source: *DBFP*, vol. 12, no. 651, 25–26 March 1935.

The object of British policy was to preserve general peace by helping to secure co-operation amongst all European countries. His Majesty's Government most earnestly wished that Germany should work with all countries for that object. They felt the future of Europe would take one of two forms.... It would either take the form of co-operation for securing continued peace – and this was the form His Majesty's Government earnestly desired. Or it would take the form of a division into camps – isolation, on the one side, and combination (which may look like encirclement) on the other.

## Document 6

The leaking of the details of the Hoare–Laval pact in December 1935 led to the fall of Sir Samuel Hoare as foreign secretary. In the following document, Chamberlain gives his view of why the scandal erupted.

Source: NC 18, Chamberlain to Ida Chamberlain, 15 December 1935.

when Sam left for Paris on Saturday the 7th. we had no idea that we would be invited to consider detailed peace proposals. I believed, and so far as I know my colleagues believed also, that he was going to stop off at Paris for a few hours on his way to Switzerland to get the discussions with the French into such a condition that we should say to the League 'Don't prejudice the chances of a favourable issue by thrusting in a particularly provocative extra sanction at this moment'. Instead of that a set of proposals was agreed.

## Document 7

There was great debate in the foreign office concerning economic appeasement. Frank Ashton-Gwatkin believed economic concessions might induce Germany to participate in a new European settlement. On 21 December 1936, Ashton-Gwatkin outlined his proposals for economic appeasement.

Source: M. Gilbert, *The Roots of Appeasement* (London 1966), pp. 212–13.

we must also seek to foster and develop the spirit and habit of international interdependence which are not only the antidote to 'nationalism' but are the approach to the solution of the ultimate problem of distribution.

Industrial interdependence can be promoted by exchange of culture, sport, tourism, etc., but above all by trade.

Intent on our national recovery we have not fully realised that the growth of industrial interdependence by trade depends almost entirely on the economic policy of Great Britain

... It is clear the economic position of Germany is not improving. Whichever way it is interpreted, the economic position is an important factor.

### Document 8

Sir Robert Vansittart, permanent under-secretary at the foreign office, was extremely sceptical about the likely success of the policy of appeasement. In the following extract, Vansittart offers a prediction of the likely course of events.

Source: *DBFP*, vol. 19, appendix 2, 'The World Situation and British Rearmament', memorandum by Sir R. Vansittart, 31 December 1936.

On any showing Germany will be ready for big mischief at least a year – and probably more – before we are ready to look after ourselves. To the Foreign Office, therefore, falls the task of holding the situation at least till 1939, and the foregoing account of the world crisis shows that there is no certainty of our being able to do so, though we are doing our utmost by negotiating with Germany, endeavouring to regain lost ground with Italy, and reducing the demands on our still exiguous strength by a treaty with Egypt.

### Document 9

Neville Chamberlain believed the foreign office was antagonistic towards the idea of improving Anglo-Italian relations. Here, Chamberlain informs his sister of his concern about foreign office hostility.

Source: NC, 18/1/1020, Chamberlain to Hilda Chamberlain, 12 September 1937.

I am not too happy about the FO who seem to have no imagination and no courage. I must say A.E. [Anthony Eden] is accepting my suggestions without grumbling, but it is wearying to have always to begin at the beginning again and sometimes even to rewrite their despatches for them. I am terribly afraid lest we should let the Anglo-Italian situation slip back to where it was before I intervened. The FO persists in seeing Musso only as a sort of Machiavelli putting on a false mask of friendship in order to further nefarious ambition. If we treat him like that we will get nowhere with him.

## Document 10

The visit of Lord Halifax to Germany in November 1937 was Chamberlain's first major initiative in the appeasement of Hitler. In another of his weekly letters to his sisters, Chamberlain offers his view on the usefulness of the visit.

Source: NC 18/1, Chamberlain to Ida Chamberlain, 26 November 1937.

The Halifax visit was from my point of view a great success because it achieved its object, that of creating an atmosphere in which it is possible to discuss with Germany the practical questions involved in a European settlement. Both Hitler and Goering said separately and emphatically, that they had no desire or intention of making war, and I think we may take that as correct, at any rate for the present. Of course they want to dominate Europe; they want as close a union with Austria as they can get without incorporating her in the Reich, and they want much the same thing for the Sudetendeutsche as we did for the Uitlanders in the Transvaal.

... But I don't see why we shouldn't say to Germany 'Give us satisfactory assurances that you won't use force to deal with Austrians and Czechoslovakians and we will give you similar assurances that we won't use force to prevent the changes you want, if you can get them by peaceful means'.

## Document 11

The chiefs of staff constantly advised the cabinet during the 1930s to follow a policy of conciliation. The following document offers a typically pessimistic appraisal of the military situation.

Source: CAB 2, 'A Comparison of the Strength of Britain and that of Certain Other Nations as at January 1939', report by the chiefs of staff, 8 December 1937.

It will be seen that our Navy, Military and Air Force in their present state of development are still far from sufficient to meet our defensive commitments, which now extend from Western Europe, through the Mediterranean to the Far East ... we cannot foresee the time when our defensive forces will be strong enough to safeguard our territory, trade and vital interests against Germany, Italy and Japan simultaneously. We cannot, therefore, exaggerate the importance from the point of view of Imperial Defence, of any political action that can be taken to reduce the number of our potential enemies and to gain the support of political allies.

## Document 12

In the following document, Oliver Harvey, Eden's private secretary, offers his view of the row between Eden and Chamberlain in January 1938 over a proposal from president Roosevelt to convene a world conference to reduce international tension.

Source: Oliver Harvey's diary, 16 January 1938, quoted in J. Harvey (ed.), *The Diplomatic Diaries of Oliver Harvey, 1937–40* (London, 1970), pp. 70–1.

I'm afraid the P.M. may have committed a colossal blunder which it is too late to retrieve. A.E. [Anthony Eden] will have to consider his position very carefully, for he obviously cannot remain responsible for foreign policy if the P.M. persists in such a line.

He cannot accept responsibility for a policy which will antagonise America. The P.M. is being advised in this folly by Horace Wilson who knows nothing about foreign affairs. He, the P.M., is temperamentally anti American, but he is also, I'm afraid, moved by some vanity of his own ventures with Hitler and Mussolini.

## Document 13

One of the most dramatic events during the early part of Chamberlain's period as prime minister was the resignation of Sir Anthony Eden, the foreign secretary. The following document is Eden's letter of resignation, which Chamberlain read out to the cabinet on 20 February 1938.

Source: CAB 23, 92, cabinet meeting, 20 February 1938.

The events of the last few days have made plain a difference between us on a decision of great importance in itself and far reaching in its consequences. I cannot recommend to Parliament a policy with which I am not in agreement. Apart from this, I have become increasingly conscious, as I know you have also, of a difference of outlook between us in respect to the international problems of the day and as to the methods by which we should seek to resolve them. It cannot be in the country's interest that those who are called upon to direct its affairs should work in an uneasy partnership, fully conscious of differences in outlook yet hoping they will not recur. This applies with a special force to the relationship between the Prime Minister and the Foreign Secretary.

### Document 14

Lord Mount Temple, president of the AGF, was a leading supporter of appeasement. In February 1938, Mount Temple gave his view of German aims.

Source: *The Times*, 26 February 1938.

German foreign policy to-day is derived from the new fundamental outlook created by the revolution. The rise of consciousness of German nationhood which is now being experienced must necessarily relate itself to the questions of Germans in Austria and Czechoslovakia. The dynamic of national liberation will not exhaust itself until these two questions are resolved. The process is inevitable. The sense of nationhood in the German mind today carries with it recognition of the 'divine right of other peoples to existence and independence'.

The integrity of the countries of Eastern Europe is equally in no danger from such a philosophy.

### Document 15

Douglas Reed was a foreign correspondent of *The Times* during the 1930s who became increasingly disillusioned with the pro-appeasement sympathies of the newspaper. In a letter to the *Times* editor, shortly after the *Anschluss*, Reed expressed his fears for the future of European peace.

Source: TA, Reed to Dawson, 16 March 1938.

I believe it is already too late. England's military defeat impends. I saw the German fighting machine enter Austria. It is terrifying. Indeed worse than anything imagined, and you will realise that is saying a great deal.... In my wildest nightmares I had not imagined something so perfectly organised.... The vital thing to remember is they want to destroy England....

In May 1936, I wrote some articles of these coming dangers which you did not use at the time because you thought there was not much in them that demanded consideration and they were too alarmist.

## Document 16

In March 1938, the British government was considering policy towards the Czech crisis. This document illustrates Chamberlain's private views on the problem.

Source: Chamberlain's diary, 20 March 1938, quoted in K. Feiling, *The Life of Neville Chamberlain* (London, 1946), pp. 347–8.

You only have to look at the map to see that nothing that France or we could do could possibly save Czechoslovakia from being overrun by the Germans, if they wanted to do it. The Austrian frontier is practically open; the great Skoda munitions works are within easy bombing distance of German aerodromes, the railways all pass through German territory, Russia is 100 miles away. Therefore, we could not help Czechoslovakia – she would simply be a pretext for going to war with Germany.

## Document 17

During September 1938, Chamberlain made three visits to Germany, in order to find a peaceful settlement of the Czech crisis. In the following document, Chamberlain reports to the cabinet on his first meeting with Hitler at Berchtesgaden.

Source: Papers of the prime minister (PRO, London), 1/266, 'Account of Conversation between Chamberlain and Hitler', 15 September 1938.

I said that I saw considerable practical difficulties about the secession of the Sudeten Germans.... Even if, for example, the areas containing 80% of Germans were taken into the Reich, there would still be a considerable number of Germans left outside, and, moreover, there would be a considerable number of Czechoslovakians in the German area and, therefore, it looks as though a solution of the problem in your [Hitler's] sense ... would require a change of boundaries.

... He [Hitler] said that percentages of Germans could not come into this. Where the Germans are in a majority the territory ought to pass to Germany, as for the rest, the Czechoslovaks in German Sudetenland should be allowed to pass out.

... So far as he [Chamberlain] was concerned he didn't give two hoots whether the Sudetens were in the Reich or out of it.

## Document 18

Clement Attlee, the Labour leader, was very critical of Chamberlain's diplomacy during the Czech crisis. This is a report of a speech by Attlee at Limehouse town hall, in September 1938.

Source: *The Times*, 19 September 1938.

It is a very melancholy thing to find one is a true prophet. The Labour movement has warned the country since 1932 that yielding to aggression in one part of the world means an increase in aggression in another. We are now paying in anxiety for a wrong foreign policy assumed since Labour was thrown out of office. I pray heaven that we will not have to pay in blood.

## Document 19

Lord Halifax, the foreign secretary, was a firm supporter of appeasement at the outset, but the terms of the Godesberg memorandum led him to have second thoughts. At a cabinet meeting on 25 September 1938, Halifax explained his worries.

Source: CAB 23/95, cabinet meeting, 25 September 1938.

[Halifax] found his opinions changing somewhat in the last day or so ... there was a distinction in principle between an orderly and disorderly transfer with all the latter implied for the minorities in the transferred areas.... Herr Hitler had given us nothing and ... was dictating terms, just as though he had won a war but without having had to fight.... So long as Nazism lasted peace would be uncertain. For this reason he did not feel that it would be right to put pressure on Czechoslovakia to accept.

## Document 20

The most famous critic of Chamberlain's appeasement within the Conservative Party was Winston Churchill. Here, he offers his verdict on the Munich settlement.

Source: *The Times*, 4 October 1938.

No one has been a more resolute and uncompromising struggler for peace than the Prime Minister. Everyone knows that. Never has there been such an intense and undaunted determination to maintain and secure peace. Nevertheless, I am not quite clear why there was so much danger of Great Britain and France being involved in war with Germany at this juncture if in fact they were ready all along to sacrifice Czechoslovakia. The terms which the Prime Minister brought back with him could have easily been agreed, I believe, through the ordinary diplomatic channels at any time during the summer. And I will say this, that I believe the Czechs left to themselves, and told they were going to get no help from the western powers, would have been able to make better terms than they have got after all the tremendous perturbation. They could hardly have had worse.

All is over. Silent, mournful, abandoned, broken, Czechoslovakia recedes into the darkness.

## Document 21

At the end of October 1938, Chamberlain informed the cabinet of what he expected to follow from the Munich agreement.

Source: CAB 23/96, cabinet meeting, 31 October 1938.

Our Foreign Policy was one of appeasement: We must aim at establishing relations with the Dictator Powers which will lead to a settlement in Europe and to a sense of stability.

There has been a good deal of talk in the country and in the press about the need for rearmament in this country. In Germany and Italy it was suspected that this rearmament was directed against them, and it was important that we should discourage these suspicions.

The Prime Minister said that he proposed to make it clear that our rearmament was directed to securing our own safety and not for purposes of aggression against other countries.... The Prime Minister hoped that it might be possible to take active steps to follow up the Munich Agreement by other measures, aimed at securing better relations. The putting into effect of the Anglo-Italian Agreement would be one step in this direction. He also hoped that some day we should be able to secure a measure of limitation of armaments, but it was too soon to say when this would be possible.

## Document 22

In a speech to the Foreign Correspondents' Association in December 1938, Chamberlain spoke of his continuing hope of appeasement.

Source: CPA, foreign policy files, 1937–39.

War to-day differs fundamentally from all the wars of the past inasmuch as to-day its first and most numerous victims are not the professional fighters, but the civilian population, the workman, and the clerk, the housewife, and, most horrible of all, the children. And when the war is over, whoever may be the victor, it leaves behind a trail of loss and suffering which two generations will not obliterate and it sows the dragon's teeth which are the seeds of fresh conflicts, fresh injustices and fresh conflicts. Such consequences are not to be lightly incurred; they ought never to be incurred unless we can be satisfied and our people are satisfied that every honourable alternative has been tried and found impossible.

## Document 23

The occupation of Prague on 15 March 1939 was the death blow to the Munich agreement. At Birmingham on 17 March 1939, Chamberlain speculated whether Hitler was aiming at world domination.

Source: *The Times*, 18 March 1939.

Germany under its present regime has sprung a series of unpleasant surprises upon the world. The Rhineland, the Austrian Anschluss, the severance of the Sudetenland – all these things shocked and affronted public opinion throughout the world. Yet however much we might take exception to the methods which were adopted in each of these cases, there was something to be said, whether on account of racial affinity or of just claims too long resisted....

But the events which have taken place this past week in complete disregard of the principle laid down by the German government itself seems to fall into a different category and must cause us all to be asking ourselves 'Is this the end of an old story, or is it the beginning of a new one? Is this the last attack on a small state, or is it to be followed by others? Is this, in fact, a step in the direction of an attempt to dominate the world by force?'

## Document 24

There was great public and political pressure on Chamberlain to conclude an Anglo-Soviet alliance in the summer of 1939. However, Chamberlain was extremely sceptical about the whole idea. Here, he outlines his private worries.

Source: Chamberlain's diary, 26 March 1939, quoted in Feiling, *Chamberlain*, p. 403.

I must confess to a most profound distrust of Russia. I have no belief whatever in her ability to maintain an effective offensive, even if she wanted to. And I distrust her motives which seem to me to have little connection with our ideas of liberty, and to be concerned only with getting everyone by the ears. Moreover, she is both hated and suspected by many smaller states, notably by Poland, Rumania and Finland.

## Document 25

Great mystery has always surrounded the reasons why Chamberlain waited almost two days after the invasion of Poland before declaring war against Germany. In the following document, Chamberlain gives his own explanation.

Source: Chamberlain's diary, 10 September 1939, quoted in Feiling, *Chamberlain*, pp. 416–17.

The final long drawn out agonies that preceded the actual declaration of war were as nearly unendurable as could be imagined. We were anxious to bring things to a head, but there were three complications – the secret communications that were going on with Goering and Hitler through a neutral intermediary, the Conference proposal of Mussolini, and the French anxiety to postpone the actual declaration as long as possible, until they could evacuate their women and children and mobilise their armies. There was very little of this that we could say to the public, and meantime the House of Commons was out of hand, torn with suspicions … [some of them believing] the government guilty of cowardice and treachery.

# Select bibliography

**Primary sources**

*Unpublished sources*

The unpublished material quoted in this volume was derived from a number of collections. The foundation of any scholarly study of the role of foreign policy at the government level is the Public Record Office, Kew, London. The most useful sources used in the research for this book were:

CAB 2 (committee of imperial defence)
CAB 23 (cabinet minutes)
CAB 24 (cabinet memoranda)
CAB 27 (committee on foreign policy)
CAB 29 (proceedings of the London reparations conference)
CAB 53 (chiefs of staff committee)
PREM 1 (covers the Chamberlain period)
PRO 30 (diary of J. Ramsay MacDonald)

Foreign office files also contain a great deal of very useful material, particularly:

FO 371 (general correspondence – political)
FO 800 (private papers series – in particular, correspondence of Frank Ashton-Gwatkin, Sir Alexander Cadogan, Lord Halifax, Sir Neville Henderson, Lord Runciman and Sir Orme Sergeant).
FO 954 (Avon – i.e. Sir Anthony Eden's – papers)

In the Treasury papers see:

T188 (the papers of Leith Ross are useful for the study of economic appeasement)

The papers of the service departments, board of trade (see, in particular, BT61 – estimates and accounts for Anglo-German trade relations), office of coordination of defence and other departments of state also contain much useful material and are also to be found in the PRO.

The following collections of private papers are also of great importance. Among the most important for this study were:

Lord Attlee (Bodleian Library, Oxford)
Stanley Baldwin (Cambridge University Library)
Sir Austen Chamberlain (Birmingham University Library)
Neville Chamberlain (Birmingham University Library)
Geoffrey Dawson (Bodleian Library, Oxford)
17th Earl of Derby (Liverpool Record Office, Central Library)
Lord Halifax (Borthwick Institute, University of York)
Lloyd George (House of Lords Record Office)
Sir John Simon (Bodleian Library, Oxford).
Lord Mount Temple (Broadlands Archive, Hartley Library, University of Southampton)

Another private collection which contains much useful material on Conservative Party foreign policy is:

Conservative Party archive (Bodleian Library, Oxford)

The greatest single collection of private papers relevant to the subject is the Library of Churchill College, Cambridge, which contains the papers of: Winston Churchill, Admiral Drax, Alfred Duff Cooper, Lord Hankey, Leslie Hore-Belisha, Sir Thomas Inskip, Lord Strang, Lord Swinton and Sir Robert Vansittart. The papers of R. A. Butler, which are also useful, are in Trinity College, Cambridge.

The best material in private papers relating to the role of press was found in:

Times archive, London.
Newspaper and periodical archive, British Library, London
Manchester Guardian archive, John Rylands Library, Manchester

Much useful material relating to British business and appeasement can be found in:

# Bibliography

Federation of British Industry papers, Modern Records Centre, University of Warwick.

For a detailed examination of primary source materials related to British foreign policy in the inter-war years see Sidney Aster (ed.), *British Foreign Policy, 1918–1945: A Guide to Research and Research Materials* (Wilmington, 1984).

## Theses

There a number of useful unpublished theses, including S. Aster, 'British Policy Towards the USSR and the Onset of the World War, March 1938–August 1939' (PhD, London University, 1969), C. J. Hill, 'The Decision Making Process in Relation to British Foreign Policy 1938–1941' (DPhil, Oxford University, 1978), A. Prazmowska, 'Anglo-Polish Relations 1938–1939' (PhD, London University, 1979), G. Van Kessel, 'The British Reaction to German Economic Expansion in Central and Eastern Europe' (PhD, London University, 1972).

## Published sources

The following from HMSO (London) contain a vast amount of useful material: E. L. Woodward and Rohan Butler (eds), *Documents on British Foreign Policy, 1919–1939* (*DBFP*), third series (1949–57); *Parliamentary Debates* (*Hansard*), House of Commons, fifth series (1918–39); *Documents on German Foreign Policy*, series D (1954–57). For other useful primary sources consult M. Gilbert, *Britain and Germany Between the Wars* (London, 1964). Another excellent set of documents is R. B. Henig (ed.), *The League of Nations* (Edinburgh, 1973).

## The press

Newspapers and periodicals are extremely important sources for the study of foreign policy. The following were consulted at the British Library, London, the Bodleian Library, Oxford, and the Liverpool Record Office: Cardiff *Western Mail*; *Daily Express*; *Daily Herald*; *Daily Mail*; *Daily Mirror*; *Daily Telegraph*; *Daily Worker*; *Economist*; *Glasgow Herald*; Leeds *Weekly Citizen*; Liverpool *Daily Post*; *Liverpool Echo*; *London Evening Standard*; *Manchester Guardian*; *New Statesman*; *News Chronicle*; *Observer*; *Spectator*; *Sunday Times*; *The Times*; *Today's Cinema*; *Tribune*; *Truth*; *Yorkshire Observer*.

# Bibliography

## Secondary sources – a bibliographical review

Note that the place of publication is London, unless stated.

The amount of published work on the policy of appeasement during the inter-war period is enormous. It remains an important topic of historical study, and will always be subject to new debate. Any survey of the secondary sources will be highly selective and will no doubt leave some scholars feeling their work has been under-represented. However, the intention has been to include material which I have found impressive and to outline studies which I believe provide much useful material for further research and study.

There are a great number of useful general and introductory works which offer an overview of the period 1918–39 and provide useful insights into the policy of appeasement, most notably: A. Adamthwaite, *The Making of the Second World War* (1977) – includes a superb selection of original documents; S. Aster, *1939: The Making of the Second World War* (1973); C. Barnett, *The Collapse of British Power* (1972); C. J. Bartlett, *British Foreign Policy in the Twentieth Century* (1989) – see especially chapter 2 for an impressive overview of the inter-war period; P. M. H. Bell, *The Origins of the Second World War* (1986); E. H. Carr, *International Relations Between the Two World Wars* (1947); D. Dilks (ed.), *Retreat from Power, Volume I, 1906–1939* (1981) – a very useful set of essays from a number of eminent scholars; D. Dilks, 'The British Foreign Office Between the Wars', in B. I. C. McKercher and D. J. Moss (eds), *Shadow and Substance in British Foreign Policy 1895–1939* (Edmonton, 1984); M. Gilbert, *The Roots of Appeasement* (1966); P. Hayes, *Modern British Foreign Policy: The Twentieth Century, 1880–1939* (1978); R. Henig, *The Origins of the Second World War* (1989); P. M. Kennedy, 'The Tradition of Appeasement in British Foreign Policy 1864–1939', *British Journal of International Studies* (1976); S. Marks, *The Illusion of Peace. International Relations, 1918–1939* (1976); G. Martel (ed.), *The Origins of the Second World War Reconsidered: The A. J. P. Taylor Debate After 15 Years* (Boston, 1986); F. McDonough, 'Why Appeasement?', in P. Catterall (ed.), *Britain 1918–1951* (Oxford, 1994); W. N. Medlicott, *British Foreign Policy Since Versailles, 1919–1963* (1968); A. Orde, *Great Britain and International Security, 1920–1926* (1978); R. A. C. Parker, *Europe, 1919–1945* (1969); W. Rock, *British Appeasement in the 1930s* (1977); A. J. P. Taylor, *The Origins of the Second World War* (1961); F. Walters, *A History of the League of Nations* (1952).

The following memoirs and diaries provide very useful contemporary accounts of the period. The role of the Labour Party is dealt with in: C. R. Attlee, *As It Happened* (1954); H. Dalton, *The Fateful Years: Memoirs, 1931–1945* (1971). The view of the TUC towards appeasement is explained in:

W. Citrine, *Men and Work* (1964). For the inside view of the role of the foreign office see: F. T. Ashton-Gwatkin, *The British Foreign Office* (1949); Earl of Avon (Anthony Eden), *Facing the Dictators* (1962); Lord Butler (R. A. Butler), *The Art of the Possible* (1971); D. Dilks (ed.), *The Diaries of Sir Alexander Cadogan, 1938–45* (1971); the Earl of Halifax, *Fullness of Days* (1957); J. Harvey (ed.), *The Diplomatic Diaries of Oliver Harvey, 1937–40* (1970); Lord Vansittart (Sir Robert Vansittart), *The Mist Procession* (1958). For the role of anti-appeasers in the Tory Party consult: J. Barnes and D. Nicholson (eds), *The Empire at Bay: The Leo Amery Diaries, 1929–45* (1988); R. Boothby, *I Fight to Live* (1947); W. S. Churchill, *The Gathering Storm* (1948); H. Macmillan, *Winds of Change* (1966); N. Nicholson, *Harold Nicolson: Diaries and Letters, Volume I 1930–39* (1967). Many useful insights into British rearmament are to be found in: Lord Chatfield, *It Might Happen Again* (1947); A. Duff Cooper, *Old Men Forget* (1953); Sir B. Liddell Hart, *The Liddell Hart Memoirs* (1965); R. Macleod and D. Kelly (eds), *The Ironside Diaries, 1937–1940* (1962); R. J. Minney, *The Private Papers of Hore-Belisha* (1960); Earl of Swinton, *I Remember* (1952). There are many useful details of Chamberlain's methods in conducting foreign policy in: Sir J. Colville, *The Fringes of Power* (1985); Neville Henderson, *Failure of a Mission* (1940); Lord Home (Alec Douglas-Home), *The Way the Wind Blows* (1976); R. R. James, *Chips: The Diaries of Sir Henry Channon* (1967); T. Jones, *A Diary with Letters, 1931–1950* (Oxford, 1954); Lord Maugham, *The Truth about the Munich Crisis* (1954); Viscount Templewood (Sir Samuel Hoare), *Nine Troubled Years* (1954). For a Soviet view on events in London during the 1930s see: I. Maisky, *Who Helped Hitler?* (1964). For a Czech view of Munich see: E. Beneš, *Memoirs of Eduard Beneš* (1954). For a contemporary account of the failed Anglo-Soviet negotiations in the summer of 1939 see: Sir W. Strang, *The Moscow Negotiations* (Leeds, 1968). There are some extremely entertaining insights into Anglo-Italian relations and the Munich conference in: M. Muggeridge (ed.), *Ciano's Diplomatic Papers* (Oxford, 1948).

Biographies provide a rich source of material on many of the leading figures. The most useful are: D. Carlton, *Anthony Eden* (1981); J. Charmley, *Duff Cooper: The Authorised Biography* (1986); Randolph S. Churchill, *The Rise and Fall of Sir Anthony Eden* (1959); I. Colvin, *Vansittart in Office* (1965); J. A. Cross, *Sir Samuel Hoare* (1977); J. A. Cross, *Lord Swinton* (Oxford, 1982); D. Dilks, *Neville Chamberlain, Volume I* (Cambridge, 1984); D. Dutton, *Simon: A Political Biography* (1992); K. Feiling, *The Life of Neville Chamberlain* (1946); M. Gilbert, *Winston S. Churchill, Volume V: The Prophet of Truth, 1922–1939* (1976); A. Horne, *Harold Macmillan, Volume I* (1988); H. M. Hyde, *Neville Chamberlain* (1976); R. R. James, *Churchill: A Study in Failure* (1970); R. R. James, *Anthony Eden* (1987); A. Lentin, *Lloyd George, Woodrow Wilson and the Guilt of Germany* (Gloucester, 1971); I. Macleod, *Neville Chamberlain* (1962); W. Manchester, *The Last Lion: W. S. Churchill, Volume II: Alone*

(Boston, 1988); D. Marquand, *Ramsay MacDonald* (1977); K. Middlemass and J. Barnes, *Baldwin* (1969); B. Pimlott, *Hugh Dalton* (1985); A. Roberts, *The Holy Fox: A Biography of Lord Halifax* (1991); W. R. Rock, *Neville Chamberlain* (1969); N. Rose, *Vansittart: Study of a Diplomat* (1978); S. Roskill, *Hankey, Man of Secrets, Volume III* (1974); A. J. P. Taylor, *Beaverbrook* (1972); K. Young, *Sir Alec Douglas-Home* (1970); K. Young, *Stanley Baldwin* (1976).

The role of Neville Chamberlain has attracted sympathetic and critical treatment. For generally favourable revisionist views consult: D. Carlton, 'Against the Grain – in Defence of Appeasement', *Policy Review* (1980); J. Charmley, *Chamberlain and the Lost Peace* (1989); D. Dilks, '"We Must Hope for the Best and Prepare for the Worst": The Prime Minister, the Cabinet and Hitler's Germany 1937–1939', *Proceedings of the British Academy* (1987); R. Douglas, 'Chamberlain and Appeasement', in W. Mommsen and L. Kettenacher (eds), *The Fascist Challenge and the Policy of Appeasement* (1983); P. M. Kennedy, *The Realities Behind Diplomacy* (1980); P. M. Kennedy, 'Appeasement', *History Today* (1982); P. M. Kennedy, *The Rise and Fall of the Great Powers* (1987); P. Taylor, 'Appeasement: Guilty Men or Guilty Conscience', *Modern History Review* (1989); D. C. Watt, 'Appeasement: The Rise of a Revisionist School?', *Political Quarterly* (1965); D. C. Watt, *How War Came: The Immediate Origins of the Second World War, 1938–39* (1989). For critical interpretations of Chamberlain consult: S. Aster, '"Guilty Men": The Case of Neville Chamberlain', in R. Boyce and E. Robertson (eds), *Paths of War: New Essays on the Origins of the Second World War* (1989); 'Cato', *The Guilty Men* (1940); I. Colvin, *The Chamberlain Cabinet* (1971); L. W. Fuchser, *Neville Chamberlain and Appeasement: A Study in the Politics of History* (1982); M. George, *The Warped Vision: British Foreign Policy, 1933–1939* (Pittsburg, 1965); K. Middlemass, *The Diplomacy of Illusion: The British Government and Germany, 1937–1939* (1972); R. A. C. Parker, *Chamberlain and Appeasement: British Policy and the Coming of the Second World War* (1993); J. Wheeler-Bennett, *Munich: Prologue to Tragedy* (1948).

For defence policy, rearmament and British intelligence see: C. M. Andrew and D. Dilks, *The Missing Dimension: Governments and Intelligence Communities in the Twentieth Century* (1984); C. M. Andrew, 'Secret Intelligence and British Foreign Policy 1900–1939', in C. M. Andrew and J. Noakes (eds), *Intelligence and International Relations, 1900–1945* (Exeter, 1987); U. Bialer, *The Shadow of the Bomber: The Fear of Air Attack and British Politics, 1932–1939* (1980); B. Bond, *British Military Policy Between the Two World Wars* (1980); F. Coghlan, 'Armaments, Economic Policy and Appeasement: The Background to British Foreign Policy 1931–37', *History* (1972); P. Dennis, *Decision by Default: Peacetime Conscription and British Defence, 1919–1939* (Durham, 1972); J. P. D. Dunbabin, 'British Rearmament in the 1930s', *Historical Journal* (1975); N. H. Gibbs, *Grand Strategy, Volume*

*I* (1976); M. Howard, *The Continental Commitment* (1972); H. Montgomery Hyde, *British Air Policy Between the Wars, 1918–1939* (1976); P. M. Kennedy, 'Appeasement and British Defence Policy', *British Journal of International Studies* (1978); R. Lamb, *The Ghosts of Peace, 1935–45* (1987); W. R. Louis, *British Strategy in the Far East, 1919–1939* (Oxford, 1971); R. A. C. Parker, 'Economics, Rearmament and Foreign Policy Before 1939 – A Preliminary Survey', *Journal of Contemporary History* (1975); R. A. C. Parker, 'British Rearmament 1936–39: Treasury, Trade Unions and Skilled Labour', *English Historical Review* (1981); R. A. C. Parker, 'The Pound Sterling, The American Treasury and British Preparations for War 1938–39', *English Historical Review* (1983); G. C. Peden, *British Rearmament and the Treasury, 1932–1939* (Edinburgh, 1979); G. C. Peden, 'A Matter of Timing: The Economic Background to British Foreign Policy, 1937–39', *History* (1984); G. Post, *Dilemmas of Appeasement: British Deterrence and Defence, 1934–37* (Ithaca, 1993); D. Richardson, *The Evolution of British Disarmament Policy in the 1920s* (1989); S. Roskill, *Naval Policy Between the Wars, 1919–1939* (1976); M. Smith, *British Air Strategy Between the Wars* (1984); R. P. Shay, *British Rearmament in the Thirties* (1977); D. C. Watt, *Too Serious a Business: European Armed Forces and the Approach to the Second World War* (1975); D. C. Watt, 'British Intelligence and the Coming of the Second World War in Europe', in E. R. May (ed.), *Knowing One's Enemies* (Princeton, 1986); A. P. Young, *The X Documents: The Secret History of Foreign Office Contacts with the German Resistance, 1937–1939* (1974).

There are number of useful studies of key events. The problem of reparations is discussed in: B. Kent, *The Politics, Economics and Diplomacy of Reparations, 1918–1932* (Oxford, 1989). For the Abyssinian affair see: G. W. Baer, *The Coming of the Italian–Ethiopian War* (1967); F. Hardie, *The Abyssinian Crisis* (1974); R. A. C. Parker, 'Great Britain, France and the Ethiopian Crisis 1935–1936', *English Historical Review* (1974). For the Anglo-German naval agreement see: H. H. Hall, 'The Origins of the Anglo-German Naval Agreement', *Historical Journal* (1976). For Britain's role in the Spanish civil war consult: J. Edwards, *The British Government and the Spanish Civil War, 1936–1939* (1979). For a detailed study of the Rhineland crisis see: J. T. Emmerson, *The Rhineland Crisis, 7 March 1936: A Study in Multilateral Diplomacy* (1977). A useful collection of essays on Britain's relations with Europe during the inter-war period can be found in: P. Catterall and C. J. Morris (eds), *Britain and the Threat to Stability in Europe 1918–45* (1993).

A number books and articles have examined important aspects of the policy of appeasement under Chamberlain from 1937 to 1939. For a summary of the historical debate see: F. McDonough, 'Guilty Man or National Saviour? The Changing Debate on Neville Chamberlain and the Policy of Appeasement', *History Review* (1995). The vexed question of the Eden–Chamberlain relationship is covered in: R. Douglas, 'Chamberlain and Eden 1937–38', *Journal of Contemporary History* (1978); A. R. Peters, *Anthony Eden at the Foreign Office 1931–1938* (Aldershot, 1986); N. Rose, 'The Resignation of Anthony Eden', *Historical Journal* (1982); V. Rothwell, *Anthony Eden: A Political Biography, 1931–1957* (Manchester, 1992). For the differences between Henderson and Vansittart on the prospects of appeasement of Nazi Germany see: A. L. Goldman, 'Two Views of Germany: Henderson vs Vansittart', *British Journal of International Studies* (1980). For the Czech crisis and Munich see: H. Auluch, 'Britain and the Sudeten Issue 1938: The Evolution of a Policy', *Journal of Contemporary History* (1983); J. W. Bruegel, *Czechoslovakia Before Munich: The German Minority Problem and German and British Appeasement* (Cambridge, 1973); R. Douglas, *In the Year of Munich* (1977); K. Eubank, *Munich* (1963); R. Kee, *Munich: The Eleventh Hour* (1988); D. Lammers, *Explaining Munich: The Search for Motive in British Foreign Policy* (1966); K. Robbins, *Munich 1938* (1968); P. W. Shroeder, 'Munich and the British Tradition', *Historical Journal* (1976); T. Taylor, *Munich: The Price of Peace* (1979); A. Teichova, *An Economic Background to Munich* (Cambridge, 1974); G. Weinberg, W. R. Rock and A. M. Ciencilia, 'The Munich Crisis Revisited', *International History Review* (1989). For the Chamberlain visit to Rome in January 1939 see: P. Stafford, 'The Chamberlain–Halifax Visit to Rome: A Reappraisal', *English Historical Review* (1983). For Anglo-Polish relations see: S. Newman, *March 1939: The British Guarantee to Poland* (Oxford, 1976); A. J. Prazmowska, 'Poland's Foreign Policy September 1938–September 1939', *Historical Journal* (1986).

There are many useful studies of Britain's foreign relations with specific countries. For Anglo-French relations see: A. Adamthwaite, *France and the Coming of the Second World War* (1977); N. Rostow, *Anglo-French Relations 1934–1936* (1984); N. Waites (ed.), *The Troubled Neighbours: Franco-British Relations in the Twentieth Century* (1971). For Anglo-American relations see: C. A. MacDonald, *The United States, Britain and Appeasement* (1981); A. Offer 'Appeasement Revisited: The U.S., Great Britain and Germany, 1933–1939', *Journal of American History* (1977); R. Ovendale, *Appeasement and the English Speaking World 1937–1939* (1975); W. Rock, *Chamberlain and Roosevelt 1937–1940* (Columbus, 1988). For Anglo-Polish relations see: A. Cienciala, *Poland and the Western Powers* (1968). For the failure of the Anglo-Soviet alliance see: D. Lammers, 'Fascism, Communism and the Foreign Office', *Journal of Contemporary History* (1971); R. Manne, 'The British Decision for an Alliance with Russia, May 1939', *Journal of Contemporary History* (1974); R. Manne, 'The Foreign Office and the Failure of the Anglo-Soviet Rapprochement', *Journal of Contemporary History* (1981). For Anglo-Japanese relations see: P. Lowe, *Great Britain and the Origins of the Pacific War: A Study of British Policy in East Asia, 1937–1941* (1977).

There are many useful micro-studies of the effect of appeasement on British politics and society. For the role of the League of Nations Union see:

# Bibliography

Donald Birn, *The League of Nations Union, 1918–1945* (1981); J. A. Thompson, 'The League of Nations Union and Promotion of the League Idea in Great Britain', *Australian Journal of Politics and History* (1972). For a good overview of pacifist groups see: M. Caedel, *Pacifism in Britain 1914–1945* (Oxford, 1980). For the impact of appeasement on party politics see the innovative – and controversial – M. Cowling, *The Impact of Hitler. British Politics and British Policy 1933–1940* (1975). For useful accounts of supporters of appeasement see: M. Gilbert and R. Gott, *The Appeasers* (1963); R. Griffiths, *Fellow Travellers of the Right: British Enthusiasts for Nazi Germany 1933–1939* (1980); S. Haxey, *Tory M.P.* (1939). For the role of the Labour Party see: J. F. Naylor, *Labour's International Policy: The Labour Party in the 1930s* (1969). For the role of Conservative opponents of Chamberlain see: N. Thompson, *The Anti-Appeasers: Conservative Opposition to Appeasement in the 1930s* (Oxford, 1971). For the role of the BUF see: C. Cross, *The Fascists in Britain* (1961); Sir Oswald Mosley, *My Life* (1968); J. Stevenson, 'Conservatism and the Failure of Fascism in Interwar Britain', in M. Blinkhorn (ed.), *Fascists and Conservatives* (1990). For the role of intellectual groups see: N. Annan, *Our Age: English Intellectuals Between the Wars, A Group Portrait* (1990); A. L. Rowse, *All Souls and Appeasement* (1961).

The question of economic appeasement is covered in: B. J. Wendt, *Economic Appeasement* (Dusseldorf, 1971), but this is available only in German. A very good English translation of a leading German contribution to the debate is: G. Schmidt, *The Politics and Economics of Appeasement, 1931–1937* (Leamington Spa, 1986). There have been a number of useful articles on the subject, including: N. Forbes, 'London Banks, the German Standstill Agreements and Economic Appeasement in the 1930s', *Economic History Review* (1987); R. F. Holland, 'The Federation of British Industry and the International Economy', *Economic History Review* (1981); C. A. MacDonald, 'Economic Appeasement and the German "Moderates" 1937–1939', *Past and Present* (1972); S. Newton, 'The Anglo-German Connection and the Political Economy of Appeasement', *Diplomacy and Statecraft* (1991); S. Newton, 'Appeasement as an Industrial Strategy 1938–41', *Contemporary Record* (1995). See also: I. Drummond, *The Floating Pound and the Sterling Area 1931–1939* (Cambridge, 1981) for the broader economic context in which foreign policy operated during the 1930s.

For the mass media, public opinion and appeasement, the following are useful: A. Adamthwaite, 'The British Government and the Media 1937–1938', *Journal of Contemporary History* (1983); R. Cockett, *Twilight of Truth: Chamberlain, Appeasement and the Manipulation of the Press 1937–1940* (1989); R. Eatwell, 'Munich, Public Opinion and the Popular Front', *Journal of Contemporary History* (1971); F. R. Gannon, *The British Press and Nazi Germany, 1936–1939* (1971); T. Harrison and C. Madge, *Britain by Mass Observation* (1986); S. Koss, *The Rise and Fall of the Political Press in Britain.*

# Bibliography

*Volume II: The Twentieth Century* (1984); P. Kyba, *Covenants Without Swords: Public Opinion and British Defence Policy* (Waterloo, 1983); J. Magarch, *The Anatomy of Power: The War Between Downing Street and the Media from Lloyd George to Callaghan* (1978); F. McDonough, 'The Times, Norman Ebbut and the Nazis, 1927–1937', *Journal of Contemporary History* (1992); F. McDonough, 'The Role of the Press in the Foreign Policy Aims of Adolf Hitler', *American Journalism* (1995); B. Morris, *The Roots of Appeasement: The British Weekly Press and Nazi Germany During the 1930s* (1991); N. Pronay, 'British Newsreels in the 1930s. 1. Audience and Producers', *History* (1971); William R. Rock, *Appeasement on Trial: British Foreign Policy and its Critics, 1938–1939* (1966); S. Rowson, 'A Statistical Survey of the Cinema Industry in Great Britain', *Journal of the Royal Historical Society* (1936); K. W. Watkins, *Britain Divided: The Effect of the Spanish Civil War on British Political Opinion* (1963); J. E. Wrench, *Geoffrey Dawson and our Times* (1955); R. J. Wybrow, *Britain Speaks Out, 1937–1987: A Social History as Seen Through Gallup* (1989).

# Index